So You Want To Be A CEO...

The Path from Middle Management to the Top Job

Thomas F. Faught

FⓄRTIS
PUBLISHING
Jacksonville, Florida ♦ Herndon, Virginia
www.Fortis-Publishing.com

So You Want To Be A CEO...
The Path from Middle Management to the Top Job

By Thomas F. Faught

ISBN 978-0-9845511-3-2 (hardcover version)

Library of Congress Control Number: 2010931758

Published by Fortis Publishing
Jacksonville, Florida—Herndon, Virginia
www.Fortis-Publishing.com

Published & Manufactured in the United States of America

DEDICATION

This book is dedicated to my children, Kellee S. (Faught) Fiola, Kimberlee J. Faught, Michael F. Faught, Mitchell T. Faught, Ryan W. F. Faught and Christopher P. Faught who have been a continual source of inspiration and support during the last several years as the manuscript was being developed.

This book also is dedicated to the paternal and related ancestors of these children from Johan Pauli Vogt (the name Vogt became Faught in the 1750s) to the present. Johann Vogt was born in 1680 in Karlovy Vary, Bohemia, Habsburg Dynasty (now a portion of the Czech Republic), and, with his wife and four children, arrived in Philadelphia, October 11, 1733; the first of the family to America.

Table of Contents

Appendices

Contents (continued)

Introduction

Simply put, the purpose of this book is to assist you in planning and executing your career path to advance from your current business responsibilities to those of senior executive leadership – to those of a Chief Executive Officer, Managing Director or similar level of responsibilities. Recognizing that times and business environments change, It is designed to meet the challenges of the 21st Century; challenges you will face as the top executive.

This book is based on my personal business experiences covering 40 plus years, and on the positive influence of a number of individuals with whom I have had the privilege of working or associating. These most considerate individuals are noted in the Acknowledgement, Appendix 'M.'

My background originated during The Great Depression, spanning President Franklin D. Roosevelt's NRA, WPA, CCC, Square Deal, etc. It was annealed during World War II; influenced by service as a Marine, and strengthened by my work as a laborer. It was shaped by western State University training and an eastern MBA education, by more than two decades of international work, by academic experience in a leading MBA program, and by several years as a senior business executive. This senior management background included that of a CEO and President of a global heavy manufacturing, engineering and construction, and systems corporation.

This working, service and academic background proved to be of considerable value during the ups and downs of personal, corporate, and family life. It also provided the basis for steadfast standards and values, affording an ethical barrier against the increasing prevaricating, cheating, obfuscating, thievery, and fraudulent global business and government events of the last 30 years or so.

Unlike the "Me" generation's questionable ethics and opportunistic management practices so evidenced by the Enrons, WorldComs, Tyco

Internationals, MCIs, AIGs and, more recently the Madoffs, Stanfords and Rothsteins of the world; the standards provided me by many worthwhile relationships underwrote the strategic soundness of "being smart rather than clever" and trust implied in such policies as "Your Word is your Bond." These individuals – whom I have attempted to emulate – worked hard, many from the bottom up; never adopting the idea "If it ain't broke, don't fix it." Consequently, as well as managing expanding enterprises, they developed new ideas and new products that resulted in new markets and considerable success for society and for themselves. The idea of "hard work" in this environment was both expected <u>and</u> respected.

These experiences have not all been successful. There have been occasions of "three steps forward, two steps back." There have been dead ends, and, along the way, there have been some failures. However, lessons learned from these events as well as from successes provide "heads up," positive, practical guidance herein for you and your career.

This book is about the value and benefits of hard work, smartly done. It is about strengthening your self-confidence, flexibility and agility, and of realizing that you'll never fully achieve your potential, but you'll always – throughout your life – be striving for that goal. You are the person who never quits.

I ask that you approach this book and study its contents as a Chief Executive Officer. When you achieve your career objective – and those supporting goals peripheral to it, I believe you will have found the premises of this book of considerable value. Although it is hoped that you will have developed a practical degree of independence and skepticism, you will be pleased to have set positive, constructive and challenging standards for those with whom you have worked and for those who will succeed you.

This book is written for people like you who already have a good assessment of themselves. Age-wise, they probably are between 30 and 45 or so, have their academic experience largely behind them, and have made a contribution in the eyes of professional individuals they respect; people other than parents and relatives. I hope that they have gained some "hard knocks" background, earning money performing some relatively menial tasks from which they gained a perspective and marked respect for the working person. It is written for people who know <u>what</u> they are rather than <u>who</u> they are.

It is for the individual who wants to make a difference, and who realizes that risks always are present in striving to achieve worthwhile goals.

You will note in this work that the word "individual" pops up frequently. This book is directed to the individual; the ambitious, constructively enthusiastic, goal-focused person who knows or has learned that decisions – good or bad – are individual acts for which they bear the responsibilities. True, often "two heads are better than one," and the individual for whom this work is targeted realizes that group discussions and deliberations frequently are useful, but that team deliberations in decision making, unless closely controlled, frequently are circuitous in nature; best left for group psychotherapy sessions. Team-based action often results in solutions of the least common denominator and too often are confined to "in the box" thinking. I recall a concern expressed several years ago by a senior executive of a leading automobile manufacturing company that his people frequently became so engrossed in team building and team thinking that few real problems were being addressed well and few solutions resulted from the time being spent.

Now, having discussed your characteristics as the targeted reader, it's only reasonable for you to ask, what does this book offer? What are its "deliverables?" Inasmuch as leadership responsibilities are comprehensive, the book's advice and guidelines are broad. Essentially, it speaks to the importance of managing your time, of disciplining yourself in planning and sticking to a career strategy, of the necessity to "set yourself apart" early and continuously, and of focusing on things you can change, not wasting your time and energy on issues over which you have little or no control. It also identifies career pitfalls which you, as the CEO should anticipate and for which, early on, you have in hand optimal alternatives or options. The book also emphasizes the importance of a family and of effective, mature family management to your career, and the nature of challenges you, as the CEO, will continue to face. Albeit different, these challenges and the way you manage them will be equally important to your continual success as a Chief Executive Officer or the leader of your organization. It also recognizes and gives attention to a major point often missed: **You, as the CEO, want to do more than merely lead, <u>you want to inspire!</u>**

Before beginning the text, I think you'll find it useful to review the thoughts and guidelines provided in the first four appendices: *Suggested Information Sources, Useful Aphorisms, The Word, and Comportment.*

Thomas F. Faught

Chapter I

Your Early Career: "The Wonder Years"

As a person considers charting his or her future career Path, three points immediately should capture their attention: One, the finite nature of time. Two, the critical importance of discipline. And three, the unequivocal serious nature of business; an endeavor no less challenging than warfare.

First, time. Life itself could be viewed in the same metrics as a horse race. Major horse races often are measured in terms of a mile and a half, or about ten furlongs (a furlong being about 220 yards or 660 feet). Comparing this to one's life, let's say that between two and three furlongs are taken to get you into the base point of a career. You've completed your formal education and gained some experience relating to your career along the way. Your career advancement now will occupy seven to eight furlongs. Your progress and increased responsibilities will depend largely on your increasing contribution, including the sharpening of your management skills. "What about retirement as an eventual aim" you might say. Retirement? Retirement is for people who have no more to contribute. Their goals become vicarious, not personal. They transfer their pleasures of success to others or possibly heroes in novels. Your commitment, motivation and career focus is much different from people looking to retiring.

Thus, as you look to the future, you must consider that approximately one-third of your life already is behind you. Two-thirds remain, or between 40 and 50 years during which time, you will make your maximum contribution and transition to leadership. Your primary career goal is to ensure that the future of your organization is much better when you depart than it was when you started. As the leader, to repeat, the successful perpetuation of your company is your primary career objective. Looking at our horse race analogy, you now have less than four furlongs to go in your business career. Within that distance, in terms of your effective career – the periods during which you are really are in control or "at the helm" – you have something less than thirty years.

6 | So You Want To Be A CEO...

When we talk about transition to leadership, we are speaking of a fundamental change in the way you work – the manner in which you approach a job and how you carry it out. In your early career, you have been recognized and awarded by your ability as an individual to take on an assignment and successfully perform it. With each success you enjoyed came greater assignment responsibility. The value of the assignments became increasingly important. To date, largely you have been a standalone machine, a doer who has emerged at the head of your respective "pack." Your success has been almost entirely related to your ability personally and individually to get the job done. You have required little assistance, and from the "get go" you have led the crowd as an outstanding individual.

However, one day you have found or will find all of this has changed. One of the people who lauded you for your success congratulates you, and tells you of a new opportunity the organization has for you. You are to become a manager. For some of you this already has happened. In a well-managed business organization, this transition is gradual. First, you, who have done so well as a self-starting individual, are asked to take on a project that involves three or four colleagues, perhaps even requiring a degree of coordination with people outside your immediate department (there's a word, "department," that's become relatively passé). At this point, whether you know it or not, you are being assessed in a new role. Your ability to get things done through other people (and simultaneously develop them) begins to receive attention, the same abilities that eventually will or will not carry you to CEO responsibilities. You may possess an MBA. You may have rated "triple A" for each and all of the work to date you have done. However, please accept the fact that all of that now is history with a capital H, from this point on you're going to be rated as a Delegator.

Speaking of history, I like to refer to a Russian's idea of a Delegator, a Manager. In 1869, some 80 years or so before the idea of "Management skills" began entering the business school's syllabi; Mr. Tolstoy finished his historic novel, "War and Peace." I should mention that Ms. Sophia Tolstoy, the author's wife, handwrote eight or nine complete manuscripts before Mr.

Tolstoy was satisfied, thus addressing the importance of a "husband-wife teamwork" relationship, we will cover later in the book.

Leo Tolstoy introduces Prince Mikhail Ilarionovich Kutuzov—and Prince Kutuzov, a historic figure, among the world's outstanding military leaders, provides an example of delegation that is difficult to match. I won't take the thrill away from you, but in a matter of hours during the Battle of Borodino, the bear rug ensconced Field Marshal Kutuzov provided about as great a lesson concerning delegation that one could imagine. In the introduction of this chapter, it was mentioned that business is no less challenging than warfare. In these four or five pages of this novel, you will come to realize this fact.

I strongly encourage you to read this work of Mr. Tolstoy. In it, you will face the complete array of the coping skills and talents of a skilled executive: stress, an excessively explosive – death dealing – environment, extreme time pressures, full realization of the impact of possible failure, and yet the guts to suck it up, and to tell a subordinate, "It's your job. You figure it out." You gotta' read this to appreciate the spectrum of challenges you will face head-on someday.

Delegation requires supreme – and calm – discipline. It's relatively easy to excuse the subordinate, and to do the job for him or her. After all, that individual talent you possess is what got you here. However, you do this once, and you fail in your job – and your responsibilities – as a manager. Also, your subordinate loses the opportunity to develop skills as well as their discipline. When you step in and permit this to occur, you are back at your same old stall.

The ability to delegate couples and uncouples simultaneously everything you have done in the past to justify in someone's mind that you deserve this initial management opportunity. It couples all of the virtues you previously have demonstrated: planning, time management, coordination, research, self-confidence, organization of the work, application of all that you've learned empirically and logically, ambition, judgment and drive. At the same time it uncouples these attributes from you, connects them to your subordinates (through your efforts and guidance), and pulls you back into an oversight and control role. Two additional attributes of the skilled manager, executive and CEO. Think of the bear rug, smile and take a deep breath.

Whether you are starting a new job or preparing yourself for career advancement, you should consider several things in the early phase of work.

Learn About Your Company

You would be surprised as to the number of intelligent, ambitious people who limit themselves to settling into their job, become familiar with their immediate organization, their associates and the challenges of their present job. Given their constructive character, they usually do quite well. However, frequently they fail to adopt a work ethic that they will need to propel their career: they fail to learn about the company in its entirety. By this, I mean its history, the size and nature of its markets. Its competition in these markets and its market share. Its reputation in these markets and within the industry. Its product development programs, its sources of materials. Its pricing practice, its financial health, the nature of its ownership, its plans for the future, its challenges –both internal and external. Its top management and its Board, and something about the families of the people who serve as supervisors, managers, executives and officers. One conclusion you might make: Does this company represent a good investment for your own money?

You might sketch the company's organization from officers and executives down to your position. Gain an understanding of the difference between the published organization information and how the organization really works. Identify probable "backups" for these higher positions, asking yourself whether such backups exist within the present organization or will they have to be hired from the outside?

What does this tell you favorably or unfavorably about the organization? With which of the possible emerging executives should you develop an acquaintance? Why? How? Plot optional career paths to senior positions and determine the development you require to qualify for these responsibilities. You should complete these tasks within the first six months you are on the job.

There is no magic to this. However, it takes time and often it requires some research and digging.

One aspect of this effort should be the development of a habit to stay informed (and keep your superior informed). This plainly is an "after working hours" task. You spend your working hours planning and performing your assigned tasks better than the capability of anyone else. You think about how the work could be done better, faster and/or at less cost. You begin, as early as possible to assist others in your area, including your manager. The continuing objective is to set yourself apart and to attract new and greater responsibilities, proving as soon as practicable that you can handle more important tasks. This points out another factor: Your career is paramount to your life – and it will continue to be so until you step aside eventually from your role as the Chief Executive Officer.

Adopt an "Apprenticeship" Mentality

To repeat, concentrate first on understanding your job and doing it right, i.e., always exceeding what is expected. Find pleasure in making solid contributions even before contemplating advancement. Early on, say in the first month or two, identify a person who really knows the business – knows what makes it tick, and get to know them well. Work for them. Help them, and seek and take their advice. They may not be blessed with your background. They may not be well spoken. However, they know the job, the people and the boss. Respect their experience, their skill and their ability to contribute more than noting their appearance or status, and let them know, by your actions, that you respect them.

This point cannot be over emphasized. Most of the people for whom or with whom you first work have seldom received the respect for which they are entitled. Most, for years, have come to work on time, done their job and gone home without recognition. Yet these are the people who make the business a success. Being the person you are you are afforded a substantial opportunity in such a relationship by demonstrating respect to these individuals. Giving a kind word, a simple courtesy – again, you'll be "setting yourself apart." These seemingly small considerations will set you apart in their minds – and the mind of your boss – as someone worth admiring and remembering. He or she may become your first mentor. People like this can provide you a considerable boost on your career path, providing, of course, that you demonstrate your worth. Because of these courtesies, opportunities frequently will come your way. I can remember, in an early job, expressing simple "thank you's" to an administrative employee was remembered and helped me career-wise a decade later.

A point within a point: Listen. Always and constantly, listen. Be on "Receive," not "Send." This reminds me of an adage attributed to the Roman Emperor Claudius, "Say not always what you know, but always know what you say." If you don't know, keep quiet and let your career competitors put their foot in their mouths.

A related point of importance: Take care in maintaining information and contacts with your mentors and supporters from day one. Also, ensure that interests and loyalties are transferred between and among these people concerning your performance. Never forget who got you here, and keep in contract with them and their families. There is a humbleness to be appreciated, and if adopted will provide you a great competitive advantage.

Avoid Comfort

This will be referenced several times as you proceed through this book, and by "comfort," I don't mean creature comforts. As you become unafraid of reasonable risks, become familiar with what others – possibly your career competitors – consider discomfort.

Too frequently people become enamored – often unconscientiously so, with the "Comfort" of titles, membership on the "Bonus Roll," the "Rug, the Jug and the Mug" aspects, the office with an outside window, the use of a company car, i.e., status. Your career path plan, which we will discuss in Chapter II, should protect you from this hurdle in large part, providing you exercise the discipline in effecting it. Sometimes you might confront the prospect of taking a step back to possibly move your career forward in the near future. This type of risk in an antithesis to most risk-adverse people (and you will find most people, consciously or unconsciously, are risk-adverse). Also, never look back after a decision has been made. People sometimes think "Oh, if I had negotiated harder or better I would have the same salary as Betty, John (or some other career competitor)." This thinking is garbage. Perhaps you would have, perhaps not. It makes no difference. Such hindsight thinking only serves to take your mind off your primary goal; career success. Stay positive and disregard "comforts" even as you obtain them. Discomfort, in this regard, strengthens your character and your individual nature.

Emphasize Your Constructive Individualist Character

You must remember how valuable you are. One might say that you are a machine – an example of the most intricate, most astonishing machine the Universe (at least until now) ever has seen. You have been granted several unique assets and opportunities in your relatively short life. Don't think the people who hire you are not aware of this. You have been employed or promoted because of your unique potential. Act like the Individual you are.

In the first phase of your new job, arrange to discuss with your superior your interest in learning as soon as practicable the progress you are making on the job, determining with him or her the date of your initial performance (and compensation) review. Suggest that, in the absence of an assignment about which a review was possible, that your three-month anniversary also be your review date. Include In your review discussion possible optional promotion paths of interest to the company and to you. If you find yourself in a job that does not have "value added" potential, identify positions with this potential, and discuss with your superior how you might program a move to such jobs. However, be aware that a "step back," as previously mentioned might be required to effect such a change. Discipline yourself that if a performance and compensation review does not occur within a six-month period, you should consider reviewing your potential career options.

Importantly, select your business colleagues carefully. Don't frequent the companionship or become identified with the organizational "chaff" which is always present in any group. The aphorism, "Birds of a feather flock together" is no more significant than during your initial employment or new job when few people know you personally, and many want to be your acquaintance. Avoiding this situation frequently poses difficult problems because of your early career in this company you may well be assigned to or with some of these "Chaff"- type people in the normal course of events. Be civil and "upbeat" to all, and be certain to handle everyone in a courteous manner so that, in the greatest stretch of imagination, no one ever can say that you are snobbish, arrogant or not caring. However, quietly maintain your independence and keep your own confidence until you've tested the relationship waters thoroughly. I repeat, this is a challenging experience and demands of you considerable tact.

In this same vein, go out of your way to help fellow employees. Be outwardly generous and kind, inwardly reserved. Make people who count dependent on you, or at least become reliant on you. A practical assessment of the character and capabilities of your colleagues – determining the "chaff" from the "wheat" – should be accomplished within the first month or two of association.

Seek opportunities from the beginning. Each evening review the happenings of the day and consider how job-related factors could be improved. Get into the habit of identifying one new improvement each night. Present and discuss with your mentor to determine practicality and how good ideas might be put forth and implemented. Initially, concentrate on profit improvements through cost reductions. Later, as your scope of responsibilities broadens, consider improvements through changes in distribution systems, product innovations, new markets, and so forth.

Insure that approaches to your assigned work are comprehensive; that no "holes" exist in the work or in the analyses supporting the work. Employ Kipling's "Six Honest Servin' Men" and Ohno's "Five Whys" in making sure that the bases are covered; that the approach you use or advocate is comprehensive and avoids blind alleys. See these references in the Suggest Reading List, Appendix 'A.'

Planning the Assignment or Task

Earlier in this Chapter, we discussed the critical importance of transitioning from a "Doer" to a "Delegator." There are several aspects to accomplishing this transition successfully, among which is successfully carrying out assignments. To accomplish this requires a plan. If the plan is not done well, the resulting work will not be done well, and you, as a first stage supervisor or manager, will not be successful.

<u>Define the Assignment</u>

This is the keystone of any piece of work. It is mandatory that the definition is clear, accurate and well understood. Usually your superior will call you into the office, inform you that his organization has a new assignment and that he wants you to lead it. Then he describes in general terms the assignment, project, task, etc., and you take notes as to the nature of the work. At the conclusion of the discussion, it may be necessary for you to ask for an idea of a completion date, and, whether or not the superior asks it, you indicate that you will flesh out the definition and give him some idea as to how you will approach it and who will do the work. Give yourself plenty of time to accomplish this step.

The "Due Date" determination always proves a hurdle. The superior usually wants it yesterday. I have found it better to advise him or her that you'll get back to them shortly with a breakdown of the work that will help determine the Due Date. If Push comes to Shove in this regard, it might be advisable to suggest attacking the assignment in phases. Here, again, your guidance primarily reflects Rudyard Kipling's famous "Servin' Men," i.e., "What,"

"Why," " When," "How," "Where" and "Who." This is the order in which Kipling presents them in his poem, and it is the order I've found most useful in planning an assignment. Of course, elaboration is needed and sometimes "How Much" is required. The 'fleshed out' definition is prepared and agreed by your superior. Now you are ready to go to work.

Assure Understanding by your Team

Insuring that all personnel involved in the work have a complete, accurate understanding of the assignment is essential. Frequently this requires having them read and discuss the work, and then repeat to you their understanding. This session represents Review Meeting One. All future Review Meetings will first be with the team and second with the superior.

- Review Meeting One
- Determine Required Data – Scope, Nature and Source
- Obtain Data
- Identify Key Findings
- Review Meeting Two
- Analyze Finding
- Develop Preliminary Conclusions
- Review Meeting Three

Now you will have consumed 1/3rd of your committed Time to complete the work

- Test Preliminary Conclusions and Develop Final Conclusions
- Draft Preliminary Recommendations
- Review Meeting Four
- Develop Final Recommendations
- Structure Implementation Steps
- Review Meeting Five
- Develop Implementation Timelines and Cost Estimates (Add 30% "cushion" to both)
- Draft "Next Steps"

- Review Meeting Six
- Finalize "Next Steps"

Now you have consumed 2/3^{rds} of your committed time needed to complete the work.

You will find that most people ignore the importance of selling the "Product," extending to midnight of the final day to finalize its contents, i.e., Recommendations, Implementation or the identity of Next Steps. You should attempt to reserve about 1/3rd of the allotted time for preparation of the report, polishing and rehearsing your presentation, etc. Rehearse, rehearse, and rehearse including your associates, your mentor and your superior in a mock Q&A. Your future career could easily depend on the quality of the work.

Honing Your Judgment

During this period in which you overcome the challenges relating to the transition from doer to delegator, to evaluating colleagues and mentors, to exercising discipline in effecting your future career plan, there's an overriding consideration demanding your attention: Strengthening your judgment. We all possess "judgment." Most of us live with the basic assumption that our judgment is good. Most of the time this is a false assumption.

Before discussing honing our judgment, we should limit somewhat the definition of judgment as it applies to our careers. "Judgment" in this case relates to (1) deciding what is important and clearly separating it from the unimportant, i.e., the trivia, (2) determining what things – even important things – we can change or control, and (3) focusing our attention and efforts accordingly. Again, history – in this instance, recent history – has something of a guide for us to in this regard. Rev. Reinhold Niebuhr, the well-known U.S. theologian (1892-1771) said, *"God, grant me the serenity to accept the things I cannot change, the courage to change the things I can, and the wisdom to know the difference."* If you are so inclined, take religion out of it. Call it a philosophy. Call it whatever you wish. The crux of this is to use your time, talent and focus constructively. This adage as well as other suggested aphorisms of value to you is shown in Appendix 'B.'

The decision you make as to what is important will position you well for several things affecting your career. For example, the need you may have always to strive for unqualified excellence may be tempered somewhat by the "80% Solution" or Arouet's 1772 adage "The Best is the Enemy of the Good." I'm not faulting a desire for excellence, indeed it is a most reputable aim. However, time limitations as well as probability considerations often require you to conclude with something other than excellence in your work. Recognize this factor. *The Word* featured in Appendix 'C,' and the related *Comportment* set forth in Appendix 'D' are among the guts of this book. I place great importance on these both for your internal development and your external perspective. Please read, memorize and, to the extent practicable, practice these tenets in your everyday life and in your career development.

In effect, the pause you require yourself to take to ensure that you are applying sound judgment, is a good example of judgment itself. Practice this. Astuteness and good judgment often are akin.

Be Aware of Anticipated Changes Affecting Your Future

While you will find few of your career competitors in this formative period of your new job developing knowledge about the company, its competitors and its industry, you will find even fewer keeping track of global factors that could affect substantially the future of your career. Too infrequently do we consider potentially changing conditions and how we might management them. Too few of us are comfortable with change; an element that is as important to our career future as the experience we have or the organization for which we have chosen to work. We should pay constant attention to what Niccolo Machiavelli had to say about change. *"There is nothing more difficult to take in hand, more perilous to conduct, or more uncertain of success, than to take the lead in the introduction of a new order or things (change), because the innovator (you) has for enemies all those who have done well under the old conditions, and only lukewarm defenders in those who may do well under the new."* What Machiavelli said some 500 years ago is just as true today. To be a success in your career you must anticipate change, accommodate it and be comfortable with the evolving results. This and other aphorisms that I believe useful are provided in Appendix 'B'.

* * *

Chapter Summary: Whether this is your first job or a change to greater career responsibilities, you are entering a new arena. The factors leading to a successful career include an awareness of the value of time – of your time and that of others. A disciplined mind that will enable you to set your course and to stick to it, a strongly individualist attitude, the importance of setting yourself apart, and the need to recognize that change – both internal and external – always will be present, and represent a factor, which you must anticipate and with which you must be comfortable. Conversely, you must overlook materialistic and egocentric factors that could become habitual, lulling you into a comfort zone—one that could destroy your career potential. Commit early on to a disciplined regime regarding the tenets of *The Word* and *Comportment.* Supplement these with increasing knowledge of business and social culture in your major markets.

Chapter II

Path to Your Goal: Thirty Years (or Less) and Counting

In the previous Chapter, we discussed elements relating to the first years of your business career or the initial period of new business responsibilities. Chapter II, beginning with that base, develops a proposed career path for the reader's consideration. A path, which again reflects the importance of discipline and flexibility.

An important caveat here: The elements described in Chapter I are tied directly to time. Thus, tied these elements and the path discussed herein may appear overall mechanical in times relationship to contents and requirements. However, time is finite, and discipline is essential to its optimum use. Changing circumstances always will affect one's life and career. However, without effective time management and discipline in implementing your plans, you and your career totally become the victims of these vagaries.

Exhibit '1', which follows, sets forth a suggested Career Path from where you are today through the step when you become the CEO or equivalent leader of your respective organization to the point at which you "pass the baton" to your CEO successor. Using these data as reference, let's begin to dissect the Plan.

The fourth or fifth anniversary of your first or new job should have provided you a solid background for the major career crossroad you will face. At this anniversary, you should evaluate several career options and make a strategic decision concerning the following:

- Remain with your present organization, planning to advance to your goals using your present path.
- Change directions either by seeking a different career area in your

present organization or move to another company.

- Move to a different type of work requiring a change in based career planning, e.g., move to consulting (versus 'line" or operating management), teaching, a "non-profit" (versus a "for-profit") organization, a globally dominant organization, a service or research versus a manufacturing or producing activity, possibly a "start-up" venture, etc.
- Consider a marriage and family involvement.

An important point here: As frustrating as your initial job or job change may become, stay with it, learning whatever you can and strengthening your reputation to the fullest in doing this work. Keep in mind that you always are learning new things and becoming acquainted with new people, both of which possibly can favorably influence your strategic career.

Exhibit '1'

Career Path to the CEO's Job

The data presented herein are of a general nature and are to be considered only as a guide, especially given your age, experience and present position. The principal purpose of this exercise is to stress – to emphasize – that time is finite and time discipline in mandatory. To achieve goals as complex as time objectives on a career path, particularly one intended to lead to leadership responsibilities of a major organization, requires continuous attention to decision points. I have attempted to identify actions steps and suggested time required to achieve them.

The Time Line

Career Timeline

1st Stage	2nd Stage	3rd (and final?) Stage	
A	B	C	D	E	F	G	H	I	J

0 1 2 3 4 5 6 7 8 9 10 11 12 13 14 15 16 17 18 19 20 21 22 23 24 25 26 27 28 29 30 31

Years

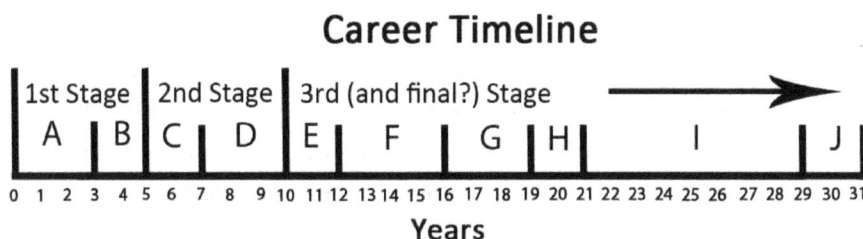

Decision and/or Action Points:

a.   36 Months (3 years): Reputation established. Challenges, recognition and visibility objectives being met. Has interest in "operations" or "advisory" (consultancy) been determined. Are you being "priced out" of the market? Getting too "comfortable"? During this period, the idea of marriage should be considered. Have you expanded your functional expertise to at least two areas? Developed fluency in at least one strategically practical foreign language? Establish a habit of reviewing The Word and Comportment weekly. This, essentially, is a period to develop a habit of the Delegator versus the Doer and in career assessment. (Twenty-eight years remaining.)

b. <u>60 Months (5 years)</u>: Fork in the Road: Stay or Change. Either way, this is a commitment point. Obtain global or international management experience. If consultancy has become your primary interest, make it a project. Develop something to sell. By this time, you would have expanded your functional expertise to at least three areas. If a marriage decision has been made, it should occur early in this period to facilitate possible relocation while your children are young and you and your prospective spouse have reached a certain maturity and each of you have acquired backgrounds to contribute ideas as to the relative importance of career, family, other interests, etc. This also would ensure that you both have sufficient years ahead to participate in developing the family. Also, from this point onward you each should participate in future career decisions. (Twenty-six years remaining.)

c. <u>84 Months (7 years)</u>: By this time, surely you have something of importance to say. By now, you should have submitted essay drafts to applicable business journals or to relevant Opinion Pages. It's important that you take action to get your name known as a constructive thinker, one who other knowledgeable individuals give their time and attention. Your thoughts are becoming increasingly respected. (Twenty-four years remaining.)

d. <u>120 Months (10 Years)</u>: A Major Decision during this period. Time to fish or cut bait. From this point onward, you are either an operating executive or an advisory executive. This doesn't restrict you from changing from one to the other sometime in the future. However, <u>at this point</u> you are building your career and your professional legacy – on one of these two broad career avenues. Entertain executive recruiting (or placement) overtures. By this time, your name (and reputation) should be on most leading "head Hunter's" candidate lists. Your target at this point would be – in the case of "operations" – a Division Manager, Superintendent, Vice President or a position with similar executive responsibilities. In the case of an "Advisory" position, Partner, Client Handling Officer, Director or a position with similar management responsibilities. This should represent your final planned, "Career Organization" move. Exceptions would be if drawn to other, more attractive opportunities by others. (Twenty-one years remaining.)

e. 144 Months (12 Years): During this period, proof of your leadership abilities either should result in continuing additional executive responsibilities – promotions, in areas of your functional expertise and/or consolidation of several of the organization's major management responsibilities under your leadership, e.g., responsibilities equivalent to those of a Vice President – Marketing, Vice President – Operations, General Partner (versus Senior Partner), etc. If this increase in responsibilities, by whatever avenue, does not occur or appear inevitable, you should move to another career opportunity (Nineteen years remaining). An additional challenge during this ambitious career period concerns the family. Children may be completing their 'teen years Now, and are considering college. It is most important that potential changes in family relationships and spousal interests be anticipated and that plans are in place before problems occur. (Nineteen years remaining.)

e. 192 Months (16 years): Elected Chief Operating Officer (COO), Chief Financial Officer (CFO), Chief Administrative Officer (CAO), Vice President – marketing, or a position with comparable responsibilities. This position should report to the President. (Fifteen years remaining.)

f. 228 Months (19 years): Elected President and Chief Operating Officer. This role should be responsible for all senior executives except, perhaps the organizations auditing and ombudsman functions, which may report to the Chief Executive Officer as well as you. (Twelve years remaining.)

g. 252 Months (21 years): Elected President and Chief Executive Officer (CEO), or President, CEO and Chairman should the organization not have an Independent Chairman First job: Set your goals and develop your plan to accomplish those. (Ten years remaining.)

h.   348 Months (29 Years): This eight-year period is when you accomplish your goals, develop your legacy, identify your successor candidates and begin their "crucible" period. (Two years remaining.)

i.   372 Months (31 years): Choose your successor, groom him or her and assure the Nos. Two and Three positions are covered well because there is a strong likelihood that at least one of your most senior and talented executives will leave for other leadership opportunities. Finish Line reached.

Time Expires. Retire, depart, and vamoose. Leave the premises. There is nothing worse for an organization than the boss staying around after his or her career with the organization is finished. Don't even expect an office and secretarial services. Travel, write a book, join Boards of Directors (not this one), become a senior golfer, do anything but interfere with this organization, directly or indirectly.

"Functional" areas, for purpose of this Career Path, are senior areas of management responsibility, primarily within the marketing, manufacturing, research and development, and/or financial sectors of an organization. Administrative functions provide valuable, necessary services, but generally, they are support activities to the successful continuum of the foregoing "Line" activities.

Activities vested in the senior executives responsible for these Functional roles might be as follow (functional alignment and reporting relations depend significantly on the type of industry and the size of the organization):

Marketing – Sales, marketing planning, brand management, advertising and promotion, after-sales service, pricing, competitor analysis, customer relations, distribution, contribution to strategic planning, etc.

Manufacturing – Production, engineering, quality control, maintenance, planning and scheduling, purchasing, vendor relations, inventory control, receiving and shipping, cost control, labor relations, facilities and process planning and development, workforce training, standard contribution to strategic planning, etc.

Research and Development – Program management, patents and copyrights, new product and/or process development, testing and evaluation, product design or formulation improvements, laboratory organization and management, product cost reduction and quality improvement, cost control, technical relations and liaison with external sources, contribution to strategic planning, etc.

Finance – Financial planning and analysis, cash management, investor relations, financial relations, banking relations, portfolio management, accounting, taxation, budgeting, foundation management, debt and equity evaluation, financial reporting, contribution to strategic planning, etc. In some instances, auditing, and strategic planning are included in the responsibilities of the Chief Financial Officer.

Administrative – legal affairs, government relations, human relations (employee relations, contract negotiation, compensation and benefits, recruiting and training, management development, public and community relations, corporate development (mergers and acquisitions), overseeing strategic planning development and corporate governance, organization development, etc. In some cases, the organization's Ombudsman responsibility is included within the Administrative function.

Referring to the suggested Career Planning Timeline, Exhibit '1', lets "flesh it out" a bit. First, you have spent anywhere from 25 to perhaps 40 years getting to where you are today. For sake of argument, let's say 30 years. This represents between 30% and 40% of your life and approximately half of the span of your professional career. Again, as you have found by this point, discipline increasingly is required if you are going to achieve your goals.

Exhibit '1' is a guide. There undoubtedly are other paths to a CEO's responsibilities (you will note that I say "responsibilities" rather than "position" because the term responsibilities characterize the nature of the work and for what you are being compensated. In my opinion, the term "position" equates too much to title, prestige, etc.). It would not be a mistake to remember that changing circumstances, even the people you meet and with whom you become acquainted, may influence your career direction as much as any initial plan. However, such changes may require another planning direction; one that also will require an objective, disciplined approach; hence, the value of what some call "networking."

Phase I – (a) in Exhibit '1' – The First Three Years

You now have been on the job for about 35 to 40 months. Your work is interesting and the product of your labor constructive. You have moved from your initial functional area, and have gained experience, or are gaining experience in at least two additional areas. You've had about a half dozen performance reviews with your supervisors or managers that have indicated that You are an outstanding employee, possibly with some "hiccups" that you have successfully overcome. By this time, you have enjoyed at least one promotion (and possibly expecting a second) and the increase in your compensation has met your goals, perhaps doubling – or coming close to doubling your initial annual base (don't be too upbeat at the thought, stay informed about the impact of inflation). Most importantly, you now are rounding out your first year or so of supervisory experience, wherein during the first year or two you primarily were a "doer." You now have become primarily a "delegator" (refer to Chapter I), responsible for managing and developing people. In fact, at this point your responsibilities as a manager (delegator) versus those of an independent contributor should be occupying at least half your working hours. You may be finding this transition challenging, but again, if you are to become a leader, it is a change you must master.

You also have demonstrated your interest in this company's success. Your suggestions and innovative ideas have evidenced that you are an "out-of-the-box," yet practical thinker. This may have taken the rather prosaic form of suggestion box creation and/or participation or procedural, personally conveyed thoughts. The aim, continuously, is to prove that you are a thinking contributor – one who sets himself (or herself) apart.

Your fine reputation, one that you had going in, has been strengthened and its recognition broadened. You have developed, through your work and thoughtfulness, good relationships with managers in your possible career path at least two organizational levels above those relating to your present responsibilities. They increasingly are beginning to ask for your participation.

By this time you know the company well, its culture and the type of talent it prizes. You have demonstrated a good file of contacts and related information. Your disciplined nature assures that you fulfill the needs of such contacts, you have kept your university, college or professional trade school and influential individuals apprised of your increasing career stature and you have become actively involved in at least one, outside-the-company business group which is well recognized and possesses at least a regional, preferably a national visibility. You also have developed a Level I (conversational) fluency in an additional, practical (potentially useful to your company) foreign language, e.g., Mandarin, Hindi, Spanish, Slavic (Greater Russian), Arabic, Farsi or Pashtun, Turkish, Niger, Bantu, etc. A truly globally oriented company often will assist you in such endeavors.

Given your personal as well as your career interest, you may contemplate marriage and a family; elements of this plan to be implemented during Phase II of your career plan. In addition, you will have identified prospects for your initial five Key Business Acquaintances who will become candidates in Phase II (the Key Business Acquaintances will be discussed in subsequent Chapters).

You will begin a strategic assessment of future global developments, drafting global environmental assumptions in Phase II, which harbor the probability of affecting business and consequently your future business career, say for the next twenty to thirty years. Examples of these assumptions could relate to demographic trends in major markets, projected natural resource developments and various national proprietary interests and controls, changes in relationships among major developing nations, possible regional or global political or military conflicts, etc. You will review these assumptions every year or two, updating accordingly.

If this appears to be considerable work for three years, it is. However, don't forget your goals, your commitment and your focus.

Phase II – (b) – The Next Two Years

This period marks a major decision point. Remain with your present organization or make a change. This commitment must be fulfilled if you are going to stay on a career path and be true to your own goals. You now have some experience, which should have afforded you "something to sell." Perhaps you have decided upon an advisory or consulting career rather than future involvement of a line management nature. However, be advised that, even with favorable and changing circumstances, the depth and/or uniqueness of your experience to date may not be of a nature to justify a partnership in a major consulting organization, and you probably should not be satisfied with a lesser position. Given that only 25 to 30 years remain in your business career, this, again, is the time to "fish or cut bait." Don't permit the slothfulness of an attractive salary or the comfort of present recognition make decisions for you. Not being an advocate, but there may not be a more propitious time for you to consider a Start-up or a new venture, assuming you are so disposed.

This two-year period also represents the time to implement plans you may have for marriage. Marriage during this time will enable you and your spouse to have pre-school age children by "Year Ten". Providing logistic flexibility in your career plan before a possible relocation could result in adjustment difficulty for them and the family (experience has shown that children possibly suffer the most in relocations between the years of 9 or 10 and 16 or 18). Such timing also should minimize the stress of a career change here. This relocation consideration is important because you should endeavor to gain international or global supervisory or management experience during this period.

An important practice for you to adopt and continuously strengthen – because you will be employing it increasingly as your career progresses – is to identify eminent individuals in your organization whom you can trust and who could form the nucleus of an organization team for you as you are promoted. You skill in learning and evaluating such people – as well as replacing them as needed – is extremely important to your career.

Another important consideration, which will be addressed further in subsequent Chapters, is your management of personal assets. You may find that your career experience to date has been so successful that you are pricing yourself out of the market. That is, compared to opportunities in other, more career attractive companies or fields, it may be necessary for you to step back somewhat compensation-wise to be attractive to other organizations that offer greater management challenges in the long term. However, inasmuch as you now have frugal habits borne of giving investment attention to needs rather than wants you should experience at most minimal restrictions in such instances.

Phase III – (c) – Three Years More

Three years in which you begin broadening your personal horizons; making a name for yourself and developing a national platform. You now have the experience to be of value to others in the business community. This is the time to whet your writing and speaking skills on topics and before audiences that will increase their awareness of you. This will help you to start being known as an emerging, knowledgeable senior industrial executive. There is a wide range of potential venues for this activity; responses to "Letters to the Editor," brief editorials in business or technical journals, essays or articles in such publications as *Business Week, Fortune, The Financial Times, Barrons,* the *Harvard Business Review,* the *Wall Street Journal,* etc.

Care, however, must be exercised. Stay away from politics, controversy and self-gratification. Play it right down the middle. How you implement this phase of your development is very important. Of course, the best way is a response to a request or a possible answer and resolution to a question. Your first entry in this regard should be structured around the contribution being made by your company, organization or senior executives. The draft of any such material must be provided in advance to company sources before being submitted for publication. Don't be concerned about your ego. It will be most effectively served as time passes, and recognition forthcoming. Consider this, partly as another way of becoming better known and respected by the company's senior executives. Even if they do not want to go forward with such an article at this time, you've made your point.

It is important that you continue this effort of national platform building throughout your career.

Phase IV – (d) – The Subsequent Two or Three Years

Another Fork in the Road, and another major career decision: Will the rest of your executive career focus on success as a Line, Operating executive or a possible senior consulting partner. You have become known both in industry and in the executive recruiting profession. You possess a decade of proven corporate and advisory experience. Your goal now is a partnership in a leading management or technical consulting firm or as an officer, director or senior executive in a corporation. This firm or industrial structure will represent your career organization, unless you become attracted away to more senior executive responsibilities in another company. Your future career at this point should be fairly well within your control. However, patience should be exercised, particularly in approaching other opportunities; a strategic evaluation of evolving options will be increasingly important. At this point, you have far too much to lose because of impatience.

Phase V – (e) – A Five-Year Perspective

During this four to five-year period, recognizing your management talent and exceptional potential, and a Board and top management awareness of what it will take to retain you, several things should be expected to occur. These include additional senior level responsibilities aligned within your organizational control, nomination to other Boards of Directors of which executive recruiting firms or your top management are aware, etc. During this time you should become, if not an executive officer, surely a member of the Executive Committee that manages the company. In essence, with your talents and potential proven, organization and functional changes as well as higher management responsibilities should be assigned based on more of the recognition of your personal character. A caution: be wary of such activities as trade associations, government committees, regional industrial development organizations, etc., unless there are clearly discernable near-term, tangible benefits to your central career path. Otherwise, these largely egocentric activities will prove a considerable waste of your time.

Consider that only 15 years or so remain of your career, if these aspects do not occur, or if your objective assessment indicate that they are not likely to occur in the immediate future (18-20 months at the outside), you should plan a career move within the next six months or so. Also, one must appreciate that the Career air becomes increasingly rarefied at this senior organization level. A number of factors can come into play in CEO's and Board promotional decisions, many of which may rest on other than objective factors. Thus, while you may stand well within your present company, it's important that you keep options continuously open to other, possible top management career opportunities. It is to your advantage to ensure that existing ones continue strong and that other, new ones are established. Loyalty is important, but flexibility, reflected in your self-confidence as to your value, is even more significant.

An additional challenge in this period concerns the family. You and your spouse now probably are in your mid-40s, and your children are completing their teenage years and approaching college age. It is an important time for family relations. Probable changes in these relationships and spousal interests should be anticipated, and plans agreed before problems occur which can adversely affect one's career and several people's lives. It is understood that you and your spouse have maintained effective communications over the years relating to all factors important to a functional family life, i.e., the rearing of the children, family values, financial matters, heath consideration, and time together, etc.

Phase VI – (f) – Tasks for the next Four Years

With some ten to twelve years now remaining in your professional career, your responsibilities now should be those of a corporate officer or an equivalent level. It is critical to you dedicated goal that, if this is not present or to occur shortly, you should assure that acquaintances in the executive placement business are aware of your possible, immediate availability. By corporate officer or an equivalent I mean the responsibilities of a vice president or executive vice present responsible for an important functional line organization, deputy managing director, deputy administrator or an analogous or higher responsibilities of senior authority, responsibility, legal accountability and frequent Board of Directors or shareholder – particularly institutional shareholder – visibility.

If not accomplished earlier, this also is the period to conclude plans for your post-career financial welfare. You should have in place a negotiated package consisting of your retirement and life insurance plan covering both you and all family members through at least the age 25 if possible, and mobility among funds allocation among the family members. This will include an investment plan for possible escrowed compensation (this subject will be further discussed in Chapter 8 relating to incentive compensation). Also retirement and benefit plans for you and your family should be on an after tax basis and include annual adjustments of inflation based on the CPI and/or other indices. The plans also should provide a post-expiration extension option at your discretion and at no cost to you. Lastly, be certain that these plans continue in effect on the same basis as agreed initially should the responsible entity be sold, merged or go out of business. In these circumstances, be certain, at your discretion, that you become a prime creditor against all assets. Consult with your financial planner and legal counselor on these matters, and do it now.

Phase VII – (g) – The Next Three Years

During this time, you will be elected or brought in from the outside to the responsibilities of President and Chief Operating Officer, or to similar No. Two executive duties. With approximately ten years remaining in your career, avoid a tendency to move quickly to affect change. Remember, in most organizations, you still have a CEO or a Chairman to whom you report, and, through them, to the Board. Also, you also have senior executives who have been competing with you for your new responsibilities, some of whom, if possible, you will want to keep and have their loyalty. In addition, there are people reporting to you and in your functional organization for which you are responsible for career and family protection.

Therefore, during the initial part of this period, be as consistent in handling your people, and as humble and magnanimous as possible, recognizing that one or more of your greatest corporate career competitors undoubtedly will depart. Your objective initially is to solidify your position and develop a loyal team that will support you in your bid for CEO responsibilities. Despite the circumstances, this positively is not the time to "slash and burn."

Being a good manager, you already have identified and developed individuals who could successfully replace you as president and chief operating officer. In the next two years or so your major task, other than carrying out your management responsibility well, is to prove to the CEO, Chairman and the leading members of the Board your abilities to smoothly bring together senior management, develop loyalties to the organization and, through them, further strengthen the company's overall performance. You further enhance your recognition as *The Organization Builder*.

During this settling in period, maintain your Personal Relations campaign. Continue to stay close to both superiors and subordinates, be generous with your praise and support and build up both. If you believe important changes are required, work them out and through the CEO, crediting him. Recognizing that, to strengthen the integrity of the organization during this period of change, the spouses and families of these individuals will need even greater personal attention than previously afforded.

Phase VIII – (h) – The Next Two and a Half Years

Here you either will be elected or brought in from the outside to be the Chief Executive Officer or CEO and President or possibly CEO and Chairman. Obviously, if you are recruited from the outside your time will be more limited to effect changes than if you were promoted from within. In the first instance, you must learn the lay of the land. In the second instance, you already know it well, and are prepared to make changes. In this regard, your leadership opportunities will be greatly enhanced, if you immediately become the CEO and President, using the Chairman as a mentor, and having the assurance of succeeding to the responsibilities of Chairman and CEO in the near future, say within a maximum of two years.

To attract a qualified individual from outside the organization for responsibilities as you have currently probably would require at least six months. It is essential that you work out this decision promptly with the CEO.

You now are in your early to mid-50s. While six or seven years remain for you until retirement (there is a 60-year-old mandatory retirement for the senior executives of many companies), the final two years or so will be occupied by successor transition activities. Thus, you really have only four of five years to make your mark; to establish your legacy, achieving the major goal of making the organization far better than you found it.

Here's your opportunity to implement those actions you long have harbored to be essential to the strategic success of the enterprise. By this time, you surely must realize that all the things in which you believe and desire to implement cannot be accomplished. However, you should have arrived at this senior-most level of responsibilities with a decided idea of the five to ten, top priority actions with which you wish to be identified. And which will lead to significant operating and cultural changes, materially strengthening the company's position and its strategic future.

You're the Man. The leader. The senior representative of the organization to whom all audiences look for standards and success. While a charismatic personality is not necessary, some aspects of this are most helpful and should be developed, e.g., you are the Front Man and it is important that your executives are aware of this fact and act accordingly. Too frequently ambitious individuals, officers or executives responsible for public affairs, such as Government Relations, Corporate publicity, etc., fill whatever void you permit to exist, and become the company spokesperson. You want ambitious people, but put a clamp on this immediately. No word goes out to any outside group, individual, organization, etc., without first being approved by you. The same rule applies to the Board of Directors, the shareholders, the financial community, the media, the government, etc. This is not a Dictatorial move. It is a move to assure that what goes out is factual, complete, objective, timely, important, consistent and legally correct. If anyone speaks for the company, it is you. It also is wise if the Directors of the Board understand and comply with this policy. You may find a review of *The Word* useful (Appendix 'C').

Make the Executive Committee of the Board your primary policy and strategic planning corporate contact—your alter ego. Unexpected events may occur that require that others might need to know your prior developed thoughts, plans, intentions, etc. This includes such things as your personal assessment and career plans for certain senior officers and executives, organization changes, merger prospects, etc. These confidential data would be shared with the Board's Executive Committee as long as you have faith in their confidence.

Phase IX – (i) – The Penultimate Year or Two

As reflected in the foregoing, your final year or two of your professional executive career largely will be occupied with selecting and grooming your successor. Evidencing the managerial acumen that got you to this pinnacle of your goals, you already have identified at least two, preferably three, candidates for this job from within the organization. The Board's Executive Committee is aware of this matter. You've done your job effectively. The Board, key members of the investment community, the company's banking interests, its institutional investors and, depending of the nature of the industry, possibly major markets already are familiar with these individuals as well as with other key executive members of the company.

While your CEO candidates, assuming they are worth their salt, also will have developed individual thoughts about potential major changes, they should share with you approximately the same thoughts about the evolving culture and philosophies of the company. The announcement regarding the identity of your successor should be made within three to six months prior to your retirement and he or she should be increasingly involved with the company's various publics. Don't saddle your successor with any promises to other executives concerning their future. It soon will be his decision.

Phase X – (j) – Prior to your 60th Year

Leave. No hanging around. Forget the practice of some companies regarding an office for their retired Chairman, President and/or CEO plus secretarial assistance, use of a company automobile, the corporate jet or an apartment, a seat on the company's Board, country club or city club dues and expenses, etc. You've had your turn in the Barrel. You're history. Make it so. And no "Kiss 'n Tell" articles or books about the company or anything related it. You might consider improving your status with what helped you accomplish your goals – your family. Being a valued grandfather will equal or exceed some of the major challenges you faced in the last thirty years.

Different situations often require different approaches. The same adage could well apply to career path development. The possible difference in viewing the career path in an entrepreneurial situation as compared to a better-established organization environment is outlined in Appendix 'E.'

* * *

Chapter Summary: Planning your career is essential to realize your goals, and discipline in your decision-making is mandatory if your planning is to be effective. This Chapter offers a suggested career plan, ensuring that you touch most of the career-developing basis along your career timeline. However, it is only a suggestion, one of several options you will have in achieving your aim at leadership responsibilities. Depending on your industrial interests, and geographic considerations, you may find an entirely different alternative meets you goals more effectively. However, almost universal aspects of any plan is the importance placed on "setting yourself apart" and the significant contribution of the family as a factor in your career team.

Chapter III

The People Challenge: Selecting, Developing, Evaluating and Leading

The people equation will be among your greatest challenges as you progress in your professional career. Herein are some thoughts on this issue and proposed guidelines in meeting this challenge.

All of us have participated in selecting people. Since our youth, we all have engaged in this process.

 Most of us also have experienced at one time or another being the person who has been selected, or rejected. Depending on circumstances, in some of these early experiences we have questioned the decisions, and have gained or lost respect for the individual making them. This aspect of respect is an important factor in the people equation. One that we will return to in this Chapter.

A significant aspect of the selection process is our own experience. Reflecting on this, we were favorably or unfavorably affected – and remember most vividly, in most cases – during our middle school and secondary school days. In many instances we can even remember the names of the instructors who determined who would be chosen as team participants responsible for developing a project or playing on a school sports team. We also, those who were so selected, recall the frustration experienced when on a Sunday evening we learned that the quality – and grade – of a project and presentation due Monday morning fell to us because some team member, chosen by a given instructor, failed to do his or her part. We soon determined, even at this relatively young age, despite alleged friendships or the proximity of our study desks, if success was to be achieved, our selection of team members, or the drive to become participants of a certain group, depended on their commitment to work hard and on their "brain power" and focus to contribute. "Popularity" soon went down the tube insofar as useful productivity was concerned.

These conclusions, in large, part, permitted you to excel in the final years of your secondary education, your college years and in your work experience to date. With continued objectivity, focused effort and refinement of thought in the people selection process, this background will significantly affect your career advancement and your success in achieving your leadership career goal.

A discussion of the people challenge is difficult without touching on related matters such as career planning, organization and relationships – and the value of a "Team" versus "Individual" approach to work. Admittedly, career planning has been largely addressed, and organization will be subsequently addressed. Suffice for now is to emphasize that, from this point forward, your principal task in achieving career advancement is how well you handle people. True, your functional and technical knowledge and expertise are important and must be kept current. However, these assets pale in importance compared to you skill in dealing with people, particularly the employees of your organization.

Sensitivity is important. As you proceed on your career path, you frequently will be inheriting a group of people with whom you have had no prior relationship. You must be aware that, given your entry as the "boss," some of these people, being disappointed in not being recognized for promotion, will be challenging, surly, and possibly downright angry; some to the point of quitting or resigning. These advances, continually facing new personnel challenges, will represent your litmus test as far as senior management is concerned. You can't fire everyone and start over. You must be capable of exercising considerable sensitivity in these situations, and yet move with alacrity in getting the job done.

Selecting and Developing People

A key to the "people selection" process is to understand the individuals' interest and objectives, and how well they correspond to the job for which they are being considered. Frequently, these people's thoughts are superficial; they don't have a definitive idea of either interests or goals. Often the "test" is by the process of elimination, that is, in determining things in which they are not interested and objectives they don't have. You are not a psychologist. However, if you don't take time at the outset to equate one's interests with the challenges of the job, the chances are that you will be searching for a replacement soon for this person, and the work is not being done.

Your people challenges is somewhat analogous to a vast lake which feeds gradually into a large, shallow river which, with an increasing current becomes narrower and more rapid until its waters pound against a dam; pounding with the force which results in a portion of this concentrated stream creating power or electric energy – equaling the success of the organization.

Initially, in your quest you will find yourself in this vast lake of people, some of whom, knowingly or unknowingly, are "in the swim" merely for the hour-to-hour or day-to-day compensation. For these people, and this often is regardless of family background or level of education, "the swim" represents only a job in which they spend their time, satisfied with attempting to do what they are told. At this nascent stage, it is easy for you, in the selection process, to eliminate these people from those contributing, or at least making a constructive effort to contribute. I'm certain you have witnessed the results if not having participated in such initial screening phase in the work experience you have had to date.

However, a crucial step now is to determine from among the individuals who have passed this first screen, those who appear to possess the potential, with development, to make further contributions – how much, and what do they need to succeed? A selection criterion that is expanded upon in *The*

Word is that it always is prudent to associate with individuals who are your equal – or, preferably, your better – in intelligence, judgment, values and commitment. Your challenge in the "people quest" is a good place to reaffirm this position.

Selection Criteria

You and your working colleagues now are out of the aforementioned "lake," and have entered the increasingly swift, focused career advancement "stream" (always remember that some of these colleagues are your career competitors). At this point, you may or may not have had supervisory responsibilities. Nevertheless, you will want to continue identifying people who have the interest and talent for making greater contributions and for assuming increasingly important management duties. You should become acquainted as soon as practicable with these people. Regardless of background, these people have potential. Your task is to identify those having the greatest potential for development.

"What makes an individual tick" is a difficult thing to identify. We all want "more," but what of and how much is not easy to determine – even for ourselves. However, it is possible – indeed, for you, mandatory – to determine criteria against which to evaluate an individual's potential through observations made during your working relationship. These criteria include the following (one might wish to quantify the relative importance of these criteria):

- <u>A Keen Interest in What Makes the Business Succeed</u> – How much time does he or she spend at their desk and in the office, as compared to the amount of time they are out in the plant, laboratory or marketplace where things are happening and on which the business depends? The only way an employee will understand the strengths or weakness of a business is to experience the work first hand – to see and feel it, and have the background to ask useful questions.

- <u>Sound Judgment</u> – Gaining an impression of the individual's judgment and analytical ability, which should enable him or her to identify and focus on the more important issues, the actual causes of an event, and determine the "Whys." This also includes "360 degree" thinking and the calmness of taking time-even under pressure-to consider the possible unintended consequences of decisions or actions, and to provide for their resolutions. See Readings suggested in Appendix 'A'.

- <u>Sagacious Rather than Astute</u> – Not to get wrapped up in hair-splitting etymology, I would strongly advise that your executive assessment criteria seek sagacity rather than astuteness. While both characteristics denote shrewdness, the latter often centers on keen perceptions and discernment <u>in which personal benefit are planned or are to be derived</u>. Yes, we want sound judgment and wisdom, but such must be directed toward the good of the organization, not to the advantage of the individual. This is a very important distinction particularly concerning executives in vitally significant positions.

- <u>Self-Expression Capability</u> – Alert, well spoken. The ability to speak and write convincingly, concisely and to the point, avoiding an enigmatic and/or sententious style which often indicates a failure to understand and deal clearly with a subject.

- <u>A Positive Attitude; Flexible</u> – One that deals objectively with the "plus" side of issues, but recognizes and is prepared to address problems that often are involved in such issues. Constantly seeks alternative or optional solutions, never admitting that something is "impossible." Works best in a non-structured, relatively laissez-faire environment. Clearly, an "out-of-the-box," non-regimented thinker; not adverse to practical risks.

- <u>Dedicated to the Work</u> – Diligent. Hard working. This is demonstrated by total absorption in the work, punctuality, the commitment to timelines, time being spent is secondary to the successful and timely completion of the assignment.

- Goal-Oriented – Knows what he or she seeks, and is objective in assessing their worth and the value of their contribution. Aware of personal strengths and weaknesses and active pursue resolutions to the latter. Strives constantly for self-improvement. Anticipates guidance and is not timid about seeking recognition – greater responsibility, visibility and reward. "Sets themself apart"; usually is far "ahead of the curve" in developing analysis and conclusions.

- Time Conscious – Evidences a keen sense of time, both their own and that of others. Thinks before speaking, centering on significant aspects of a problem or solution. Demonstrates a talent (Judgment) for identifying the "Pros" and "Cons" of issues. Listens.

- Respectful of Others – Demonstrates honest, open respect for others and for himself. Cordial, courteous and relaxed in dealings with others. Acknowledges the value of others' opinions. Avoids patronizing behavior, even the remote appearance of such.

- An Affable Personality – Pleasant "to be around." Exhibits an interest and an ability to work with others. A cheerful and calming influence. Frank defends his or her positions well, yet in a quiet manner.

- Appearance – His or her self-respect and their respect for their working environment are reflected in their appropriate dress and professional bearing.

Surely, unqualified ethical and moral behavior is a basic requirement, superseding all of the foregoing criteria. These are difficult traits to determine. Frequently one's tendency to take short cuts, generalize results, adopt a clever rather than a smart behavior and evidence astuteness provides Red Flags in the ethical and moral area.

References, Resumes, Recruiting and "Out-Sourcing"

At some point in your management career, it may appear easier to go outside the organization and recruit executive talent. However, this never is as easy as it appears. One faces both internal and external challenges in going outside. Internally there are executives to mollify; individuals who believe they possess the exact background and skills which you seek for the subject responsibilities.

Externally, in spite of a prospect's known background, references, resumes, recruiters' assessments, news releases, etc., you will never truly know the capabilities of the selected candidate until he or she has been on the job for several months – and then it may be too late. Perhaps the background and talent of an outsider are excellent. However, every corporate culture and management environment is different, and the individual's characteristics in one business situation may not work well, or be successful, in another.

When you consider the alternative of going outside for executive talent or seeking the solution from inside the company, recall the idiom, "The Devil you know (probably) is better than the Devil you don't know." Unless all relatively outstanding talent inside the company has been tested and found wanting, or a management redirection is required immediately, I have found it better to develop an outstanding insider as quickly as possible and give him or her "the nod." It may or may not prove out, but you've given your initial attention to providing an executive inside the organization with the opportunity, and this action will be respected both inside and outside the organization. You have given truth to the often stated (and sometimes overlooked) policy of "We promote from inside the company."

Sometime executive search firms are retained for intelligence purposes, for example, to determine the nature of available management talent, what types and amounts of compensation are being paid, what benefit packages are being offered, etc. These data are particularly valuable regarding competitors, and it permits you to determine how smart these organizations are for your future reference.

A time to consider bringing onboard outside personnel or using out-sourcing firms makes considerable sense when less than full-time jobs are involved. This could be done, for example, if it is reasonably apparent that the scope or nature of the work, and the number of employees assigned, probably will change within a year or two. This approach provides increased work security for your regular people and helps maintain a stable workforce. However, conversely, assurance of quality work by outsiders can pose a problem, one about which consideration must be given – and financial and reputational risks offset. For instances, if you are positioned as a Prime Contractor, you may want to require that all Subcontractors, highly qualified by previous work, insure 90% of their respective costs for their respective portions of the job being bid before your final submission.

A step applicable both to the selection and to the development process is one requiring each of the company people reporting to you have, as a strategic management responsibility, the task of identifying two individuals within their area of responsibility who are, or shortly could be, prepared to succeed them. This subject is explored further in Chapter VII.

Developing Executives

In discussing approaches to executive development, it is advisable to review what you believe is required to be a good manager. Managing well requires the ability to handle complexity and tolerate ambiguity, to make oneself a figure on whom subordinates can depend, to control one's emotions, to set ambitious yet achievable performance goals (and insist that responsible individuals meet them), to judge subordinates frequently and honestly and to depend on others and ensure that they may depend on you. Most unsuccessful executives lack these traits instead of lacking specific knowledge relating to the business. Nurturing these management traits in promising individuals is among the principal objectives of an effective development effort. Before progressing further, you should evaluate yourself against these "check lists."

It is interesting to note that the success of a business and one's career is based on deception, particularly to the outside world, especially concerning anything relating to your competitors. Hence, when you and your company are posed for successful action, you reflect that you appear unable; when nearing conclusions, decisions or actions, you adopt a view of inaction or appear some distance from reaching these points. Conversely, when any of these aspects are hampered, you appear more advanced than you are. The idea, not unlike Sun Tzu, the Chinese strategist's premises concerning warfare, you confuse your competitor (adversary), you hold out bait to entice them or (mis)direct them, you feign disorder and confusion, then you crush them. It isn't pretty, it's not conventional wisdom and it surely is not "political correctness," but it can be wonderfully successful. Someone once said something about "Everything's fair in love and war." They should have included business. Make certain these thoughts are imbedded in your executive development curriculum.

Compatible cultures and values are a great asset in management (or personnel) development. If your organization's top management has reservations about such things as in-house training sessions, career transfer opportunities, job opening publications, industrial psychological counseling, visibility with senior management, "off campus" management development programs, executive educational opportunities, portable benefits, etc., you may confront serious problems in attempting to identify and develop management talent. Indeed, given these provisos, you may well have selected the wrong company for your career. In your selection of career opportunities, you may wish to discuss this point with company recruiting representatives.

Study the individuals who are relevant to your job and your organization. This includes each person for whom and to whom you are responsible, viz., the people who report to you and your boss (and his boss). Also, consider the individuals who have peripheral responsibilities that influence your effectiveness, and who you may later draw on. You might find it beneficial to review these backgrounds periodically, noting changes in your initial impressions.

In developing an individual, target what he or she requires to exceed the probable and achieve the possible.

Work Assignments – The obvious goal of a work assignment is to get the job done. However, you should also consider the work assignment as an excellent management development tool. In this regard, get the team together for assignment discussion, and note the impact of the discussion on the individuals and the nature of the contributions each make. How do they react, and more importantly, why? Are contributions of value? Who appears to be the "informal group leader?" Do they see the assignment as an opportunity or merely a piece of work? What aspects "pique" their interest?

When developing an assignment, look beyond to whom you will give the job (this may change).

Discuss the proposed work with more than one potential candidate. Get their views as to the assignment's importance, its scope, the adequacy of the proposed goals, major hurdles that they envision, the product (or "deliverable") they see, and their initial thoughts as to the approach to be used (how much Individual versus Team effort?) and the time it would take.

These all are significant considerations. However, again of equal importance are their reactions. Do they really understand the assignment? Do they ask good questions or do the leap to conclusions in an effort to demonstrate their "smarts" and mental agility? Are they eager, reluctant? Are their views comprehensive and aspects prioritized? Do they see more challenges than value in the work? Are time estimates practical? What about their "body language," what does this tell you?

Interestingly, some assignments are best accomplished by individuals who already are overloaded. One advantage of assigning work to overloaded people is that their time constraints do not permit them to be bogged down in details. Usually, being of necessity conscience of their time, they also will develop a more effective plan. In addition, they frequently understand the value of using – and directing or managing – others, and in determining which individuals would be best to use in the project. Chapter I includes the process of carrying out an effective assignment plan.

Identify Needs That Can Be Met Quickly – Personnel interested in development gain much if such development can be gained – and progress assessed – over a reasonably short time. Examples could be engagement in diverse work assignments, possible "team lead" responsibilities, in-house study possibilities and single semester coursework at local universities. Conversely, it is not too meaningful to an ambitious individual possessing interest and reasonable practical talent to be told that he or she would benefit from a "college education." Surely, over time, given the potential you have identified, such a goal can be fulfilled, perhaps even with company financial support, but this doesn't answer his or her interest in some form of immediate improvement.

"Individual" Versus "Team" Work – Team effort is valuable, particularly in project work involving the input of several disciplines. However, it is difficult to evaluate the contribution of individual team members, except perhaps that of the team leader. Hence, it is difficult to chart the developing of any given individual. Thus, as far as development is concerned, attempt as often as possible to assign work so that an individual's contribution can be practically evaluated. Take the opportunity also to further review the candidate during discussion of the assignment, and examine his input.

Frankly, my experience indicates that the pendulum has swung too far toward "Team," "Group," "Work Shop," and "Collective" emphasis both in carry out normal, relatively continuous management functions or in "one time" project assignments. Essentially, I want to hold an individual responsible for a job. If such an individual wishes to assign parts of a project to others on a "one time" basis, and if the work justifies such an approach (and schedules can be met), fine. However, she or he still is considered the manager of the work, and it is understood that they are to be individually accountable for its success.

<u>Communicate</u> – People work best when they know what is happening, and "where the company's going." Your esteem as a manager also will be enhanced by providing answers frequently to these questions or concerns. You will find also that people in other organizations will want to work for you – to be on your team – simply for the reason that you let your people know "what's up." It is an interesting point that, for whatever reason, many executives overlook the importance of this aspect of management. Again, here you'll enjoy a competitive advantage.

I would suggest that your communicating efforts start with a brief weekly meeting – limited if possible to thirty minutes each Friday morning. This will enable you to cover the happenings of the week and things of possible interest for the ensuing week. You should acknowledge the outstanding performance of individuals at this time. Be sure to provide a few minutes for <u>each person to have an opportunity</u> for questions and comments. It is not necessary for them to contribute, but you should give them the opportunity. Slides, Power Points, etc., are not required; they are not welcome. This is an informal meeting. Keep it that way. These brief sessions also enable the employees to become better acquainted, it marks you as a supervisor who cares and it helps to keep you informed as well as them. While it may appear as a detail, I've found that a round table with no "head" helps to keep the meeting informal and relaxed. People, from habit, usually gravitate to the same seats, but that's no great problem.

To the extent possible, from your first day on the job as a supervisor, manager, etc., implement an "open door" policy; an evident indication that you always have time for your people, that you are not aloof and that you are not secretive. Some people believe a closed door indicates a superior status, while just the opposite is true. Also, begin immediately a "walkabout." You'll be surprised how much you will learn, and how much credit will accrue to you for such a small indication of interest. These actions will strengthen your knowledge of the job, keep you current, and will demonstrate your confidence in your ability to understand and appreciate the people's contribution.

Also, avoid contact through a spokesperson. Make a practice of answering your own phone. Having such intermediaries is among the most supercilious things an executive can do. Also, drive your own car. If you are that enfeebled, that you can't, you shouldn't have the job. Eliminate such affectations.

Relating to communications, when you come across a news article that you believe would be of interest to an employee – peer, subordinate or superior, or an acquaintance outside the organization, clip it or attach it to an E-mail and send it along. Make this a habit. It will help to make him or her a more informed person and, again, will show your people that you think beyond your own personal interests.

Avoid contacts through electronic devices to the greatest degree possible. If there is no escape from this, make certain your recorded messages are current and inform the caller where and when – and by what number – you can be immediately contacted. The individual contacting you or your company is using their valuable time and deserves to speak directly with a human being. They are not calling to listen to "changes in menus," the latest musical recording, to remember how to spell and index some person's last name on a key pad, or to engage in pressing a series of buttons. Employing such technologies gives the impression that the company cares more for a slight reduction in overhead expense than it does for the caller's interest; the "caller" may well be a customer. This slovenliness has become the greatest insult to common courtesy that industry has yet inflicted.

Personal Reviews – A year should not pass without your employees receiving a formal review of their performance and their compensation. Your better people, and your "direct reports," will expect and deserve reviews that are more frequent. Stay ahead of the expectations of your key people. Surprise them with relatively frequent conversations of their work and how their responsibilities "fit" and relate to the overall progress of the organization. Be sure to include your ideas regarding what you believe they need, and get their response. Caution: If your employees have to ask you about a review, you and your subordinate supervisors may not be doing as good a development job as you think. Also, encourage them to read their reviews, and include their comments if they wish. There are no secrets between you in this management development relationship. While it should never be necessary to mention, never lie. It's better to tell the truth directly and exclusively to an employee and suffer the consequences, if there are any, than to lie to them. If you lie to them, expect the same in return.

Trust and Loyalty – Trust and loyalty go hand in hand. They also are reciprocal. If you trust your people and prove loyal to them, usually – not always, but usually – they will trust you and reciprocate your loyalty. One thing I have found useful is to be aware of other more demanding and visible responsibilities for which they qualify, advise them of such and provide support to them in possibly making a change. Another is to assign work that is more challenging to the better people, tasks that offer greater management growth potential and probabilities of greater visibility to senior executives. Permit them to prepare and make the presentations, confining your participation to oversight of preparatory rehearsals.

Praise and Criticism – We all are aware of the importance of these two factors in the development of people – both those with whom we associate and ourselves. However, how praise and criticism are handled mark the difference between helping you along your career path, and causing non-productive resentment and disrespect. Recognizing this difference, the adage "Praise in public, criticize in private" continues as the guideline in this regard. Two things are mandatory: Makes sure of your facts, and keep emotions out of it.

In meetings, note your thoughts about these matters, maintain a positive composure, and reserve comments and actions for another time – this includes your body language. Never even tend to ignore a meeting participant who may not be contributing to the extent you think constructive, nor project a disregard for his or her comments. Take time to get the facts, post-meeting, and chose a time to discuss this matter – favorable or unfavorable – with the subject. If it's praise, there's always plenty of time to acknowledge it publicly. If it's criticism, you keep it private.

In commenting on matters relating to criticism, afford the subject time in a relaxed environment to explain their actions and position. Limit your questions and comments, enabling the responses to be of a kind that can help him or her, and your organization. Your job is to make them a better person – a more valued contributor, not to denigrate them. You are a mentor. You are responsible for making things better. You are not being paid to demonstrate how stern or "right," you are – or your possible degree of embarrassment.

In matters of praise, depending on the nature and importance of the work being praised, consider the consequences of sending a letter of acknowledgement to your superior, copying the employee. Also, as applicable, copy individuals if they are referenced in the correspondence.

Two matters here: Action, in either instance, should be taken expeditiously, and, as always, determine what possible "unintended consequences" are involved in the optional actions you are considering. This approach also will ensure that you take the time to think and to approach these matters in a calm, constructive disposition. Another point, also included in *The Word*: Never begin something that you don't intend to continue forever, including how you employ praise and criticism.

Your actions and attitude are the main instruments in these matters that convey the organization's culture. Second to the manner in which you praise or criticize a given effort or product, is the Performance Appraisal. It also is learning on the job activity. As an addendum to this periodic appraisal, determine what specifics please or displease your superior. Often, admitted or not, these could be subjective factors. Nevertheless, they are important and deserve inclusion. The Performance Appraisal should be an education tool, not provided only to justify an award or record a chastisement. A couple of points here: In all of these matters, it helps to remember "Those who stop being better, stop being good." Also, "If you are satisfied, you are going backwards."

Test Performance – In addition to formal appraisal or evaluations, let the employees know that occasionally their actions become subjects of "tests." For example, while travelling I would contact our various offices to determine personally the quality of telephone (or now E-mail) responses our customers, suppliers, shareholder, financial analysts, et al were receiving. After all, often this can significantly affect your business and the impression one gets of the company by their response (including swiftness) and how they handle such calls. You undoubtedly can determine other ways to "test" the various functions of your organization.

Relating to how well the organization projects impressions. Be personally involved in approaches and methods of advertising and public relations. Yes, it is true you have marketing managers and possibly others responsible for these activities. However, again, you must be aware of "how" these programs are being put together and their effect on your markets and the public. This is of particular consequences in the global arena.

Spouse Involvement – A spouse may well recognize better than his or her partner your career competitors' characteristic behavior, e.g., the way he or she usually manifest the impacts of pressure or stress, anxiety, the need for quick response, etc. Your spouse can be your greatest friend and career colleague, if you permit them to participate in what is affecting or can affect you. Thus, without divulging trade secrets, etc., it is to your advantage to keep the "home folks" appraised concerning the company, its business, management, the markets, products and services, and your job. If you experience discomfort sharing these data with your spouse, perhaps you have a problem – perhaps you are the problem.

A caution: Troubled spousal and family relationships are not rare occurrences. You may recognize symptoms of such, and you may – depending on circumstances – provide some counsel to employees indicating such systems. However, unless you are a qualified marriage counselor (and most of us are not), it is best to bring someone into the situation who is experienced in these matters and knows what to do. For example, this could be the company's human resources director or manager. One thing for sure:

Don't do anything or counsel with anyone about a possible employee problem without first discussing the matter with him or her, and obtaining his or her permission.

Friendships versus Acquaintanceships

As John Donne, the 17th century English poet and clergyman, said, "No man is an island…"

While, without the biblical connotations of the Reverend Donne, this fact is as true today as ever before. In business and commerce particularly, relationships – strong, professional, confidential relationships are imperative. Recognizing that we all are different, you should examine what you have found to be your needs in this regards, and determine how such relationships are to be established and maintained. I would emphasize that maintaining relationships frequently is more difficult – certainly more time consuming – than establishing them.

Key Business Acquaintances – In broaching this matter, I appreciate that it has received little notice. Indeed, except on an infrequent, ad hoc basis, I don't believe that many business leaders employ this practice. However, I have found it most helpful and thus I provide the idea to you for your consideration. I would say at the outset that it requires time and some cost.

Frequently, the job of a business leader is said to be "lonely." It is. You have few people, almost no one publicly, in whom you may confide, and if you are not cautious, you find yourself depending too frequently on your own, sometimes limited, counsel. To be successful, business leaders, such as you are becoming, need personal "sounding boards." I call these individuals "Key Business Acquaintances."

We are not talking about members of the Board of Directors or your key executives; nor are these individuals' casual acquaintances or friends. We are talking about professional members of a personal advisory group; five individuals who know you better than, in some instances, you know yourself.

They operate with you based on "client privilege," even in the legal sense, and they are compensated well and directly by you. You look to these people to help you excel, to keep you out of trouble and to defend you professionally should trouble arise. Their background and acquaintances position them to ask the right questions and to acquaint you with others of a like ilk should this become necessary. Frequently, these advisors will be positioned well to be aware of competitors' actions, if not competitors' plans. Obviously, these people have outstanding reputations.

An Attorney

Despite what Shakespeare said about lawyers, in this increasingly litigious and government involved business world, a close working and personal relationship with an experienced, skilled, continually well-informed attorney is essential. This individual is a professional who has a broad, diverse legal practice and specialized legal contacts in corporate, contracts, and international law. She or he also should have civil and, if possible, criminal litigation experience, or be closely associated with those who do. An adept, business-oriented attorney is invaluable as an advisor, a possible source of Board candidates, and contacts with local, state and federal politicians; people of significance to your industry and business. As much as one might disdain politicians, don't discount their potential power, influence and importance to your business and your career.

A Banker (or a Financier)

Obviously, this individual will prove useful in procuring funds, providing credit and in counseling on possible refinancing strategies, i.e., banker's work. He's not your company's banker, but can advise you on anticipated changing conditions, etc., in this area. His or her ability to anticipate events of a financing or economic nature is most important. This individual may be looked to for advice on structuring deals, identifying Board or partnership candidates, evaluating changes within the global banking community, assisting in due diligence challenges and providing counsel on possible upcoming actions by the Fed or state banking interests.

An Accountant (the CPA)

Adept in the practical aspects of corporate governance, public disclosures, FASB and SEC nuances, auditing and tax issues, this key acquaintance can be useful in ensuring optimum and practical degrees of transparency, tax and fiscal approaches and in defining the changing financial reporting requirements. Both this individual and the Attorney should help in removing the vagaries of laws and regulations with which you, the CEO and the business may become involved. As with your attorney, an important strength that this individual offers is their ability to "get behind the law" to determine the maximum degree of "doability."

A Media Specialist

This key acquaintance has grown up with the media and the people who are their principal influences. He or she is apolitical, hopefully, and can insulate you in the camps of all Political Parties and those of their supporters. This individual is not a so-called "spin doctor." But a person to whom you can look to review and recommend how best to tell your story and that of the company. To help you as you progress in your career concerning optimal news releases and possible upcoming news topics, this should assure you and the company most effective visibility, including the possible reactions of your competitors.

A Physician

Capable of providing both physical and mental health counsel, this person can assist both you, as the emerging CEO, and your top management. Key managers are the organization's most important asset. This key acquaintance can help to assure their continued optimum performance. Also, importantly, he or she will not risk infringing on other executives' responsibilities, which, because of the nature of their normal work, this is a risk against which your other Key Acquaintances must guard against.

The Physician, in this sense, is far more than being a Doctor. He or she serves as a personal counselor regarding emotional as well as physical matters (see the foregoing "Spouse" section). He or she also may serve the organization in the industrial psychological area as my Key Acquaintance did. The extent to which you wish the Physician's counsel to apply to others of your management team will be your call. However, few things carry more mystery or fear – particularly with the financial and banking community – than health questions about the people who manage the companies in which these financiers have investments or ownership interests. Because of a preconception that, even given the stress of the job, most executives are healthy, an illness can come as a shock to the traders and financiers, and the stock being adversely affected. Hence, any involvement of a Physician with management must be prudently handled, and this individual must be a person on whom you can depend in this regard.

As in the case of all of these key relationships, you must keep them informed beyond the data -provided by the 10-K, the 10-Q, other reports and news releases. "No surprises" is the rule with these professionals as it is with the Board. Also, in selecting these *consigliore*, or their replacements, you must anticipate that occasions will arise requiring two or more to work together. Thus, it is important in your selection process to determine how well these professionals can cooperate among themselves.

Friendships and Business Careers

A word here about "acquaintances" and "friends" relating to business is appropriate.

Acquaintanceships and friendships are not the same. "Friends" should never be involved in business affairs. Friends are fine. Your spouse is your "friend," probably your best friend. Your dog is your "friend." People with whom you are emotionally involved or with whom you might trust with your life probably are your "friends." However, not a person with whom you are involved in a business or in business dealings.

In my relationships, I endeavor to keep "friends" and "acquaintances" apart. They are two different kinds of relationships. Experience indicates frequently and clearly that when one involves friends in business dealings, one is courting problems if not a disaster. The activities of business are as close to a totally objective, selfish situation as one can encounter. Friendship, on the other hand, largely consists of subjectivity – a significant degree of emotion that will contaminate the objectivity required in a business. Sometimes things are done because of the fear of damaging a friendship that is totally opposed to decisions needed for a business. An example could be providing lower prices – possibly at cost or below cost – than are provided the market in general just because of a friendship. Another example is the possibility of hiring someone for a given senior responsibility, making allowance for his or her qualifications because they are a friend. Once such subjective emotion enters the equation, you are plainly on the downward slope.

With friends, one relaxes, enjoys social intercourse, may have a glass of wine, engage in trivial conversation, share a sporting event, take vacations and, even, if one is somewhat masochistic, engages in totally emotionally based discussions about politics or religion. However, again, this is not the business environment.

Recall *The Word*, inasmuch as time is of the utmost importance to your career, don't waste it on anyone or anything for which you don't have the greatest respect. I'm sure you've heard the comment, as have I, "I don't like him, but I respect him." In considering relationships, first determine your "respect factor." If your "respect factor" isn't there, or is fuzzy, stop. The adage that "birds of a feather flock together," or "you can tell him (or her) by the company he (or she) keeps" may appear to be generalizations. However, they are worth remembering and deserve to be kept foremost in your mind as you evaluate people. Strive to develop acquaintanceships – and even friendships – with Individuals (note the capital 'I'") who are equal to, preferably better than you are; better in terms of intelligence, judgment, knowledge ambition or values. We always are in the "learning" mode, and, for the time we spend, we should expect to learn – to improve ourselves – both from friends and acquaintances.

<u>Remember Those Who Got You Where You Are</u>

In considering principal relationships, you should accord attention to the people responsible for you being where you are today. I call this my "Mentor List." These people had the greatest influence on you during your formative years. Their values, character, demands, expectations, etc., or the lack thereof, molded you. Their influence likely was as important as the traits that you inherited. They could have been authors affecting your thoughts indirectly, or they could have been teachers, family members, employers or even fellow employees. They deserve your attention; even those whose negative actions influenced you to think positively; to strengthen yourself.

If you aren't doing it already, develop a habit – a courtesy – to keep in contact with these people, or, should they be deceased, with their surviving family members; letting them know how greatly you respect their forbearers. It certainly will provide a prideful moment for them, perhaps even giving them an incentive boost to do better. It's a positive practice, and, given the vagaries of life, who knows when such Individuals might again prove valuable to you?

Given this background, if you haven't done it to date, this is a good time to develop your "support file," recognizing that this will be a dynamic source, requiring frequent review; yet another advantage of the computer. To make this file useful you should at least keep current as to the addresses of these individuals, and hopefully notes regarding changes in careers, families and interests. Annual exchanges are among the most effective ways of accomplishing this, which also keeps your progress and status in front of them.

<u>Politicians and Others</u>

While discussing relationships, a word about politicians and similar types.

As in most cases, I have found that politicians come in three varieties: Good, Not So Good and Bad. Sometimes, the good politicians become "statesmen;"

leaders who have the character and interests that carry them to matters of truly national, state or local concerns which are above the political Party struggles that typify the usual pork-oriented, vote groveling "ward heelers." Experience with the U.S. Congress provides examples of individuals fitting the mold as Statesmen. These include (or have included), in my opinion, such people as Sam Nunn, Richard Lugar, Jeff Bingaman, Warren Rudman, Mike Mansfield, Daniel Moynihan, Ernest Hollings, Phil Gramm, Charles Grassley, Richard Shelby and Max Baucus. I'm sure there are others, but these are the individuals about whom I'm aware that advocate more for the good of the nation than for their political Party or for themselves. The highest priority of most politicians is to keep their jobs, and most will do almost anything to do so. After all, upwards of $200,000 per year plus perks isn't bad for the limited effort and pontification required of them. To remain in office and stay on the dole, despite what these people say, they don't want your ideas, most of which they couldn't grasp anyway. They want your support, viz., your money.

The political arena, include the vagueness of legislation and some of the laws, always poses dangers for the businessperson. Thus, while you may wish to support certain issues, be wary of becoming identified with the political individual their representatives and their aides. Their basic values differ from yours, and their values and principles are constantly changing, depending on the wind's direction and intensity. You'll never know when something negative in their background or actions will become public, and, if you are identified with them, you (and yours) may be subject to the same criticism.

This point will be revisited later, however for now I also would advise that you avoid subjectively based "causes." Obviously, it is your responsibility and duty to become involved if political considerations may affect your business and the welfare of your employees and stockholders. However, always take the high ground, and consider possible unintended consequences before deciding how to enter the fray.

* * *

A final point on developing people and on relationships: That point is <u>you</u>. Whether or not you realize it, and perhaps accredited to your humbleness you may not recognize it, for some time you have been identified as a member of a rather special group, an elite class. Because of your status and the inferred advantages you have, you are a target. Your increasingly significant industrial and public visibility, your intelligence, ambition and potential for ever greater success subject you to increasing envy, jealousy, gossip lies and false friendships. "Constant care" should be your watch phrase: skepticism bordering on a healthy suspicion. Be civil, be humble but be wary. Consider carefully before taking positions, and with whom you may take them, making certain that thoughts or actions you are considering supporting cannot be misinterpreted to your detriment and that of your organization.

As stated previously, an important aspect in both your relationships and to your career is to keep informed. If you are well informed, you can avoid being misled.

* * *

Chapter Summary: Developing people and taking care of the nature and type of relationships you establish – and maintain – are critical to your career plan and to its success. In the one – selecting and developing people – you give of yourself to develop and support your people so that they can and will support you; enhancing your career. In the other – establishing and permitting relationships to develop – you exercise judgment tempered with caution. Again, if you seek acquaintanceships and friendships with individuals equal to or better than yourself, experience indicates that you generally will be well off. Also, be very reticent in involving friends in business affairs. Social and business affairs differ greatly, and one must be constantly aware of this difference in the subjectivity and objectivity character of these two worlds. Lastly, take care concerning the working backgrounds of people being selected. For example, the effectiveness and potential of people, no matter what their professional or technical skills may be who have long worked in a bureaucratic or similarly restricted environment, may not meet your future needs.

Chapter IV
The CEO: What it Takes. Luck? You Make Your Own

Earlier you were asked to approach the subject matter of this book as if you were the CEO; an executive with a "CEO mentality," a leader's mind set. Here we focus on the Chief Executive Officer's job, which should provide you a good idea of the seriousness of your leadership's frame of mind and actions related to your career path.

As mentioned in the previous chapter, the leader, CEO or otherwise, is a lonely post. Not to romanticize this truism, the job is lonely, but this is only one characteristic defining the responsibilities of the CEO. There are several other aspects of greater importance. Besides, if an individual is incapable of effectively operating solo on many occasions, they probably should not aspire to leadership.

The CEO, first, is the individual most accountable for the successful longevity of the organization, be it a professional firm, an industrial corporation or a not-for-profit institution. You will note that the word "accountable" is used instead of "responsible." In my definition (and I admit this is largely opinion), "accountable" connotes complete, unqualified responsibility. You are accountable – answerable – for the success, you achieve, and for the commitment, you have made, in performing the responsibilities of your job. You give an account of the discharge of your responsibilities. As the CEO, you are accountable. While, "being only human, one will make mistakes," may represent an excuse for some people, you as a leader are accountable for such mistakes; and if you make too many, you will no longer be given the responsibility to make more.

The leader's failure cannot justifiably be attributed to the economy, the weather, a family argument, the demise of a major customer – or banker, volatile exchange rates, competitive factors, a supplier's defect or government actions or interventions. These factors all characterize the environment – the circumstances –in which business is conducted, and it is the CEO's job to have the vision to anticipate their impact and to already have implemented actions to overcome them. You, supposedly, have been made accountable for senior level responsibilities because of your experience, intelligence, maturity, courage and resulting vision. These factors have led you on your path to becoming the CEO. These are the reasons why others have confidence in you. These are the reasons for your better than average compensation and future career opportunities. Your vision and managerial capabilities underwrite your skills in "what if" planning. President Truman's alleged statement the "The buck stops here," certain applies in this case.

Now that we have established that you, as the evolving CEO, are held accountable for your actions, let's examine the principal audiences to which you are accountable:

Shareholders

People have several options available to them as to where they put their money. They invest in the securities – the equity or debt instruments – of organizations to have profit making and cash generating prospects that, over time, should offer better returns than they could obtain elsewhere. Therefore, the CEO is responsible for generating earnings for the shareholder greater than the proverbial "lil' old lady from Dubuque" can realize from her bank savings account, CDs or other low risk investments. There are vast varieties of investment instruments against which you as the CEO can measure your success in this regard, ranging from Treasuries to Junk Bonds to those available in Start-up ventures. An essential objective is to provide your investors a return notably higher than inflation. In this regard, it is interesting to note that one Dollar invested in the 1982 market is worth today, in terms of purchasing power. Fifty cents. Thus, the CEO should set business goals needed to realize a base stock price increase of at least the anticipated annual inflation rate just to maintain the shareholders' purchasing power.

The Chief Executive Officer also is accountable for enhancing the asset value of the company. These assets include the organization's management capabilities. This is required to ensure that the business is conducted in an honest and ethical manner, and for making sure, that periodic information due the shareholders is accurate, reflecting the full and true account of current business activities. This element of transparency should be well beyond the general nature of government and industrial association reporting requirements. The data should reflect clearly what you believe to be right, the same information on which you and your family would depend.

The leader also is accountable for ensuring all parties that the company's money is spent in a sensible, frugal manner. He or she is expected to control the spending of company funds, and the assumption of debt, as if it was his own money. However, given the values of inhabitants of the executive suite of companies in recent past years, such as Enron, WorldCom, Tyco International, ImClone, Adelphia, Dynegy and the Madoff group – to name only a few, one truly becomes skeptical if past values of trust have not been lost. If you are the type of person justifying the trust of your shareholders, employees, customers, suppliers and others you must re-think matters of morals and ethics, and reflect the higher values in all for which you are accountable. The era in which "My word is my bond" has not ended. It just needs good people to restore it.

Security "buy backs," spin offs and some acquisitions, varying dividend actions (defined as "policies"), changes in incentive compensation practices, Board members' inertia, inattention to the media, etc., all relate to shareholders' interests. These subjects will be covered in subsequent Chapters. However, suffice at this point to say that you will be "above Caesar's Wife" in matters of ethics and trusts in such matters.

A word concerning dividends at this point is appropriate. The idea was current during the final decades of the Twentieth Century that the payment of dividends was a policy for the corporate weak of heart. This view was not based solely on the change in U.S. Federal tax policy that made share "buy-backs" more attractive than dividend payments. Managements long have thought that it is far better to plough back funds into the business than to distribute funds as dividends. However, research[1] in recent years indicates that this premise just doesn't wash. This is demonstrated by merely dividing a company's earnings yield (the inverse of the Price-Earnings Ratio) into the dividend yield and the retained earnings yield. For example, between 1950 and 1960 – dealing with somewhat dated information – U.S. firms traded on an earnings yield of 15.8%, consisting of a dividend yield of 8.8% and a retained earnings yield of 7.0%. Assuming that the cash the companies retained was put to work profitably, the real dividend growth rate at least should equal the retained earnings yield. However, the only decade in which this occurred was in the 1960s when a retained earnings yield of 2.6% translated into real dividend growth of 2.8%. In the 1950s, a retained earnings yield of 7.0% generated real dividend growth of 2.6%. In the 1970s, the returns respectively were 2.8% and (1.3)%. In the 1980s, they were 8.4% and 1.8%, and in the 1990s, 3.3% and 1.3%.

Why didn't the expected happen? It seems, not unlike our politicians, when executives have cash – retained earnings – they want to do "something" with it. "With it" translates to making acquisitions, buying back securities, investing in new projects, expanding into new marketing or research areas, etc. However, on average – at least historically – it appears that these investments do not realize anticipated returns. In spite of double taxation, etc., my advice would be for you to interrogate your finance people thoroughly before discounting the shareholder value of paying dividends. There must be some reasons, other than sharing the wealth that GE, Merck Alcoa, Air Products, ExxonMobil and smaller companies such as Amerigas continue to pay dividends.

Looking at a company's shareholder populations, make shareholder structuring part of your strategic plan. It is my experience that few corporate leaders give proper attention to the makeup of their shareholding population; a population when business problems occur (and they will), may

---

[1] Research by Mr. James Montier of Dresdner Kleinwort Wasserstein.

lead to potential challenges accompanied by a considerable expenditure of time. As the CEO of a publicly traded company, consider the proportional composition of shareholders according to their respective interests. You'll have opportunities to adjust this makeup each time you put forth a public offering, a secondary, a buy back, a convertible issue, etc. Such a strategic plan also will provide you a good guide to riding herd over your investment bankers and underwriters when offerings are being structured.

Employees

First off, let's define terms. By employee, I mean men and women whose contributions are compensated by the hour, the week or the month, who do not have supervisory or management roles. They may be of high skill levels, perhaps the highest skill levels, but they are not accountable for managing other individuals.

Every time I discuss "employees", I recall the expression of Newton[2], "To every action there always is an equal and opposite reaction." His expression related to science, specifically to the motion of particles. However, in my opinion, it also describes well the history of industrial labor relations. A history on which you, as the future CEO, should constantly reflect and keep in mind in dealing with your people.

In the 1880s to 1900s in the United States, corporate management largely considered the people who worked for them, and, incidentally, helped make America the world's manufacturing powerhouse that it was to become, as mere assets. With the possible exception of owner-managers such as Henry Ford, executives looked at their workers not unlike plant and equipment. Hours of work and the relatively meager pay for such labor meant little, the "more for less" being the mantra of the times.

---

[2] *Philosophiae Naturalis Principia Mathametica*, Sir Isaac Newton, July 5, 1687

Eventually, a reaction set in. Many workers began to assert themselves, realizing after some time that group action on their part was the only way to change the inequities of the labor environment. These were terrible periods for the workers. Battles occurred in which many were disabled, even killed. However, the groups formed unions of labor. They exercised their power – sometimes considered illegal –and engaged in strikes, crippling industrial output, and, more importantly, establishing a long-term division between labor and management–an equal and opposite reaction. Admittedly, applying hindsight, had the 19th Century U.S. owner-managers considered and resolved the Law of Unintended Consequences, there is a strong likelihood that ensuring corporate loyalties and pride could have resulted in a team mentality between management and employees that could have led to continued world dominance by leading U.S. manufacturing companies.

Your job is to use your head and exercise sound judgment to overcome the current entitlement mentality, and to "bring back" yesteryear in terms of individual values and ethics, if not for industrial America, then for your own organizations.

I don't think it's any surprise to you, but it's something you must constantly remember, that your people work for different things. They are not all inspired as are you for continued challenges and advancement. Some work merely to "get out of the house." Some work for the wages involved; some, indeed, for the pride they have to do a good job, but consider of equal importance, time spent – sometimes considered as "quality time" – outside the office or the plant. Your job is to obtain the highest possible productivity from these people and concurrently burnish their self-respect and pleasure in putting forth labor in an organization that honors and acknowledges their contribution to its success. Loyalty is important and considered a valuable contribution to the success of the organization.

Fortunately, executives like Mr. Warren Buffett, who represent the best of executive and investment talent, value and ethics, exist who provide us examples for our own development and future success.

Again, the employees' interest benefits from the <u>selfishness</u> of the true leader. If the leader, in our case the CEO, accomplishes his or her self-centered interests and success, more jobs and advancement opportunities will develop for the company's employees. However, too often this is not happening in current corporate actions. In today's business world we see abundant evidence of the results of reportedly "concerned" and/or "caring" senior executives who, as soon as their failures of vision and planning become apparent, furlough or discharge employees with little warning or compensation all in the name of "restructuring." For these reported "sound management practices," Boards of Directors continue to support the Chairman, will be fairly and equitably treated, that job security is ensured to the extent that the individual performs well and shareholders' interest is protected, and that the employee is brought into the picture and kept informed of matters of interest to them and to their families. Those within the organization who strive for improvement and advancement must understand that compensation is merit-based and that <u>everyone</u> in this regard will be treated fairly.

To repeat, incompetent, uncaring and, yes, unselfish managements in the past have brought on a major threat to continued industrial progress. Government intervention and trade labor union movements, which now represent more of a political party than a help to America's working men and women, have taken hold and gained increased power on the industrial scene; filling a vacuum that poor management historically created. A most unfortunate consequence of these occurrences has been the intervention of politicians whose ignorance of business and related economics are legend. They increasingly stumble all over themselves, taking failing actions against business all for gaining votes and financial rewards.

These past poor management practices have opened the door to such politically-motivated constraints as the Fair Employment Practice Act, the Sherman Antitrust Act, the National Labor Relations Board, the Security & Exchange Commission, the Glass-Steagall Act, the Social Security Act, regulations on project contract awards, many activities of the Internal Revenue Service and related laws and regulations controlling business and industry. All are cumbersome, time-consuming and expensive. We as business executives brought these issues on ourselves, providing the politicians the power that has harmed American business. However, as witnessed by the corporate graft, theft, bribery, etc., during this past decade or so, we only continue to dig the grave deeper.

President and/or CEO, in many cases increasing his incentive compensation payments for allegedly taking these "constructive actions". These executives strictly are "fair weather" executives who are unable or unwilling to meet and overcome the challenges of adversity, and, what is worse, they are protected by Boards that are equally risk averse.

Returning to the subject of loyalty, the leader has an important responsibility in developing and maintaining this aspect of sound employee relations. The leader or CEO accomplishes this by indicating clearly and continuously that he or she and their senior management respect the employee. By this, I don't mean a Christmas Eve tour through the offices or the plant to shake hands, although in the absence of something of greater value, at least this act is helpful. I do mean an honest awareness of the employee who, not unlike yourself, from time to time harbors a non-company related problem that requires your attention and honest concern. You and your management must become familiar with your employees in the same manner discussed earlier regarding your major shareholders and customers.

You must provide employment stability to the greatest of your ability. You, as the emerging business leader, must demonstrate respect for the skills and contribution – and ideas – of the people. This also includes affording them the best working conditions and your confidence in them, trusting them to perform the work as you have permitted them to understand it, and in keeping them informed. To continue to reemphasize what by this time should have become obvious, no one should endure surprises. This aspect of business practices applies to your employees as much as to your shareholders, Board members, customers or clients and management. A quarterly meeting with the employees, something akin to a "fireside chat," by you will go far to meeting this requirement as well as strengthen loyalty.

Like it or not, there's also a senior mentor or even that of a "father figure" that frequently goes with the job of leader. You may be asked from time to time to provide counsel, and you should do so. As the 360° executive, you will evidence awareness that you and your managers are concerned about your people. Perhaps it is a hackneyed expression, but you should reflect that, in a professional, job-related way, you are "family." However, on the other hand, you should never impose – or give the impression of desiring to impose – on the free time of your executives or employees. I always remember people who had experienced being laborers in the Detroit, Michigan, manufacturing era of the 1920s and 1930s recalling when asking an individual what he did the response was "I'm an Ford man," not a welder, not a member of the UAW-CIO, not simply a worker, but "a Ford man." You could do far worse as a leader than striving to gain this type of relationship with your employees.

The only thing that sets you apart as the CEO from your managers and employees is your accountability for certain senior responsibilities and, perhaps your senior career goals. Aside from these things, you will remember – and show it – that you are no better than anyone else in your organization. You, like everyone else "put your pants on, one leg at a time." Keep your ego in check. I realize that you will have much to do, but in your relationships with the employees, a productive idea is to have some form of quarterly or annual meeting, bringing management and employees together. Perhaps, this could be an annual affair with an awards ceremony prior to the annual shareholders' meeting – maybe including Board members. However, as reflected earlier, don't start something that you do not intend to continue forever – in bad times as well as good.

Should your employees necessarily become shareholders? It may provide the leader a degree of comfort and pleasure – read ego enhancement – to know that employees are buying the company's stock. However, I have found that this is a personal matter, a decision left entirely to the employee. Also, if your securities are to be included in pension plan investment or funding, they should, at most, represent a minor part of the plan's investment.

Management
_____

By my definition, "management" encompasses all individuals responsible for assigning and supervising the work of others. As the CEO, you are accountable for the selection and development of key executives as well as their managers and supervisors. The manner in which you organize to carry out this work and the strategic direction of the company will be addressed later. However, suffice to say now, you don't adopt a certain type of organization and then slot your people in it. Organizations are dynamic. If they are not changing, the business is not growing.

Contrary to the comfort of many leaders, you, as the CEO, do not want executives who agree with you without valid purpose. Most "yes" men are so either because they believe agreement garners them favor in the leader's eyes or they are too lazy to do the analysis and identify conclusions and recommendations that are of value even though such disagree with the leader's ideas. Diversity of background also is of value and, if experience and talent are present, should be given attention. However, the executive group should be ground in similar values, certainly in ethics and morals. These should include basic agreement and support for the free enterprise system, the free market, a merit-based philosophy, a strong, focused work ethic, family values, respect for the opinions of others, the value of time (both theirs and others), and the respect for being smart rather than clever.

Objectivity coupled with clear, comprehensive vision and independent thinking is key to business success. Effective decision-making cannot be accomplished without these factors. These characteristics should be a part of each of your senior executives, and should be mandatory in all individuals you slate for higher responsibilities. These traits also are required in the people in firms that your company retains for out-sourcing duties, e.g., auditors, consultants, investment and commercial bankers, legal firms, etc. Given the degree of familiarity that often occurs between inside and outside people, you should ensure that such firms providing outside assistance are rotated frequently, assuming, of course, that such organizations chosen for rotation are equally competent.

By your own attitude and practices advise your key people that, being an independent-thinking organization, such things as industrially-accepted (or politically-accepted) standards of acceptability or of performance are not good enough for your company. I refer specifically as examples, to GAAP, FASB and similar "Standards." Your acceptance of results and integrity are geared to measurements well within these criteria; your measurements being tailored to your company's specific industry, methods of operations, changing global business environment, etc. It is your responsibility to ensure that outside auditors and legal advisors are aware of this and are qualified to provide such service.

A point concerning your personal working relationships: Consider retaining outside professional management relations counsel. This type of expertise is invaluable in checking your personal effectiveness – and that of your senior people – in working with each other. I have found this type of assistance keeps egos in check and identifies relationship problems for solution before they become barriers. Your key physician acquaintance, described earlier, could be helpful in identifying such counsel for your consideration.

The Board of Directors

You, as the CEO, are beholden to the Board of Directors. While Chapter V addresses the specifics and the challenges of this CEO-Board relationship, as a "basic" it is important now for you to recognize that the Board is not a "self-standing, self-motivating, all seeing organization" as one might conclude from the media, books, film, etc. You, as the CEO (or the organization's leader), are responsible for the effectiveness of this group. You ensure that its members receive required information in a timely and comprehensive manner, that recommendations concerning vacancies are provided and encouraged in advance of needs, that management discipline and the awareness of the importance of time is recognized, and that they become familiar with your plans – operational, organizational, executive development and business changes – so that their deliberations most favorably influence the company's future.

Bankers

The CEO is responsible to ensure that the most qualified banks – both commercial and investment banks – are chosen to serve the company, that they are aware of the nature of the company's business and that they are kept sufficiently informed to provide optimum and timely service.

A couple of points concerning banks and financial positions: First, as to banks–borrow before you need it. This includes establishing and maintaining lines of credit. Settle for attractive, not "ego busting" credit ratings. For example, currently interest rates investors are paying for an S&P AAA-rated debt issues are only slightly less that AA+. This minor delta is prevalent in most other evaluations within investment rated issues. Hence, while remaining above Investment Grades, be wary of paying for more than you need. Second, in terms of your financial structure of your Balance Sheet, don't be so conservative regarding the company's debt capacity that you expose being acquired, the payment being based on using your company's own debt capability.

Community

Be certain that the characteristics of the community or communities in which your company operates are consistent and compatible with the company's long-term interest and its people's values. Too many organizations continue to remain in an area in which either they or the community has outlived their respective usefulness. Community environments change. You must ensure that these changes, such as tax and fiscal issues, labor relations, the labor pool, politically based restrictions, services, educational availability and quality, resources and the overall life style, are anticipated and plans are in place for their resolutions. Also, ensure that no commitments are made to communities that are not compatible with the interests of your company, and are not well within your most conservative operating plans – time wise – for the area.

Stay out of politics or politically based actions unless it clearly is within the strategic interests of the company.

<u>Altruism and Other Related Considerations</u>

As referenced earlier, among the most positive contributions a CEO can make to all of this various audiences is to pursue a policy of unqualified <u>selfishness</u>. People and communities of value don't want to be helped. They want opportunity. Obviously, this policy must be implemented within reason. If situations occur in which the public, through no fault of its own, faces crises, assistance must be provided. However, this assistance is to be measured and controlled, insuring desired results are obtained. A "good word" is not a sufficient reason for company time or funds being expended.

Unless you are the leader of a not-for-profit, charity-based organization or a company engaged in related products or services, stay away from "causes" and their implications. Should the company's shareholders or employees – or the CEO's spouse, wish to spend time and/or money on such matters; it certainly is their right to do so. However, to emphasize, unless solid results can be identified and factually supported that will favorably affects the company's "bottom line" (including market share, cash flow, its EBIT, employee development, etc.) within a reasonable period of time, say a couple of years, forget it. Experience has shown that even with these criteria, enough altruistic issues will get through management perusal, unfortunately, to provide a good citizen impression to the cause-oriented public. With these failings, "the fat is in the fire." You can expect further contacts, seeking the same benefits. Recall, again, "don't start something, you don't intend to do forever".

<u>Your Public Image versus Your Private (Strategically Productive) Self</u>

The selection of a "celebrity CEO" frequently can work wonders regarding share price. However, the longer term value to the company – and its securities, unless the person's experience and management skills equal his or her celebrity status, is questionable. This point well may answer the question as to why so many companies experienced trouble in the post-1980s era during which time few of the executives "on their way up" faced and overcame adversity. Without experiencing and overcoming problems – often "game breaking" problems, few individuals have the background to succeed in business over the long term. It's interesting to note that in recent, typical years, between 120 and 200 CEO openings occurred in the largest 1,000 companies, the vast majority being due to normal retirements. Roughly, one-third of the replacements came from outside these organizations. Fortunately, you, while possibly having some celebrity status and charismatic features, are a serious, goal-oriented business leader.

Also, the career path to becoming a CEO has changed. In the past management usually controlled the succession process. The new CEO normally was promoted from within, usually the choice being the outgoing incumbent with the agreement of the Board (which, in many cases, also had been chosen by the CEO). The change that has occurred largely has been the result of changes in the stockholding composition, and to no small degree increased shareholder activism. For example, in the 1950s less than 10% of U.S. common equities were owned by institutional investors (of the type earlier described). Today, such investor organizations hold over half outstanding common shares. In the 1980s, as corporate profits declined, the major intuitional investors acted to dislodge management groups, which were seen as entrenched, self-satisfied and underperforming. These institutional investors, joined by others, became increasingly active in financing leveraged buyouts by private equity firms and replaced previous managements, people who mishandled adversity. As states enacted anti-takeover laws, the focus of these investors shifted to the boards of directors.

Among the early so-called charismatic executives was Mr. Lee Iacocca. He was given credit, a considerable amount self-declared, for "saving Chrysler." Few media and fewer people acknowledged the fact that his efforts were supported by $2 Billion federally guaranteed loans provided to bailout the company nor the significant United Auto Workers' (UAW) givebacks to protect its political interests. The image of the CEO gained traction during this period from an image of a capable business planner and administrator to an ego-driven, well publicized, flamboyant individual; one often with grandiose, political ambitions. In the past two decades many (not all) businesses have attempted to redefine themselves. The objective became less the apparently profane task of making money to one involved in well publicized goals of creating vision, mission, changed directions, etc.; the corporate officers identified by the media as recognized leaders even as their companies were going down the drain. The evidence of the results now is well known.

Dr. Max Weber, the noted German sociologist, indicates that charisma and rationality cannot coexist. Mr. Jack Welch, the former leader of General Electric, was another charismatic, 20th Century, ego-driven Chairman and CEO. However, it has now been acknowledged that the well-publicized "Eighty consecutive quarters of earnings improvements" could not have been realized without taking into account some accounting liberties. There is little proof of a stable "CEO effect" in this situation as some writers termed it. In most cases the person at the top, in spite of all the publicity, matters much less than the impact of relevant business conditions If conditions are favorable, as often is the case between periodic financial crises, the CEO can claim business success. However, if conditions are not favorable, it usually is reported as totally due to the adverse market environment. One seldom hears of the failure of the celebrity CEO in these instances to anticipate such conditions and consequently to weather the storm successfully.

Charisma can be bulletproof. By definition, it is impervious to rationality. Even so, charismatic authority is a precarious, profoundly vulnerable thing. In fact, allegiance to charismatic leaders is antithetical to an open society in which most companies operate. The somewhat atavistic corporate quest for charismatic CEOs, a fashion supported my several major executive recruiting firms in the past two three decades, with its deference to the personality and so called vision of particular individuals, comes with considerable risks of abuse, misconduct and incompetence, particularly over the long term; a period seldom realized.

An interesting perspective on the factors involved in the selection and grooming of a CEO can be obtained in reviewing the ATT situation in 1997. This involved a Board of Directors, Messrs. Armstrong, Zeglis, Allen, et al and a major U.S. executive recruiting firm. It also brings into focus the impact of earlier government intervention. All in all, a point of interesting reality.

Obviously, every organization and environment is different. The reputation, culture and market image of a company sometimes rest on the name and/or background of the founder, and previous senior officers. This is true particularly in some start-up or merger situations that may benefit from the identity and public visibility of, for example, a well-known, well-regarded investor or their firm. In other instances, companies of long standing and possessing successful histories, including withstanding crisis environments, do not require such "personality" identifications to standout.

Charisma may avail some leaders an edge, but it doesn't compare to the experience and management skills they require for long-term success. Evaluate now, as you proceed on your career path the pros and cons of strengthening your personal image beyond that of a professional, merit-oriented, successful manager. Challenges in leading a company can come in many forms from many directions. For example, the unfavorable impact of problems – implied or real – made public by a divisive Board, a potential hostile takeover, hiccups in product quality, the release of a "Kiss and Tell" publication, all may be lessened or eliminated if the CEO has a well-known, previously established, favorable image. However, your objective in possibly developing or strengthening a public persona is to make available to your various publics your abilities as a serious, experienced, broad gauged, ethical business executive. It is not for advancing your ego or your popularity. An applicable Chinese adage is "One who is full of oneself often is an empty vessel." Also, permit us to be frank. Such a public role may not be in keeping with your character. Let's not waste time trying to be someone we're not when we have much more of value to sell. In this regard, remember that your key objective as a business leader in a successful enterprise that will live far beyond your career years. Thus, your goal is a company which success is attributed to its advanced products and services, its market position, its continued financial strength, its ethical and moral character and your successors' capabilities – not your personal identity.

As business success justifies media attention, let your key people stand in the spot light; let them get the recognition. If problems or failures occur, you take the heat. I would refer you to James Burke, the Chairman of Johnson & Johnson who in the 1980s publicly handled the Tylenol product poison challenge personally – and very effectively. He assumed the blame for inadequate measures, and, by doing so, further strengthened the morale and cohesiveness of his management organization and the image of his company. You might note J&J's position today.

You Set the Pace and the Standards

As in every organization or group, each has a "character" or a "culture." Just as in outstanding military organizations, the dedicated, courageous leader leads, so it is in business. The CEO establishes or maintains the character and culture of the company, sets the standards and becomes the example. You will want strong, self-initiative oriented individuals as managers; confident people who are comfortable with change and willing to take reasonable risks – people who clearly operate "outside the box." Treat them that way. Compensate them well. Personally and frequently, acknowledge their participations and the contributions of their families. We will consider incentive compensation and the plans required to make it practical and reasonable in a later Chapter. However, as a guide in this regard, incentive compensation must be a highly significant portion of the executive's total compensation if it is to be a true incentive. The payout must apply to more than one or two years to make it truly of strategic worth.

You company is not a benevolent organization. Executives are compensated well, based on their strategic contributions to the company and to its shareholders. Thus, think long and hard before considering such so called "perks" as company furnished automobiles, business and first class air transportation, executive (and Board) monetary "advances" or loans, country (or city) club memberships and dues, sports event "boxes" or tickets, the ownership or use of corporate jets, and so forth. Paternalism is for groups that want to be comfortable and dependent on others – people who depend on "entitlements." What you want, and the type of people you want to attract and develop, are hard driving, no nonsense, objective thinking, merit-oriented, take-no-prisoners, independent executives. Don't permit policies to seep in which detract from this objective, notwithstanding what other organizations may do. In this sense, remember that your team takes its lead from you. A solid, constructive rule is to treat time and expenditures of company funds as you do your own. For example, do your personnel during vacations fly other than economy class. Do they reside at 4 or 5-star hotels? Do they or their families "wine and dine" at 3-Star restaurants? This answer is no and neither should they – or you – do so on the job. However, if they do, perhaps you have the wrong people working for you. Actions such a frugality and direct, constructive focus on your job, surprisingly will garner attention by people who count, because so few of your competitors sail on this same course.

You, progressing to your career goal to become a CEO, set the pace. Your purpose in the successful achievement and perpetuity of the organization. Anything that does not relate directly to that purpose is irrelevant. Leave publicity, affectation and ostentation to such as the film actors, fashion "leaders," and "taking heads" that depend on tabloids for their careers or to others who have little else for which to live. Ostentation brings problems: Customers and clients will resent their monies being spent frivolously, and will lose respect for you and your company if such occurs. Vendor, witnessing this behavior, quickly will get the idea that they can charge you a tad more for supplies and equipment. Conversely, this is an example of a culture you should consider in selecting a company for your career.

A final word about "Luck." You make your own. The better prepared you are, the more observant and sensitive you are to opportunities. The harder you work, the luckier you'll be.

A major word of caution: The first two months or so after you become the CEO – the leader; be particularly sensitive to what you do, how you do it, and to whom. This is especially true if you are coming in from outside the organization. You'll want to retain your senior executives until you decide on a separation. You will want this to be your decision, not theirs. Some of these people believe deeply, as do their families, that they should have been named to the top job. Some others possibly will take a "wait and see" attitude to determine the cut of your jib. Many questions, some asked and some implied, will influence the "executive suite" until they understand and appreciate your direction, methods, management style, etc. Don't expect universal agreement immediately. This will take time, as you prove to your senior people why you got the job. You should anticipate that, even given day-to-day contact, this would require at least two months or so. Don't hurry the process by other than your normal leadership way of managing things.

* * *

Chapter Summary: The information in this Chapter marks in some ways the transition of the executive to the accountability of one who has assumed the CEO's responsibilities, i.e., in addresses those still "on the way" career wise and those that "have arrived." It stresses accountability versus responsibility, it identifies the CEO's principal audiences and suggests how each should be treated, it emphasizes the importance of impressions – good and bad – as one moves along in his or her career of setting oneself apart all along the way, and when you arrive.

Chapter V

The Board and the CEO: It's Your Job To Make it Work

Yes, the CEO reports to the Board, specifically to its Chairman. Yes, the principal job of the Board is to represent the shareholders. This is fine and provides a good explanation when one is engaged in drafting Corporate Governance 101. However, make no mistake about it, the strength and effectiveness of the Board in large measure rests with you, the Chief Executive Officer.

If you examine Boards closely, you are struck by the number of CEOs sitting on them. One also is struck, particularly in larger corporations, by how many of the Directors on Boards are senior executives of very well-known organizations and surprised, as further analysis indicates, how many Board's on which these people sit. A requisite in this case is a minimum of four hours reading and studying the materials for each of from six to eight Board meetings annually, reflecting on past performance and considering these data vis-à-vis the company's strategic plan. Also, there's the strategic plan itself, plus the 10-Ks and 10-Qs, a couple of site visits and a shareholders' meeting annually to consider; let alone the occasional "special" or "executive" meeting and Board Committee meetings. Simple mathematics suggests that this all translates, in the most efficient terms, to roughly a month a year for a Director to serve on a single Board. This is in addition to the time required to lead – hopefully successfully – his or her own company.

Now, who interfaces with the Board in the interim? Who usually sets the board agendum and the meeting schedule? Who ensures that the Board meetings data are well organized provided the Directors in a timely fashion (say, two weeks prior to a Board or Committee meeting) and is FACTUAL and OBJECTIVE? Who keeps the Directors apprised of events that could affect the company and its future? Who leads in identifying individuals you might be prospects for future Board membership? Who makes the final review of the Board minutes and other material for distribution to the Board? To these, and many other Board-related questions, the answer is YOU. In fact, contrary to what some others in the public, the government or academic institutions may espouse, the Chief Executive Officer is the "stem-winder" that makes the Board effective and sets the course for the organization, including its standards, values, future direction, etc. This in addition to everything else for which the CEO is responsible, including managing the corporation, developing individuals, husbanding and acting as the senior steward of its assets, and meeting the payroll.

It is a good bet that you, as the Chief Executive Officer, could "inherit" your Board of Directors. This is true particularly if you are brought in from the outside. This is a more difficult situation than would be the case if you were engaged in a start-up, but it isn't all bad, and depends on your predecessor and, should there be one other than yourself, the Chairman.

In essence, your Board of Directors should be qualified to be your advisor and counselor. To perform these very important tasks the individual Directors must possess successful, currently ongoing leadership experience and have the spirit, energy and enthusiasm to support you and your management team to achieve success. Above all, they must possess sound judgment. While you don't want advice based on cutting corners or engaging in illegal, unethical or inappropriate practices, you don't want Directors who are risk adverse. Also, they should accept their roles as individuals and be diligent in keeping informed; an activity for which you will be significantly responsible. And, as aforementioned, even though currently carrying out their own senior executive responsibilities, they should have time to fulfill their Director's duties. You should not have to worry about quorums inasmuch as the Board meetings, etc. schedules will be established well in advance (six months would not be considered too early).

These are among the criteria you will seek in the Board. I mean YOU will seek in the Board. Again, in spite of so-called "Conventional Wisdom," as the company's Chief Executive Officer (whether or not you also are its Chairman), you personally are the individual that will expect the most and get the most out of your board. If you fall back to await happenings, you will not be the executive you think you are. Specifics regarding what you will want in your Directors on the Board (Qualifications) and what you want your Board to do (Responsibilities) are outlined in Appendices 'F' and 'G.' Given experience that indicates that you as the CEO in fact will be largely responsible for the success of the Board, these qualifications and responsibilities may differ from those provided by other, more formal sources.

Properly shaped and managed, the Board becomes the CEO's whetstone. He increasingly uses it to sharpen his vision and strategic direction. In this context, the relationship become as a hand and glove. Through constant nurturing, the Board becomes an active, continuous catalyst, eventually becoming enthusiastic in being used for this constructive purpose.

As much benefit as in formal Board meetings is the interim counseling, the CEO obtains in one-on-one "luncheon" counseling. In fact, given the differences in individual Director's traits, some prefer the confidential environment of such closeness to the openness of the Board meetings to achieve such ends.

Changes in Board membership undoubtedly will be necessary. However, caution is needed. Some aspects of the Board should be "Grandfathered." For example, changes in the number of members, qualifications, age and/or status for retirement, the number of other Board seats already occupied by a Director, shareholder status and compensation can be made, but probably will not affect present members. To keep the Directors' interest and attention – and to keep you apprised of their thinking – Board prospects should be reviewed with them annually.

They should be expected to identify prospects, but the drive to do so probably will require you to put forward some possibilities.

You will be the sole interface between the Board and the Company's management. You will be solely responsible for management or executive contacts with the Directors. While the company's General Counsel, may act as the Secretary to the Board and provide legal advice for which he or she is qualified and upon being requested, they are not a Board member. As with other management members of the company, they have no direct contact with the Directors except through you. Assuming you are the company's President and Chief Executive Officer, there will be no other member of management except you on the Board of Directors (this assumes the Chairman is an independent Director, not a member of the company's management). This is not a "Grandfathered" situation.

Regardless of whether you inherit a Board or have the opportunity to help establish one from the beginning, the first thing you must do is "grab the helm." You must be capable of articulating clearly and concisely the direction in which you plan to take the company, what alternatives or options you are considering and, in approximate terms, the time and investment involved. This will be the first occasion in which you may encounter head winds from the Board or, if not you, the Chairman. However, if you are to do the job, you must prevail. You, in addition to the foregoing, are the connection between the advisors on the Board and the managers of the company. The vision of the organization's future is yours. While it may be challenged (and, if you have a good Board, probably will be), and may require some modification, it is still your course to set and carry out. This definitely is a game breaker. If you are not the skipper of this ship, move on.

The next thing to establish is the sanctity or objectivity of the company's strategic plan. This is the "bible," the single document outlining the future of the company and how it is to be achieved (see Chapter VI). This document is to be reviewed and approved annually by the Board. Everything of significance relating to the company's future development and success is set forth in this Plan, viz., the purpose and goals of each business activity, the objectives to be achieved, executive compensation, incentive award plans, the relationships with management, customers, employees, the unions, the financial community, the government and the corporate governance. The reference Chapter spells out all of this.

The review of the strategic plan dictates the schedule and timing of one of the Board of Directors' meetings. The critique of the 10-K, the 10-Qs and the annual report (and shareholders' annual meeting) determines the timing of an additional five or six meeting. In talking about Board meetings, I would suggest that one be scheduled sometime between mid-December and mid-January for the social purpose of bringing the Directors and their spouses together with the company's senior executives and their spouses. True, you will want to have your senior executives lead Board discussions from time to time relating to major projects, contracts, etc., for which these individuals are or will be responsible. However, on one occasion, at least, the spouses of these people, on who so much depends, should be provided the opportunity to socialize with the Board members, other senior executives and their spouses. To make these occasions meaningful and to ensure that all attendees appreciate that they are considered a part of the success of the organization, the agendum should include a review of the company, its performance and, in general, its plans.

You should engage the Board beyond the context of the periodic meetings. The idea of having them author draft papers intended for publication or reporting on the general tenor of competition in various areas of the company's business could be considered; things that bring them closer to the workings of the company and its management. However, this is a thin line; one that should be engaged cautiously because you don't want even to come close to giving the Directors the idea that they are participating in the management of the company. I have found that providing them articles about the industries in which the company is engaged, about competition, about related technologies or those which could be of interest vis-à-vis the company's strategic direction, and having them assess such data proves beneficial to achieving desired Director-Management closeness. These approaches also tend to excite the more reticent members to engage more in deliberations and decision-making.

As to the size of the Board and the number of Board Committees, I believe the general idea of the fewer the better. Considering the Board of a mature company, I believe the number of Directors should be limited to a maximum of nine, including the Chairman. Why no more than nine? The reason, not in any order of importance, first is economy. We will address the costs later in the chapter, but you want to concentrate on quality, and in today's market – discounting the exorbitant and asinine millions of dollars in an Executive's compensation – it is not beyond the pale that a qualified Director will cost between $75,000 and $100,000 in an annual fee (2009 Dollars), plus D&O liability Insurance, travel expenses, possible supplementary staff expenses, etc. Second, experience has shown that a fewer number frequently avoids the "informal group leader" syndrome. In other words, one hopes to people the Board with individuals who think for themselves, exercise independence in their counsel and decision-making, and bring to deliberations their own, personal backgrounds and experience, regardless of the relative corporate rank of the Board's membership. The fewer number tends to encourage each Director to think and act on his or her own, not hiding behind someone else for whatever reason and exhibiting "me-to-ism." Seven or nine members also assure in most instances an effective quorum. Third, numbers beyond this often become unwieldy. You must establish and maintain contact with the Directors in the interim between meetings. This can become a time consuming effort. Also, the more Directors you have the more tendencies there is for "block action," an addendum to "me-to-ism." Seven to nine well-informed, conscientious individuals with diverse management experience are capable of identifying most matters of Board and management interest. This relatively limited number of Directors also eliminates the need for an Executive Committee of the Board. In essence, the Board is the Executive Committee, and I believe will function more effectively with your direct, personal guidance and direction.

Speaking of an Executive Committee leads us to a discussion of the proposed Board Committees needed by a company in today's world. It's no great truism to say that it is not so much the number of committees as it is the manner in which they act, the independence they have and the judgment, objectivity and honesty of the members. I would advocate four Board Committees, i.e., the Audit Committee, the Finance (and Budget?) Committee, the Nominating Committee and the Compensation Committee.

Please recall the adage to which someone allegedly referred: You always can add something, but it's devilishly difficult to take something away. Incidentally, to provide continuity I would suggest that each Board Committee Chairman's term be for a minimum of three years. No Committee Chairman should Chair another Board Committee, and all Directors should participate on one or more Board Committees. Depending on backgrounds and experience, Committee Chairmanships should involve all members.

Don't let current events stampede you into doing something stupid. If you have good, honest, trusted people – it's up to you to make sure of this, all of the Ethics, Political Action, By-Laws, Governance and Policy Committees become superfluous. Bending somewhat to the apparent traits of some businesses, it should be accepted that the Audit Committee is the fulcrum of the Board's Committee structure.

The Audit Committee and its Chairman have <u>direct contact</u> with the company's outside auditing firm as well as the senior executive directly responsible for the company's internal auditing activity. This is an exception to the previously stated "management and executive contact" rule. To insure that you and your financial executive know what's going on, the Audit Committee Chairman will be responsible for keeping you apprised of what's going on but no one interferes with his or her direct contact with the auditors. The specific responsibilities of the Audit Committee, as well as those of the other committees, are well documented, and it is assumed that its Chairman has the experience to ensure that the annual audit program, etc., is well planned, conducted and controlled. Hence, we will not take space here for such specifics.

An important point: Nothing will happen about the business or the management about which the Board, in its entirety will not be advised within eight hours of its occurrence – preferably within less time than that. Also, while it seems understood, it needs emphasizing that no press release will be issued or other media entertained without prior knowledge given the Board, again in its entirety. Please notice there is no qualification, e.g., "material" happening, etc. The meaning is that <u>nothing</u> will occur without such relatively immediate advisory.

Here it's important to note that you should not be satisfied with assurances that your company is "being operated in line with generally accepted accounting principles (GAAP)" or any other "generally accepted" industry, SEC or legal criteria. Habits are hard to break and tough ones ever harder to establish, particularly when it effects compensation, but this is what you as the CEO must do. The Board's Audit Committee, the outside and internal auditors, you and your chief financial officer will operate well within anything required by Sarbanes-Oxley, forgetting "material" aspects; you will attain these goals for <u>all</u> aspects. In effect, as you have done throughout your career development, you will set yourself apart as a leader, bringing discipline and strict, unambiguous "cause and effect" results in all that your company, your Board, your management, your auditors and you do. Anticipate, for this example to be established, it's going to cost money. And forget the promised "secrecy of disclosure." In these matters, as a public company you will be operating with the government, and matters known to the government, SEC or otherwise, soon become public knowledge. If you and your management – for whom you are responsible – do your job correctly, you should harbor no concerns about providing the auditors a signed Management Representation Letter.

Digressing somewhat, and repeating a point made in an early chapter, I want to emphasize the importance of "accounting adjustments" and providing "earnings estimates" or "earnings guidance." As for adjustments, each one every quarter must be vetted by the outside auditor. This includes such items as status of contract revenues, costs, cash flow and EBIT, over or under retirement fund accruals, tax payment escrows and payments, etc. Again, forget "accepted industry practices." Stick to "cause and effect" in timing, amounts and administration.

As to providing earnings estimates, I don't know when or where this practice began, but DON'T. The securities market has financial analysts who supposedly know their business. Let them do their job. Even if they don't want to follow your company because you refuse to do their job for them, they'll have to due to the demands of the investors. This is very important. Publicizing earnings estimates leads to many things, most of them bad. One makes an estimate as to what is going to result in the next quarter, and everyone stretches actual results to make the company and the boss look good. Can it—don't make estimates.

Next, let's examine the makeup of an effective Board. First, the Directors should currently be engaged in senior executive roles in ongoing, successful companies. Second, for a number of reasons, all the individuals should be of relatively equal rank or status, preferably CEOs, presidents or executive vice presidents or equivalent of their organizations, depending on the size of the companies and their nature. Third, top financial, legal, operations and marketing experience should be represented. Fourth, while somewhat dependent on several factors, the age, health and available time of the Board member should permit him or her to serve for at least five years before mandatory Board retirement, say 62 years of age. Fifth, examining the company's strategic direction, if the plan is to take the organization in a different direction, say globally rather than domestic and/or technologically rather than commodities bent, experience in these areas should be considered, even if it results in expansion of the Board. Now, this well could be considered a "dream team." In all likelihood, it will require time to develop. However, as in the strategic plan, strategic considerations for the evolving Board are requisites.

A number of shareholder activist are running around making demands on the Boards and management of publicly owned companies. These demands, for the most part, strike for greater transparency, honesty, truthfulness, better management and stronger controls. Reasonable thought has been given most of these proposals. However, as usual, many are weak when it comes to considering unintended consequences, and evidence little understanding of what makes a company tick – successfully. Examples of these proposals range from requiring an independent (non-executive or non-management) Chairman of the Board to the shareholders having prior input on the retirement or termination payment of senior executives. Setting this spectrum of proposals aside, the one with which I strongly disagree relates to doing away with the "staggered" Board as relates to Board of Directors' election; the idea being when things don't go well, "throw the rascals – all of them – out."

A "staggered" Board, or Classes of Directors in the election scenario, however, makes considerable sense. The most important aspect is continuum or the availability of corporate knowledge. A Board of nine Directors, given retirements, illness, deaths, changing circumstances of the members, etc., will experience considerable – possibly total – turnover within a reasonable time. Also, during this period there will be significant changes in the senior executive cadre. If the entire Board can be voted in or out every year, little remains of the experiences of oversight and corrections existing previously. This is more than whistling in the dark. It is a fact. A "Staggered" Board is a most useful and valuable instrument in assuring that past mistakes are not repeated and that past lessons learned are constantly remembered.

Keep records. The other side of "ensure no surprises" and "keeping people – including you – informed," is "Gee, I didn't know that," and "No one told me about this." It's not a matter of obfuscation or faultfinding. In the majority of instances, it merely is our faulty memories. Everyone is busy. Thoughts conveyed, in the heat of ongoing activities, particularly nuances, often are lost or misconstrued. I have found that it is helpful for me and helpful for the Board Director to keep records of our exchanges, particularly between Board meetings where the minutes should accurately, if concisely, reflect what has and is transpiring, including the votes. Today e-mail probably is the best answer; the telephone and personal conversations probably the worst. If a telephone must be used, I record the conversation, advising the other party that such is being done confidentially and for our mutual benefit. If a personal conversation with a Director occurs, and if it is convenient, I have involved the company's General Counsel, or appropriate member of my Five Personal Advisors (see Chapter V), depending on the degree of confidentiality and the nature of the discussion. Trust is fundamental.

However, this fundamental is mandatory, or you or the Board member should not have your job.

Speaking of maintaining records, among the most important record between the CEO and the Board is the minutes of Board meetings. In the increasingly litigious environment between business and the Courts, the Board of Director minutes frequently are solicited to prove or disprove evidence of executives' irresponsibility or wrongdoing. Thus, as the CEO, one of your major Board-Management jobs is to ensure that the minutes accurately reflect deliberations of the Board regarding related management decisions.

In this process among the first things about which to be certain is that the minutes contain information concerning each topics on the Board meeting's agendum — no gaps. Minutes omitting references to applicable agendum topics, even the most inconsequential, lead only to inquiries. Returning to the previous discussion of Rudyard Kipling's "Six Servin' Men,' the topics described in the minutes should be concisely stated, addressing in cryptic terms (a) What was the subject?, (b) Why it was being addressed at this time?, (c) What were the positions (if such were taken), and their sources?, (d) Who voiced or voted for which?, (e) What were the anticipated results and/or impact, including values, risks, etc.?, (f) What was the proposed and agreed upon timeline for action and completion?, and who will be responsible for such action, follow-up, etc.? It is important that Directors abstaining or recusing be identified as well as their respective reasons.

All of these administrative specifics lead to a couple of cautions: One — Be certain both the agenda and the minutes are brief. Data must be sufficient to ensure comprehension by the Directors and responsible executives, but information beyond these basic data only can result in concentric circles in the pools of misunderstanding or misinterpretations, sometimes intentional. Two — inasmuch as the Directors will be responsible for approving the minutes, I suggest that the only notes taken carried from the meetings relating to Board matters be those of the Secretary to the Board; notes required to draft the related minutes. The Directors should resolve all understandings of information prior to the meeting's adjournment. No "loose ends" should exist.

The job of redacting these notes, drafting the minutes, and – subject to the CEO's review and approval – distributing them to the Directors is exclusively that of the Secretary to the Board who generally is the company's General (legal) Counsel.

The same process is applicable concerning such documents as the aforementioned, 10-K, 10-Q, annual report text and financials, etc. The idea again, is to stay way ahead of any official policy or shareholders' expectations in managing and controlling the activities of the company.

Should the Director be compensated other than his or her annual fee, and their Committee Chairman's or participant's fee? Should Directors participate in the company's bonus or incentive compensation plan? Should Board members be encouraged to be stockholders?

Should Board members, in fulfilling their Director's duties, follow the company's expense plan for its senior executives or should they be entitled to more senior level accommodations?

What about the expenses generated by their accompanying spouses? Should the company underwrite club memberships for its Directors? Should the company pay for the total D&O Liability Insurance, and other such benefits, for Directors?

Undoubtedly, for some, there are simple "yes" or "no" answers to these questions. However, these matters are more complex than they might first appear. The environment is the determining factor. You want – indeed, need – top quality advisors on your Board. There is considerable competition for such talent and experience, and, with increasing government intervention, there is a degree of reluctance on the part of many people to serve on Boards. As an aside, just look at our national government. There are many highly qualified, experienced individuals who would most effectively lead our national government, but the personal cost, liability and hassle in their estimation are too great.

Given the objectivity you seek in your Directors and the frailties of human nature, I do not advocate any part of the Director's compensation being dependent on the results of the company or the existences of the stock market. The Directors of the Board should be compensated for the use of their experience, judgment and intelligence, and the time given to the subject company's deliberations. The amount of this fee for Board membership, committee participation and leadership, etc., should be based partly on the size of the company, the complexity of operations and markets, and on competition for such talent in the marketplace. I believe that some form of retirement plan should be provided, that a monetary provision should be provided in instances of change or transfer of ownership, and that annual inflation adjustments incorporated in all fees and benefits (as with retirement and separation plans and life insurance provisions of subject executives).

The discussion thus far relates largely to ongoing, relatively well-established companies. What about situations involving "Start-up" situations?

The Start-up situation, in many ways, is unique. In other ways, quite similar to the CEO's job in an ongoing organization. The difference is largely time and timing. The person carrying out the leadership or co-leadership role in a start-up is a very busy individual. In many ways, I believe the term "multi-faceted" must have originated when someone first set out to describe the leader's role in a Start-up organization.

Start-ups can come in many types and hues. Some are based on a better product in an existing market (recall the maker of a better mousetrap?). They may involve an existing product, or a variety of such, for a new, or different market, or a new product for an existing market, or a new product for a new market, and so forth. They may consist of a service instead of a manufactured product, and with that, one can envision a plethora of possibilities.

Whatever the product or service, from a management standpoint the most difficult job involves a new idea, product or service, somewhat regardless of the market. Early on there's the business plan. The idea generators call him or her entrepreneur if you wish, must first make sure that their idea makes sense, will attract customers, be priced "right, and attract financers. Such original thinkers have much on their plate before they begin contemplating Boards of Directors. Among these challenges may well be one of convincing potential customers that they need this new idea, and worse yet, that it may cost something.

As a start-up advances from the idea generators to the next level, the business plan necessarily includes ideas of how much money will be necessary to get the product or service launched and still keep the proverbial wolf away from the entrepreneur's door until he or she, or they can begin generating enough money on which to live. Speaking of "time and timing," we now have seen several months pass, and our thinking is beginning to mature. First thought: This whole venture is going to require much more time than initially anticipated. This will become particularly evident if government involvement is required, Second thought (following closely on the heels of the first, if not tripping over them): This idea, as great as we believe it to be, is going to require more money than was first contemplated. Consequently, there is very little money available for other than test marketing, further product development and obtaining oversight in developing a saleable business plan.

Now, experience shows that even with the thinker's spouse or mother-in-law taking care of "the books," outside counsel from someone becomes necessary. This may evolve from the need for guidance concerning patents, copyrights and/or trademarks. It may relate to how "this thing" is to be priced, what after-sales service and/or maintenance will be needed, what guarantees will be necessary, and so forth. The operating word soon becomes "advisor," and I mean here someone beyond the people potential investors may have on the scene. Usually, as the entry script, advisors include an attorney, an accountant, "finders" to open the doors to prospective investors and possibly eventual customers.

An exigency becomes how to compensate these 'advisors?' Now, given the continuing scarcity of money, and the fact that such advisors seldom are available for the long term, one wants a compensation approach that does not involve money. One way is to an option grant or a similar award, the amount and timing depending on the nature and length of service provided. This could range from quite small to an equivalent of the amount paid the investor for the funds brought in. The exercise could be three to five years out.

Along in this process, for taxes, personal liability and other reasons, the originators of the new product, service, etc., probably would begin giving some thought to the manner of incorporation. Here's the first step in planning for a more permanent counseling approach that may entail a Board of Directors. A major decision point occurs about this time. Are the start-up creators intending to take this activity public, develop it to a certain level and then sell it, sell it before going through an IPO and the work that this will entail, or plan to develop it into a major, ongoing business, providing the management and direction for the strategic future?

"Not to rain on anyone's parade," but often – more frequently than anticipated – the talent required to develop a new product, to put together a new business, or even to turn around an ongoing business is different – frequently considerably different – than the experience and skills needed to strategically direct and manage an organization. It is wise to consider this challenge as one determines how he or she sees the start-up developing in the near future. As the entrepreneur gives thought to the composition of a Board of Directors, thought should be given the possibility of selecting one or more candidates who eventually could manage the business.

From this point onward, the challenges of the leader of the organization in terms of the Board of Directors, relationships, responsibilities, qualifications, etc., are not much different from those of the CEO in an ongoing, relatively mature business. Also, the Start-up leader possibly has the advantage of selecting his or her own Board, thus side stepping the challenges of dealing with an inherited body.

Speaking of maintaining records, as mentioned previously, among the most important record between the CEO and the Board is the minutes of Board meetings. In the increasingly litigious environment between business and the Courts, the Board of Director minutes frequently are solicited to prove or disprove evidence of executives' irresponsibility or wrongdoing. Thus, as the CEO, one of your major Board-Management jobs is to ensure that the minutes accurately reflect deliberations of the Board regarding related management decisions.

All of these administrative specifics lead to a couple of cautions: One – Be certain both the agenda and the minutes are brief. Obviously, data must be sufficient to ensure comprehension by the Directors and responsible executives, but information beyond these basic data only can result in concentric circles in the pools of misunderstanding or misinterpretations, sometimes intentional. Two – inasmuch as the Directors will be responsible for approving the minutes, I strongly suggest that the only notes taken during the meetings relating to Board matters be those of the Secretary to the Board; notes required to draft the related minutes. Relating to these cautions is the aphorism that "One should not cut corners, should not make assumptions and should not stick one's nose in other people's business."

The job of redacting these notes, drafting the minutes, and – subject to the CEO's review and approval – distributing them to the Directors is exclusively that of the Secretary to the Board who generally is the company's General (legal) Counsel.

The same process is applicable concerning such documents as the aforementioned, 10-K, 10-Q, annual report text and financials, etc. The idea again, is to stay way ahead of any official policy or shareholders' expectations in managing and controlling the activities of the company.

* * *

Chapter Summary: Your Board of Directors essentially is what you make of it. Its integrity, ability to provide you effective counsel and to act efficiently on behalf of the shareholders depends of the time and dedication you – the

CEO – devote to it. Forget the "conventional wisdom." While not being acknowledged as such, you are the skipper.

Chapter VI

The Strategic Plan: Commitment, Guide or Myth?

Whether or not it was recognized as such, we all have been immersed in the strategic planning process for some time. Our first impressions of this process could well have occurred during our pre-high school math or economics classes. It was termed "extrapolation." The two or three-point based extrapolation became so fixed in our minds that, when one spoke of looking into the future, many of the early strategic planning attempts merely involved projecting trends from the past.

While strategic planning should consider the past – to historic results, and involve attempts not to repeat past mistakes, our strategic planning must be based on specific goals, influenced by how we anticipate future events that may influence our plan – favorable or unfavorable. Don't be fooled. In preparation, the Strategic Plan may appear as only another mechanical process in the world of business directive, instructions, doctrine, laws, regulations, etc. However, as you get into it and realize the Plan's value, you will appreciate how essential it is to the success of the business and to your career.

The CEO's accountability for the success of the company has been mentioned earlier. An element of that success is his or her ability concerning vision, and this ability becomes an important aspect of strategic planning. Before proceeding further, you should consider the strategic plan as the "Bible," the "Koran," of your business. It may be taken as a guide for others, but for you it is a fundamental for the success of the endeavor. "Strategic" in the planning sense means long term—a plan for the next five to eight years – a commitment.

The "vision" you employ addresses future factors that could affect the Plan, factors during the next ten to twenty years that possibly or probably would affect management's efforts to achieve its various goals. The importance of the strategic plan is reflected in the CEO's time taken in the planning process.

After the Plan is up and running, after the key members of your team are acquainted with its importance and it nuances, you will find that overseeing the Plan, its modifications, etc. will occupy about a quarter of your time – and that's after it is implemented. An upfront example of strategic planning is the effort you already have put forth in planning your career path to the CEO's responsibilities.

It is of the utmost importance that your senior people, and through them their executives, etc. understand the significance you place on the Strategic Plan and the continuous process required to insure its effectiveness. They also should understand at the outset that their future corporate success – compensation and promotions – would depend on the degree to which their portions of the Plan are achieved. Again, you set the pace. Your actions will convince them of your words.

A caution: If you are coming into an organization from the outside, particularly as a senior executive, especially the CEO, determine before making your final decision how serious the company is about strategic planning. Of course, you can't very well pursue this subject with management personnel, but you certainly can question the Board in depth about this and several other things. Identify what the company is doing – or seriously planning to do – now that it wasn't doing five or six years ago. Determine what amount of senior executives' compensation is tied to successfully accomplishing major strategic tasks. Review the recent annual strategic plans. Are the tasks strategic? Are individuals held accountable? You might find that you should "keep your powder dry," and look elsewhere, particularly if you would have fewer than seven or eight years left in your career.

Again, strategic planning is important. However, while you may have time to quickly strengthen a plan and how it is administered, it is doubtful if you would have the time, given all the other work you will have, to train people to think strategically and start a plan from Ground Zero. Remember Machiavelli and what he said about change. If you don't remember, check the Appendix dealing with Useful Aphorisms. You also would be wise to determine why this company needs a new senior executive. "Old dogs" seldom can learn new tricks and the attitudes of people, especially those comfortable with their jobs and not heretofore expected to exercise more than their day-to-day, well "in-the-box" thinking, are difficult to change. True, you are accountable for leaving your successor a better situation than the one you have found, but you also are accountable for making progress, not in engaging in training people with only a problematic chance of success.

Moving on to the Plan...

The Company's Raison d'être and its Goals

The initial phase in the strategic planning process involves a couple of basic things: Validate the company's purpose, its raison d'être, and its major Strategic Goals. This is no easy task. First, you are looking several years into the future in considering what the company should be doing. A good point of reference it seems to me is to place yourself in the position of one who owned and managed a leading buggy whip manufacturer in the late 1880s. Should this executive have foreseen the advent and rapidly growing importance of the automobile or, of secondary importance, the railroad? This purpose or mission should involve the thinking of your Board, your top management and, if existing, some of your various advisors.

In my opinion, strategic planning merely is the mechanics the CEO uses to bring his or her vision into clear focus and down to quantitative, measurable terms, including specific responsibilities. If a strategic plan or the strategic planning process is not essentially the result of extensive and soundly annealed vision and results in clearly understood and universally endorsed responsibilities for constructive action, it is worthless. Also, without being tested thoroughly, one's "vision" is only ethereal. At best, because vision deals with the future, and the future, by definition is uncertain; accomplishing such vision must involve alternatives and options in the planning process. In particular, the CEO, in setting forth his vision of the organization's future must deal with the character, eccentricities and moral shortcomings of men and women. One need look no further than what has occurred in recent decades to appreciate the risks of this uncertainty.

Your well-developed vision and the organization's capability to realize its full potential must not be negatively impacted by human complacency or inability. Thus, after your vision has been established as the keystone of the strategic plan, you will assess that your principal "human assets" are up to the job of carrying through with the Plan and achieving your vision.

Next, with your strategic purpose established, you must decide on the major Strategic Goals necessary to achieve this purpose, again for the long term. A point to inject here: The Strategic Plan is not static. It is dynamic, subject to annual review and modification – possibly significant change. Your Strategic Goals represent the most important "Whats" are required to underwrite – to achieve – the organization's purpose. Emphasizing their importance, they should be few in number, possibly more than three, probably fewer than five or six. Like so many other elements, it's always easier to add rather than delete.

The Strategic Goals of organizations differ widely. They depend on many things such as the current position of a company in terms of its industries and its environmental factors. It depends on the importance of technology to the long-term success of the enterprise, what it wants to achieve, and several other relatively unique considerations. However, one major Goal universal to most organizations is that of ensuring that the managerial talent and organization strength continues to be capable of supporting your other major goals. I would suggest that, whatever the nature and number of your major Strategic Goals, this is one of them, and it, as the rest, be reviewed, updated and possibly modified during your annual review with your management and with the Board of Directors.

Up to this point, the purpose and especially the goals are drafts. They may eventually become figuratively etched in stone (for a year), but not until they are subjected to an annealing process. This process requires the identification and comparative evaluation of several long-term, broad future conditions. We may call these key Strategic Assumptions for our purposes here.

Key Strategic Assumptions

The key Strategic Assumptions provide a twenty to thirty-year framework within which the purpose and goals of your strategic plan are finalized. These assumptions, global in nature, encompass the forecast of all factors that could affect your company, from wars to worldwide natural disasters, and everything in between. I have found that assigning your senior people to developing these assumptions, including their probability or possibility of occurring is an excellent way to strengthen their strategic interests and plan involvement. It also affords you a perspective of which of these top executives justify further development and responsibilities, and which might not be with the company for the long haul.

The starting point in developing these assumptions is to identify specifically what factors each of your businesses depend for success. Recent history might help in making these determinations. Examples of these factors may include natural resource availability – globally or domestic, status of labor contracts and labor relations, tariff, import and/or export restrictions or other government actions, tax and fiscal legislation, results of ongoing research and development, global sanctions, natural disasters, timely availability of qualified people, global or regional wars, internecine conflicts or political or economic changes in market or supply areas or in distribution routes, delays or accelerates in new product or service availabilities, unforeseen quality or maintenance problems, energy restrictions or cost changes, and competitors' actions, which could be myriad. Both Kipling's "Six Servin' Men" and Taiichi Ohno's "Five Whys" could come in handy here.

Next is to prioritize these factors by their importance to the success of your major products and services and to their respective markets – global as well as domestic. As a guideline for your consideration, especially in the formative years of strategic planning, I normally drop factors below the top five identified priorities.

After your senior executives, with your counsel and the joint application of "Kentucky Windage," determine these factors and their priorities, the next step is to determine what can be anticipated regarding the trends and magnitudes of these factors for the ensuing twenty to thirty years – certainly no small task. This involves deciding on Probabilities versus Possibilities, and applying "What If" considerations.

Normally, I am skeptical about the value of outside help in business matters. However, in getting off the ground in the strategic planning process, you may want to consider such help in this key development work. However, both concerning opinions of your senior people and those of whatever consultants they retain, understand that their thoughts are just thoughts, not facts. As one makes projections or predictions, and their probabilities or possibilities, they are very dependent on experience and judgment until time permits facts to emerge. Experience and judgment are supreme. Therefore, test the historic success of consultants you consider before retaining them.

Objectives Relating to Goals

After all of this, you now can return to finalizing your purpose and goals (the "What" and the "Why" elements), and determining your objectives (the overall "How" element) needed to meet your goals. This also addresses the general framework of planning, implementing and/or achieving these objectives within the company's five-to-eight year Strategic Plan period. You must appreciate that, depending on the scope and nature of these objectives, during this Strategic Planning period, it is possible that some of your truly strategically focused objectives may not be partially or fully achieved. Remember, don't accept a group's day-to-day work as a strategic objective –or, as we will discuss subsequently – a strategic task.

An important consideration in defining these objectives is the degree to which they depend on outside participation or influence. For example, the Strategic Plan Objectives of a firm such as GE Capital or GE Energy Financial Services could well depend – perhaps almost totally depend – on the success of other General Electric Business Units or business and economic circumstances completely divorced from the Corporation's control. Inasmuch as your Board and your shareholders look to you, the Company's CEO, as being accountable for planning, implementing and successful achieving these strategic objectives, they should depend on you and your senior management for success. The faults or failing of outsiders or outside influences are not an excuse.

Your plan will evolve with time. At the beginning, to ensure attention and comprehensiveness, limit the number of objectives, say, to three or four, on average, for each strategic goal. For example, if you start with four goals, you might have 12 to 16 objectives. The specific number is not relevant. However, the fewer number, in effect, forces you and your senior people to focus on the most important goals and objectives. Let say that these apply to strategies involving your organization's Marketing, Manufacturing, Finance and Administrative units and you. The Administrative unit includes Human Resources, Legal Affairs, strategic Planning and Corporate Development, and so forth.

The Purpose, Goals and Objectives of the Strategic Plan, annealed by the anticipated impact of the key Strategic Assumptions, previously a draft, now are finalized for the first year of the plan's effect. Perhaps the nature of the final assumptions and your choice of direction to overcome probable or possible negative influences permit you and your senior management to accelerate the accomplishment of your objectives, resulting in more favorable, ambitious results for the organization.

Frequently, in various organizations it has been found that managements sometime consider the foregoing to represent The Strategic Plan. However, this is not the case. A strategic plan is a dynamic action plan, aimed at achieving positive results. The foregoing should be considered only as Phase One of a for-profit Strategic Road Map.

A caution: Referring again to Sun Tzu (see Chapter III), you should be certain in identifying what would be a considerable competitive challenge first to soundly estimate the costs, examples would be a new product development or a new market entry. When your company engages in actual competition, if success is a long time in coming, assets become dull and management (and shareholder) enthusiasm is dampened. If you lay long-term siege to a competitor's strategy, you will exhaust your strength. Again, if the campaign is protracted your career resources and/or those of your company will not be equal to the strain. At this point, when your assets are dull, your ardor dampened, your strength exhausted and your funds spent, other competitors will arise to take advantages of your circumstances. Then you or no one else, however prudent, skilled and ambitious will be able to overcome the adverse consequences that must ensue. In competition, be it against other career challenging individuals or against companies, let your greatest strategic objectives, particularly those characterized by major uncertainties, be focused on rapid success, not lengthy campaigns. Make this a test of all of your major strategic objectives, and advise your management and the Board of such a test screen.

Establishing Strategic Tasks

Phase Two, which follows, expands on the "What" is to done, but also emphasizes and concentrates on the "How," "When," Where," and "Who" aspects of the planning process.

Strategic tasks must relate, if not be tied to, objectives, not unlike those that are tied to the organization's goals. If they do not, either the tasks or the objectives are wrong or ill-timed and usually it is the tasks. Incidentally, there is nothing magic about the use of the words *Goals, Objectives,* or *Tasks.* They just happen to be used herein to describe the strategic planning process. Use whatever words make sense to you and your management, just so all understand and the executives are dedicated to accomplishing successfully the company's strategic aims.

Not emphasizing grammar, but I have found that a Strategic Task, like any piece of work, must be clearly described, and that means it leads off – it starts – with an action verb. For example, some simple action verbs are *Make, Develop, Write, Buy, Sell, Design, Train, Build, Hire,* and possibly

Transfer are easily understood. While words such as *Manage, Coordinate, Finalize, Deliberate, Re-Work, Analyze, Determine, Document, Research, Identify, Implement, Accelerate, Direct, Activate, Discuss,* and *Evaluate* are verbs, but they are mushy, subject to much interpretation and difficult to measure. They also mean different thing to different people. It should not be necessary to qualify an action verb for any reasonably intelligent person to understand the scope, nature and aim of the task.

Strategic Tasks also must have a clearly stated beginning and ending point – A Start and a Finish. They must be concise, yet sufficiently lengthy to ensure understanding. Importantly, the objective to which this task relates must be indicated, and what would be the impact if this task were deleted. The task definition must include a timeline noting when the job will start, when it will be completed, what interruptions are to be expected in its process and the amount of time such interruptions will require, where the work is to be done, when it will begin and who is accountable for each step in the process. The timeline should be verbally explained as to "Why so long?" "How is it possible to accomplish so fast?" "What alternative or optional methods exist to accelerate the process?" "What is the cost in money and manpower?" "Are funds available or can they be made available?" "What are the anticipated financial returns?" "What other tasks must be begun or completed before the steps in this Task can commence or move ahead?" "Does the Timeline for this Task indicate these relationships?" "Are qualified people, and appropriate equipment and facilities available at the time required for the work involved in this Task?" "Are outside talents or assistance required?" "Are times required to obtain such assistance indicated in the Task's Timeline?" "What is the Timeline for the expenditure of funds?"

The Plan must identify the executive who is accountable for the effective completion of the task. This includes taking into account that he or she understands the magnitude of the work, is qualified and has the time to accomplish the task, including the required coordination and participation with other parties involved in it. Also, a backup should be identified as in any other area of business responsibility.

You, as the organization's senior executive, are accountable for approving the Strategic Plan and gaining the understanding and approval of the Board. Nothing of significance or material is permitted to occur outside of the approved Strategic Plan until reviewed with the Board.

The Control Mechanism

Each calendar quarter the CEO meets with key executives to review their progress and their task work for that quarter. I have found that it is advisable to have the senior executives responsible for Finance and Legal Affairs attend these meetings, and to have the minutes recorded. Subsequent to these "one-on-one" sessions, all appropriate parties sit in on a summary discussion. I have called these meetings my Quarterly Operating Plan Review, or the QOPR. While the primary purpose of the QOPR is to review progress and problems, and decide on changes and solutions. Another result is that it provides you with yet another opportunity to assess your key people. To determine who thinks clearly about the present and the future and the risk-taking nature of individuals, to evaluate their guts and their "sweat coefficient," their calmness in stress and adversity (there always will be some of both), and their maturity, skill and judgment in working with their fellow senior executives. These meetings, particularly the second session, should conclude with decisions as to possible problems for the upcoming quarter and for the ensuing year.

These reviews should also give you evidence you may need to make possible management and organization changes for the success of the strategic future of the company. This is a continuous responsibility for you. While the subject is a three-month review, you are constantly focusing on the future and the competency of these key people to make it successful. What do they need to bring out their full potential? As was stated earlier, people are your greatest challenge. And these quarterly reviews, not unlike your weekly executive meetings, provide a forum for assessing strengths and weaknesses, and considering changes.

Hold these quarterly reviews at the company's operating centers, not always in the headquarters' executive conference room. Go to them instead of having them continually coming to you. After all, they are doing the work and making the money. You merely are providing direction and oversight – again, this is not an ego thing.

Some senior executives have their Strategic Plan open on their desk, reflecting its importance and its continued use as a reference. One caveat in your planning: envision your market as a chess or a checker board. Consider it finite. It is just <u>so large</u>. You and your competitors are fighting within – and for – this territory. In planning your strategy, in setting your sights, don't you or your senior executives start dreaming of your markets expanding. Think, instead, that it may indeed become smaller, and what the company will do if such occurs. This will remove a major "open door" for the continually optimistic executive who visualizes a Utopian market condition as an avenue for overcoming his competitive challenges. However, also make it a challenge for your better executives to seek approaches to enlarge your market for both your present and future products and services.

The Plan's intention is to provide the basis for improvements within the organization and its businesses – such tasks should involve practical "stretch" in achieving truly strategic (long-term) results. Take care, especially in the formative period of the strategic planning process, to ensure that some executives do not attempt to "low ball" their targets, providing themselves a "comfort quotient" for their committed tasks. You should be sufficiently aware of the potential of the executives so that you may be skeptical of such advances made by certain executives. If comfort factors are to be considered because of the nature of the work, it is your responsibility as the CEO and of the Board to do so, not the executives. A method to counter such attempts is to require draft information to be submitted early enough to permit tests to be conducted on related data before final reviews are made, and to conclude the formal reviews with corporate-wide discussions of how prospective challenges or problems as identified barriers to higher expectations can be overcome. Also, be aware of the possibility of multiple pockets of reserves up the chain of reporting relationships. Let no one reduce a commitment without thoroughly examining optional paths and convincing you (and other executives) of the impracticality of the higher targets.

Strategic Plans should aim at more than one level of performance. For example, you might wish to consider having three levels, such as, Expected, Exceptional and Outstanding. There's certainly nothing profound about specific wording. Some business acquaintances have chosen other terms, such as Anticipated, Notable and Conspicuous. However, whatever definitions are chosen, the important factors are that the two higher level targets reflect growth significantly above the baseline in terms of (a) Cash Flow, (b) Return on Invested Capital and (4) Market Share. It also is important that the executives whose compensation is subject to Board review, understand these optional strategic targets and the impact of success on their incentive compensation and that of their top people.

The strategic plan encompasses more than projected targets concerning ongoing markets, operations, product lines and/or investments. It is a comprehensive expansion diagram <u>for the future</u>. It sets forth the organization's projected position, which the Board must understand (and approve), simultaneously assuring with confidence that the company's financial capabilities, at reasonable costs, will be adequate to underwrite the needs both of growth anticipated in the Plan and possibly unforeseen consequences. By such understanding, opportunism, sometimes spawned by failures, can be avoided. Take examples that we've witnessed over past recent years. Managements, some of which are taking the lemmings approach to stay under the radarscope of the media and the financial community, continue to "restructure." This is an increasingly blatant euphemism for closing plants, cutting product lines, firing employees, repurchasing stock, spinning off businesses, obtaining federal and state government funds, and setting up "off sheet" shell organizations as dumping grounds for debt, bad loans and so forth.

Thus, the CEO and the Board must be confident that the Plan anticipates well the strategic needs of the organization and addresses them within the Plan. With the Board's approval, this Plan becomes the company's comprehensive, "all-in" future road map. If, for example, management's plan to enter a potential major foreign market receives Board approval, and an acquisition is deemed an optimal way to enter this market, the specific nature of the acquisition – criteria, possible identify, etc., – is included in the Plan, as well as the method and timing of the acquisition – and possible challenges such an acquisition may represent. These requirements should cause you and your management to pause before proposing to the Board a possible, hastily conceived acquisition, divestiture or some type of "restructuring" to compensate for some failure in meeting previously committed planned goals or objectives.

In this regard, earlier in this decade it was interesting to note that a major, well-managed U.S. Company was negotiating for the sale of its share in a European white goods manufacturer to a European white goods manufacturer, making this European producer the third largest in Europe. It also was interesting to note that the sale would have been for less than was paid by the U.S. Company for this share twenty years earlier; that the U.S. firm long had been a leader in the global white goods market, and had long had the ambition to become a major player in the European white goods market. Thus, we see that even major, reputably well-managed Companies appear at time to violate its own strategic direction.

In summary, there are five points to look to in developing, implementing and modifying Strategic Plans:

1. A strategy can be formulated only after desired objectives have been determined and agreed. The Strategic Plan is an extension of the organization's annual business plan. It is a dynamic ("living") document, reviewed and probably modified and approved annually.

2. The Strategic Plan is the basis for the highly incentive-driven executive compensation plan.

3. The organization's Strategic Plan is "classified." It is as confidential as any business document can be. It is known only to the Board, the CEO, the President and the several most senior executives—those responsible for marketing, operations, finance, administration and the legal counsel. While the CEO may discuss the organization's general growth strategy with outsiders (financial, technical and similar interests and the media), the Plan itself, including its Goals and Objectives remain confidential.

4. In addition to Strategic Assumptions, the Strategic Planning process contains considerations for "What If" factors and the "possible" or "probable" degree of such assumptions and "What If" factors occurring. These also relate to reasonably anticipated competitors' actions based on the strategic steps planned by your company.

5. The screen for validating a Task, for determining whether it is a true Strategic Task – is the degree to which it is relevant to a Strategic Objective, as the objectives are to the organization's Strategic Goals. If it is not relevant to such objectives, it is undeserving of the assets required for its implementation. Also, its priority vis-à-vis the use of funds, time, facilities and so forth, is measured in terms of its importance to the accomplishment of the Objective.

In looking back to earlier subjects highlighted in this book, you should determine early on in each career move the degree to which your management responsibilities relate to the key strategic considerations of your organization. Visibility and impact are important to your career's progress. Thus, if these responsibilities do not have an identifiable, significant relationship, you may wish to consider near future moves to ones that do.

* * *

Chapter Summary: The Strategic Plan is a commitment by you and each of your senior executives. It is far more than a guide or a myth. It is a dynamic, some might say a "living" – instrument. It is the Road Map of "What" the organization plans to accomplish strategically, "Why" it has set these goals and supporting objectives, "How" accomplishment is to take place, "When" it will occur (identifying each major step and its timeline), "where" the work will take place, and "Who" specifically will be accountable as well as who else will be responsible for participating and contributing to the success of the step. Looking from the bottom up, each Task supports an Objective and each Objective supports a Goal. Otherwise, the task or objective is irrelevant. The tasks are reviewed by management quarterly in terms of progress and possible change in priority and direction. The Goals, Objectives and Tasks are reviewed annually by management and the Board to ensure continued relevancy. One goal of most organizations (I can't think of any to which this doesn't apply) is to ensure the presence of managerial and organization competence to support effectively the organization's other major goals. **The success in achieving obligated tasks relates directly to management's strategically oriented Incentive Compensation Plan.**

Chapter VII

Organization Dynamics: People and "Checks & Balances" are Key

Thus far, we've discussed your path to CEO responsibilities, the Chief Executive's job itself, the Board of Directors function and relationships, the challenge you are having and will have in selecting, training and developing people – as well as evaluating and leading them – and the nuance of strategic planning. Now comes the point when we put these assets all together in a smooth running system: The Organization.

As in most aspects of business, there is nothing mysterious about the subject of organization. It's merely the way people's responsibilities, efforts and talents are put together to get a job done. However, while there is no mystery, there are approaches to putting people and functions together which are more effective than other ways.

We've all been subject to organization charts. You know those relatively formal diagrams that supposedly picture how functions relate and who is responsible for what and, after some experience, we realize that nothing happens that way. The trouble with these charts is that they lead us to believe that these "structures" depict how the company works. Few things are further from the truth. I've been in management of seven different organizations – Ford Motor Company, Booz, Allen & Hamilton, Gould Inc., Schaefer, Dravo, Boyden Associates, the Pentagon and our own firm, FMG Ltd. Except, perhaps, for Booz, Allen & Hamilton and FMG Ltd., I've yet to see organization relationships function as they are outlined on such charts. Also, these last two firms functioned largely and efficiently in the absence of any published diagrams.

The fact is that people – good, experienced, qualified people, in carrying out their responsibilities – including the accomplishment of their strategic plan tasks, establish relatively effective working relationships among themselves.

Yes, the neatly placed names and titles within the organization chart squares are interesting, and provide some inputs for business cards, etc. However, it's those lines connecting the squares that are misleading. Some of these are solid lines, some dotted and some even are doubled and/or colored. Among the principal conclusions that our people may draw from these connecting lines is that by "connecting the dots," they might determine to what job their next promotion could lead. However, there are other purposes for structuring an organization, and these are the objective of this chapter. Also considered are the different approaches to organizing an enterprise, what relationships exists and how they might evolve.

Key Purposes

<u>Getting the Job Done Efficiently</u> – We all are aware of the basic jobs involved in a business. The work begins with designing or developing a product or service for a given market and concludes with the receipt and application of money paid for such a product or service. In between these beginnings and endings are the steps of manufacturing or providing, promoting, selling, servicing, handling the systems required for costing, billing and getting the funds into the organization's account, as well as hiring or selecting and paying the employees, suppliers, etc. And, increasingly so in our litigious society, keeping accurate data and reports to avoid legal troubles.

Now, to ensure that "all the bases – or jobs – are covered," and we aren't missing or duplicating any required activity, these jobs are assigned to people. Each individual has something they are supposed to do and for which they are paid; that is, except for our wives, husbands, mothers, fathers or other family relatives who we expect to keep the books, etc., for nothing.

Depending on how difficult or complicated the jobs are, and how many different skills are required, we sometimes assign them to different people. Inasmuch as, in some cases, the owner or the most experienced person in the organization frequently knows more about the work than some other employees, he or she has the job of telling the assigned people what is expected of them and, in some instances, how to do the work; perhaps coincidentally training them at the same time. In other words, being the Boss.

In essence, while these relationships are yet to be sketched or computerized, we have the beginnings of an organization. Loosely, we've organized verbally to accomplish the work, and since we don't have two or more people doing the same job, we've avoided duplication, as long as they remember who is supposed to do what.

We then set these relationships to paper, so that everyone understands who is doing what, to whom each person is responsible, and who is accountable for assigning jobs, controlling performance, and – hopefully – training and developing his or her people. With this step, we no longer must depend on memory. We have an organization chart; one usually is useful just about, as long as it has taken to produce it.

Checks & Balances – This purpose, as noted in the Chapter title, is a "Key" to the organization plan. As more and more of our products or services are sold, it becomes necessary – assuming we are successful – to produce or provide more and more. Hence, we must plan the work, schedule deliveries or installations and perhaps take care of "after sales" service. The person making the product, while responsible for a production program, may not be too keen to vary or adjust his or her output according to some sales-oriented schedule arranged by someone else. This is particularly objectionable if the producer or developer is being paid for the quantity (and quality) of their product. Thus, for this and other reasons, the delivery-scheduling job, tied to sales, can't very well be made the responsibility of the person making the product. Hence, this job necessarily must report to someone else to ensure a type of "Checks & Balance."

However, a system ensuring that in a company is just as important as it is in a government organization, for which the term originally was intended. Montesquieu (aka Charles-Louis de Secondat) in the 1740s was concerned about the potential of a concentration of power in government, particularly, at the time, the government of France. His government organization philosophy centered on the Separation of Powers to resolve this concern. His thought took the form of separating actions so that power could not be concentrated or centralized in one department or one person.

In a business enterprise, as we've witnessed in the past couple of decades, this separation of power is at least as important as it is in a government. However, for somewhat different reasons as we've seen in the foregoing discussion. Thus, in organizing a business you will want to ensure that the people who handle the money, who "account" for it, are not the same people who spend it. Hence, a major purpose of an organization structure or design is to guard against potential of fraud, theft, etc. That is why the executive who wants to use funds must convince another executive of the validity of the requirement, the reputation of the supplier or whomever, and that he or she will receive applicable quality and delivery time for the price being quoted, i.e., an example of checks & balance. I'm sure you have seen several other examples during your experience for this Separation of Power.

Functional Alignment – Related functions, those either technically or managerially related, should be closely associated and report to the same supervisor, manager, etc. Not to confuse functional alignment and the foregoing checks & balances, functional alignment should not occur if a check & balance relationship exists. An example could occur within a manufacturing organization by placing the management responsibility for production and for quality control under the same individual. While these functions are related in that they both concern production, the checks & balances criterion may well be the more important. The same organization alignment challenge may be in a situation involving production and equipment maintenance. This decision depends on the nature of the industry and the process, and frequently becomes a matter of judgment. The Glass-Steagall Act highlights the Government's approach to this problem in the financial community in which the separation of investment banking from investment analysis was legally mandated.

Span of Control – This purpose, stated in a rather fancy phrase, means that one person cannot be responsible for supervising too many people and still get his or her own work accomplished effectively. In other words, there are limits to one's Span of Control. This especially is true if the jobs of people reporting to a single individual are complex or quite different. Hence, the need to break up the number of jobs – shown as "boxes" on organization charts – which are the responsibility of a single individual, be they a foreman, supervisor, manager or senior executive.

I have found a good way of determining this so-called "span of control" is first to determine the time required by the "delegator" to do his or her own job and then establish the number of people they can supervise. Suggestions about such numbers of subordinate positions are easy to make, but difficult to prove. However, having more than six individuals performing <u>different but related</u> functions reporting directly to a single "delegator" may appear excessive, especially given the training, developing and evaluating job of the "Boss." For example, on an automobile assembly line this could well exceed three or four times this number reporting directly to a single line foreman.

<u>Managerial Development</u> – The organization should be designed to enhance career promotional opportunities. Within reason, don't let your desire for a flat structure create "dead end" advancement chances for your people. Ambitious individuals – the kind of people you want – desire to have an idea of the nature and scope of future career opportunities that might be available to them. There should be multiple functional avenues across the company for these people to consider.

Top management certainly is a factor in the managerial development purpose of organization planning. I realize there are several controversial positions regarding the advisability or inadvisability of having a non-executive or non-management Chairman of the Board. While I favor the position that the Chairman <u>should be</u> a management member, I could come down on either side of this argument. However, both from the point of view of executive development and the division of senior management responsibilities, particularly but not limited to a publicly-owned company, I advocate strongly that there should be a position of Senior Executive Officer and a position of President and Chief Operating Officer; duties being somewhat akin to a "Mister Outside" and a "Mister Inside," but not totally.

The President and Chief Operating Officer largely would be responsible for running the company in line with the Goals, Objectives and Task commitments in the Strategic Plan. His or her running the company would be carried out with the oversight, counsel and frequent, possibly daily review and instruction by the CEO. As applicable, he might accompany the CEO on the latter's "outside" activities, mainly to achieve face-time with some of these communities and to provide a second view of interpretations of these outside communities.

The Chief Executive Officer would be, in my judgment, responsible for Board relationships (including the Board's Secretary), relationships with the financial and investment communities, Legal affairs (including government affairs), audit activities (including the internal audit management), media relations, the Ombudsman and company operations through the President and Chief Operating Officer. No one will engage the Board except the CEO or through him, without his prior approval.

Communications – The organization, as well as the related facilities, should encourage communications. People responsible for similar work, particularly if it requires frequently working together, should be collocated both among themselves and with their supervisor, manager or executive. The job is done best when immediate communications are available both verbal and physical between the people doing the work and the people directing and controlling the work.

Pushing Down Executive Responsibilities – Efforts should be made within the organization structure to "push down" executive responsibilities to the lowest level, particularly when they concern the developing of an integral business. In some organization, Business Units, Divisions and Profit Centers, etc., are established in which the integrity of a separate business can be identified in toto as nearly as possible. This enables an executive to be accountable for at least the marketing, manufacturing, product development, controllership and management development of a business, drawing on the corporate organization for legal, financing, and other ancillary and administrative support. In addition to being more precise concerning P&L accountability, this purpose also could relate to the foregoing Management Development purpose.

Flexibility & Agility

Early on, we discussed the need for successful business people to be comfortable with change, and, in effect, uncomfortable with the status quo and similar matters where change matters. The same applies to organizational relationships and how you structure the organization to accommodate anticipated change – and risks. Too often, as in the matter of strategic planning, issues are left as they are, and the realization of the importance—sometimes the critical importance—of change is ignored. This applies to your people as well as to your markets and the global business environment.

Let's remember a fundamental principal: "People first" in organization relationships and planning. You undoubtedly have recognized the different traits among people, even management individuals with MBA degrees. We all are aware that some people inherently are better than others are in developing, maintaining and exploiting people relationships. It isn't such the number of people with whom they are acquainted, but the types of people they know. Other people, again talented and experienced, concentrate – even in their free hours – on obtaining information, perhaps because of a personal need for facts. These people are as valuable as the first group in making an information contribution to the organization. And we know of other individual traits, all of which are valuable to a company and its organization. You may have done a spectacular job in separating the wheat from the chaff in forming and manning your organization, but, again, people change – they come and go, and change mental direction and alacrity of decision-making. Also, circumstances change sometime faster and differently than we realize. An aspect of this is technology. I can recall not too long ago, because of the changes in the importance of information technology, the CIO

(Chief Information Officer) was considered to head the Financial organization of several major corporations.

The organization – its structure and its relationships – should be reviewed annually as an integral part of the strategic plan review. Changing circumstances may make such reviews more frequent. Each executive responsible for proposing and implementing approved tasks should also make it a point to develop a strategic (at least a three to five-year) outlook regarding changes in his or her organization.

Organization Structures

Essentially, there are two basic approaches to organization structures: Hierarchal and Matrix. Each is characterized as much by the nature of personal and functional relationships as the design of the structures. Most organizations lean more toward one or the other of these approaches. Between these two basic types, there are as many variants as there are organizations. As you are aware, the former is one in which there is a relative formal, fixed (depicted mainly by solid line) reporting relationship, the latter being more "team" oriented, with reporting and working relationships being more informal (depicted by dotted lines, solid lines and, at times, broken lines).

The Matrix structure, both because of its informality and because of greater flexibility, is most useful in the early stages of a businesses' development and because the fewer people involved have greater familiarity with each other's strengths, weaknesses, given responsibilities, and manner of operating. Also, the Matrix approach could be of value in larger, older, well-established organizations for these same reasons.

The Hierarchal structure is of greatest value when changes in personnel (particularly in management), the nature of business or the global environment are relatively frequent. In such an environment, the Hierarchal approach, in its formality, provides an element of greater continuity than is reasonable to expect from the looser, more informal matrix structure.

As organizations become larger, more complex and develop in an environment more sensitive to changes in cultures and other environments, they tend to shift to a more formal structure in which the description of individual responsibilities, authorities and reporting relationships is more clearly defined.

Organization Efficiency

Among the major aspects of organization planning, and a reflection of your personal values, is you're aim for a "lean and mean" structure, eliminating any aspects of bureaucracy.

While the foregoing Span of Control discussion may be considered as an element of organization efficiency, it is a "Top, Down" consideration. From a cost and efficiency standpoint, an equal or better impact is realized from a "Bottom, Up" assessment. A determination of the following three factors should assure you of optimum efficiency in planning the organization:

1. Create or approve no position before determining:

    a.   The purpose of the work and its longevity. If the longevity cannot be determined, perhaps no organizational position is required. Positions should be determined for work needed for an indeterminable time. If the time can be determined, look for a short-term solution, e.g., out-sourcing, the use of a consultant or possibly a committee function.

    b.   If the work is necessary for an indeterminable time, is it justifiably unique from a checks and balance perspective to be effected by single positions, or is in sufficiently general to be based on a division among like talent of an eight to ten hour daily work schedule. Note here that you are forcing a determination of the number of employees required as well as the nature of the work. For example, you might question your Chief Financial Officer, "Why the need for more than one Cost Analyst?" And don't accept the response, "Oh, there's just too much work for one person." Constantly encourage your executives to require an elimination of so-called "excessive" workload so that jobs can be accomplished by minimum numbers of people. Make them squeak. Make administrative cost reductions an annual part of their Strategic Plans.

c.   The degree of necessity. Some jobs are more important to your organization for the success and longevity of the company than others are. If you are a manufacturing firm making heavy steel products, you might find that the position of a welder is more important than an M&A Analyst, regardless of the compensation, etc. Based on such a priority assessment, you might consider eliminating them and/or assigning such activities to an outside agency.

Tie layoffs, furloughs and demotions as well as hiring and promotions to anticipated market and EBIT conditions. Don't wait for the impact of adverse results to take action. Assess and rank your approved (point 'c.' above) jobs accordingly.

d.   Avoid adding layers of management in an attempt to solve problems. Make changes internally before adding to the organization. Find out what is wrong and change the executive or reporting relationships before adding additional functions.

Sociology and Organization

In the fourth paragraph of this chapter, I alluded to the importance of the impact of "good people" in matters of organization. General Georges Doriot, the Professor of Manufacturing at the Harvard Business School, in the 1950s explored sociology and its possible impact on corporate organization relationships. In fact, having had the opportunity to have been among his students in 1952-53, I was impressed how the General considered sociology as a good test in developing an effective organization structure, i.e., reporting relationships, etc. As an important aside, the General actually was Professor of Successful Management Practices. "Manufacturing" was only an academic leveling term and just a point of reference.

In discussing an approach to an emerging start-up in the then nascent electronics industry, the General related a situation in which a new general manager approached the organization structure subject with the following steps. First, while depending initially on the structure in place, this executive had a survey conducted in which managers and supervisors were asked with which individuals they consulted most frequently. Second, whom they looked to for expert input, and third who among the group either increased or diminished their interest and energy levels. The analysis of these survey data provided the general manager a sound idea of how the work really was accomplished among his employees. This information proved of great value in determining and assessing the informal working relationships among the company's key people as compared to the reporting relationships, etc., outlined in the company's formal organization chart. It also provided information as to potential "back up" capabilities. In short, General Doriot provided additional credence that the people quotient is the greatest factor in effective organization relationships.

More recently, in the February 27, 2006 edition of *Business Week* the thoughts of General Doriot and others received further attention in an article entitled, *The Office Chart That Really Counts*, proving further that sociology and the use of social network analysis continues to gain traction as a management tool in organization planning are related fields.

Committees

A characteristic of bureaucracies is their rush to form committees or add additional, new layers or echelons to an organization when their members or their staffs think a problem might be developing. An outstanding example was the 2005 Federal Government's creation of an "Office of National

Intelligence" instead of requiring the already fifteen or sixteen Government-sponsored Intelligence agencies to do the required coordination of information job. And, parenthetically, in most instances the nation's federal and state politicians have no idea of the problem they are addressing or the cost in the taxpayers' money they spend. The same approach exists when organizations attempt to eliminate "stove piping" in business deliberations or decision-making.

Leave bureaucracies to the politicians and to most Government Employees who are mired in the dogmas of Policies, Concepts, Doctrine, Regulations, Instructions and other, well "Inside-the-Box" thinking. You are an Individual – a thinking Individual – who realizes tomorrow, will be different from today, and will require different thinking, even some thinking that might involve risk.

This all gets down to avoiding committees whenever and wherever possible. Within the business organization, unlike the Board of Directors, Standing Committees should be avoided. The essential job of the manager includes coordinating with other appropriate people in identifying and solving problems. These are ad hoc meetings, perhaps–perish the thought—even after hours. "Stove Piping" and other negative actions should have been overcome at the first echelon or line of management. You don't need people to form committees to do the work for which they already are responsible – and accountable.

Now, there are sound purposes for some committees and committee-based action. However, recognize that these situations are exceptional. Not unlike project work or consulting assignment, these committee actions have definite Start and Stop points. For example, corporate-wide decisions about a possible involvement in a major contract or a business acquisition or merger, could well justify the formation of a committee. However, hold your executives to a timetable for a product, a deliverable, or a decision and ensure that the committee is terminated at that time.

People and the Organization

Too often, companies become enamored with their organization structure; the status quo. They seem to implicitly assume that their tradition proves the structure's usefulness. The appear to adopt a "One Size Fits All" mentality regarding organization relationships, changes occurring only when business units are added or spun off, or on the occasion of a major, high impact crisis.

Repeating a point – a point worth emphasizing: <u>An organization is dynamic</u>. It bears frequent analysis to assure that changes in technology, business conditions and its senior people do not require organization changes.

Let's return to the CEO's position and responsibilities within the organization, and to the different traits of individuals. The talents and experience of a CEO may be outstanding in a period in which a hard-hitting, drastic "turn around" is required of the business. However, the needs in this position may change, and various organization-reporting relationships may require revision, as the business re-achieves stability and a favorable growth curve begins. I'm not saying that this is a certainty, but certainly, it can – and has frequently, happened.

In media jargon this takes on the Board's language as, ".....a change in management style was believed necessary," even though the company never was in a better marketing and financial position, and the shareholders were never more pleased. This happens.

Organization Conundrums

Conundrums well may develop in organizations that relate both to the structure and to senior people. Some major challenges could be resolved, if the future develops according to your vision and to your strategic assumptions. However, as illustrated in the following example, the problem is:

A major chemical manufacturing company is expanding abroad. It establishes its first foreign sales office, headed by an aggressive, ambitious thinking individual; the kind of executive talent you want. Through his efforts, the company's sales in this new foreign market are increasing handsomely. In fact, now, they are resulting in foreign inventory and delivery pressures. At the same time, the corporation's domestic sales also are increasing well. There is only one manufacturing facility for the products in question and it is located domestically. Sales volume in the domestic market, based on its market share and recent experience, is anticipated to continue to expand. However, such volume in the foreign market also is expected to experience outstanding growth, although experience in the foreign market is comparatively slight. The Vice President of Manufacturing, to date, has favored domestic deliveries over those to the foreign market, the brands and products being slightly different. His decision is based on the expected higher return seen in domestic production, deliveries and sales. The combined markets at this point and in the near future will not be sufficient to expand or construct new facilities. The company, because of certain serious proprietary considerations, opposes using a licensed producer. There are many more aspects to this conundrum, but this affords an idea of its complexity.

Naturally, with time, this puzzle possibly can be solved, but it points to the relationships of senior executives, the importance of the Strategic Plan, the organization's marketing, manufacturing and financial structure, the importance of the executive incentive compensation plan and how these factors all are entwined in the successful management of a business.

Chapter Summary: Organizations are dynamic, changing with business circumstances, people, technology and time. Organizations should be reviewed for change annually with each review of the Strategic Plan, or more frequent as unforeseen events occur or are anticipated. Checks & Balances are a characteristic of a good organization, followed by management development opportunities, efficiencies, "push down" decision making, effective "span of control," etc. Ensure that organization improvements are included in executives' Strategic Plan Tasks. Avoid bureaucratic thinking as a plague, e.g., "stove pipe" thinking, standing committees, restricted (read, dogma directed) thinking and so forth. Consider the relative advantages and disadvantages of Hierarchal versus Matrix structures for your specific organization in its specific phase of development. Evaluate both "Top, Down" and "Bottom, Up" aspects in planning your organization. Look to "outside" and "inside" requirements in designing organization divisions between your most senior management.

Chapter VIII

The Big "M" and True Incentive Comp: What They Are and What They're Not

We seek business and career success in a meritocratic environment; one that equates high contribution to high rewards. Rewards acknowledging performance beyond the expected may take many forms. For example, a personal, meaningful letter from your superior will go far in strengthening your motivation – The Big "M." There also may be time off for the employee to be with his or her family. If the performance and qualifications justify it, there is a career promotion, and there always are monetary awards, e.g., base compensation increases, bonuses, options and so forth.

Motivation

We all have personally experienced motivation – being motivated, or we wouldn't be here. Motivation takes many forms, but the honest and sincere providing of one's time and attention for the performance of someone else probably is among the best motivation, and certainly is where it starts. However, even a "thank you" must be honest and sincere or it becomes a standard response of a person who is neither honest nor sincere – a phony.

Unfortunately, people like this are in every organization, and you as the leader must insure that the bus (your company) leaving the station – destined for greater things and more success – leaves this baggage behind. There is no place for phonies in your organization.

Among my greatest motivators was a quiet, calm deliberate manager for whom I worked as a teenaged laborer. He always set the standard of what a leader should be. He did not rely on money, time off, or similar rewards for motivation. He only most sincerely acknowledged a job well done and occasionally and honestly asked my opinion as to how the job could be improved. Just the fact that he asked me such a question stimulated me. I begin thinking, "how the work could be done better?" He took the time, often in relatively hectic environments, to discuss my responses. He patiently – another major leadership characteristic – discussed the pros and cons of my ideas, most of which turned to be "cons," and explained the positive and negative aspects of these idea from a management perspective. This gentleman is included among the individuals acknowledged in the book. He long since has passed. However, I still strive to perform as he in my relationships with people. In the sociologist's term, this surely was an example of Key Experiences as proposed in a paper by Professor Gad Yair.

Another aspect of this type of motivation is the idea that you are one of the few recipients of such time and attention. Fortunately, for you and your career, this concept that you are "setting yourself apart" takes hold before you realized that this man treated everyone who deserved accolades the same. Your spirits and degree of self-confidence permanently were strengthened even as the years passed and your realization of this man's motivation to others became evident.

It seems somewhat ironic, but from to time-to-time we must remember that motivation in a business has a purpose. It isn't primarily to "make people feel good," including ourselves, or to meet some altruistic desire.

Motivation in a business context primarily is to increase productivity – the output, quality and creativity of our work and that of our people.

As the leader, mostly through your own actions, you are responsible for pulling others along, focusing them in their motivation practices – and sincerity. Many people have talents and experience exceeding yours and mine. However, their lack of attention and caring and acknowledging of what others do – to what others accomplish, limits the potential strength of their organizations and the potential advancement of their careers. Again, like ethics and morale values, I believe you will find that this productivity-oriented, "human caring" trait results more from empirical knowledge than academic training. One possibly could say, admittedly with some reservation, that it is more inherent than learned.

A most valuable result of a well-motivated organization – of well-motivated people – is loyalty beyond one's imagination. Had the famed business leaders of the mid-1800s to mid-1900s understood and practiced honest and sincere recognition of the labors of their people, no doubt the loyalty of the employees would have centered on their respective organizations instead of them being forced to seek alternatives as outside labor unions. This single management weakness set U.S. industry back in the 1900s, and the results are still evident.

Motivation and, more specifically, motivation and productivity, have been subjects of study for a long time. The Hawthorne experiments of the late 1920s and early 1930s and the unique productivity and compensation practices of the Lincoln Electric Company beginning in 1930s certainly are worth your time in understanding the value and application of motivation. Other theories and research, such as Theory 'Y', Theory 'Z,' Extrinsic and/or Intrinsic motivation (Two Factor Motivation Hygiene Theory), Self-determination Theory, Drive Reduction Theory, Key Experiences, Need Hierarchy Theory, Achievement Motivation, Expectancy Theory, Attribution Theory, etc., also have proved constructive in understanding motivation and productivity both in the industrial and other venues. [3]

To summarize this vital subject – vital to your executive career, the principal result of most of this work centers on the fact that (1) all people are different, motivated differently, and (2) time and attention, fairly, honestly and continuously employed, are essential in any positive motivation practice. I'm not a sociologist or psychologist, but I have experienced the following in my management relationships, several of which tie back to our discussion of developing people in Chapter III.

---

[3] Also, reference outstanding views on this subject in articles and research by Edward Deci, Fritz Heider, Frederick Herzberg, Steven Kerr, Christopher Argyris Remsis Likert, Abraham Maslow, Elton Mayo, David McClelland, Douglas McGregor, Richard Ryan, Victor Vroom, Gad Yair, et al. These data further buttress the fact that your people are vastly different, and require different motivational approaches.

- A balance of Intrinsic and Extrinsic motivation is best, both from a tactical and strategic viewpoint. Even considering the value of an incentive compensation program, I believe intrinsic awards are more enduring, hence strategically rewarding than extrinsic rewards in an industrial career environment.

- Acknowledgment of an outstanding performance – however "rewarded" – should be immediate. You'd be surprised how the value of such acknowledgement erodes over even a brief lapse of time.

- Recognize that the factors motivating your people may change over their career. However, the respect you show for the individual continues as a prime motivational factor.

- Praise the individual for his or her outstanding achievement both publically, among other employees, and in calm, sit down, "One-on-One" discussion. Recall that more people, often individuals with considerable potential, leave their jobs because they do not believe their work is appreciated than because of compensation, benefits, perks, etc. Forget Employee Recognition Programs, except possibly for entries in the newsletter. They tend to detract from truly recognized outstanding achievement.

- Many individuals prove most productive immediately prior to a scheduled deadline. For various reasons, some justified, they have difficulty providing the best focus to a job until that deadline threatens. To compensate for these challenges, consider establishing milestones along the way, leading to a conclusion or end state.

- Good people are most pleased when they, and their work, are progressing toward a recognized goal. Give these people, who usually are busy, new and difficult challenges and they will be more enthusiastic. You may be surprised how contagious this is.

- Conversely, don't let people stagnate, particularly the individuals you have assessed as having outstanding potential. Each time an individual advances, "raise the bar" and keep them going. As in all cases, this applies to you as well.

- Accept different approaches. Provide guidance and counsel, but let people do the job their way. The objective is to achieve the goal successfully, not show how much you know. Make it clear what you want and when you want it. Let them exercise creativity. That's how new ideas and career opportunities are born.

- Take care in assigning work to a "Team" versus an "Individual." Team approaches have become a mantra, sometimes to an organization's detriment. If work requires a team, rotate its leadership.

- Make sure that the motivation factor meets the individual's motivating needs. "Different folks need different strokes."

- Sincere interest and concern for your people, and the belief that you will support them in any reasonable way will lift spirits and cause them to achieve even greater heights.

- Never provide an award for an achievement that is within the job's normal expectations. The nature and amount of the reward must relate to the significance of the achievement, and be so recognized. Also, the motivational award is for results, not for effort.

- Employ both tactical and strategic (immediate or short-term and long-term) objectives in setting tasks for your people. This helps guide the action process and creates an environment in which the people must anticipate factor, which will influence their future work – and their future career.

- Demonstrate that you care more for rewarding your executives than in rewarding yourself. However, never consider a reward for others that holds no value for you.

- Appeal to an Individual's selfish or self-centered interests. Provide them the opportunity to earn more for themselves by earning more for you (see Lincoln Electric's experience).

These 15 key motivational points complement the people development suggested addressed in Chapter III such as communicating, being the example, and ensuring criticism is constructive and carried out in private. This listing certainly isn't all-inclusive. I'm sure that your experience could add several other, equally important points. However, regardless of the specifics, until consideration is given such factors, and they are implemented in your management practices, you will not achieve the increased productivity and constructive working environment you seek.

Incentive Compensation

Incentive Compensation is tied closely with the company's Strategic Plan. In fact, it is based on the long-term accomplishment of the executive's tasks related to the Plan's Objectives (which are in support of the organization's Strategic Goals). Incentive compensation programs just don't happen. They are the result of considerable work and, if effective, will have considerable impact of the long-term success of the company. Thus, consider this subject carefully. In a business, there are few facets that deserve the caution "Don't start something that you don't intend to continue forever" than an executive Incentive Compensation Plan.

The incentive plan, if properly planned, developed, communicated and administered, can work wonders for a company. In establishing such a Plan, the Chairman and Chief Executive Officer and the Board of Directors should retain appropriate legal, tax and professional compensation counsel. However, I would propose the following characteristics for your consideration:

- Strategic Plan Assumptions, Goals, Objectives and Tasks must be thoroughly developed, annealed and understood by all Incentive Plan participants, especially the senior Human Resources (aka Personnel), legal and Finance people who will be responsible for the Compensation's Plan success.

- The functional alignment of the company's Organization Structure must accommodate the executive's commitment to accomplish his or her Strategic Tasks without excessively influence (read "interruption") by outside agencies, including executives or business units within the company.

- Annual review and possible modifications in the Strategic Plan and the Organization Structure must include the impact on the Incentive Compensation Plan, with necessary and understood changes understood by all Com Plan participants. Again, this is an annual job.

- The Board and the company's shareholder must understand that incentive-based compensation will relate and be paid only for performance greater than could reasonably be realized without such an incentive-based program.

- The Incentive Compensation Plan will be strategically-oriented with the participant's compensation accruing on annual results and the payout being based on a three to five-year schedule (see Exhibit '2').

- Incentive compensation will relate both to the performance of the respective Business Units, Profit Centers, Divisions, etc. and to the performance of the entire corporation (reflecting shareholder interest).

- Incentive Compensation Plan participation would be restricted initially only to the corporation's senior executives and to those executives having Profit & Loss responsibility for the results of their totally integrated operation.

- The Corporation's "Senior Executives" will include the Chairman, Chief Executive Officer, President, Chief Operating Officer, Chief Financial Officer, Chief Administrative Officer and/or positions of equivalent levels of responsibility as determined by the Board of Directors. Executives in management positions reporting to the Incentive Compensation Plan participants would qualify for Annual Bonus Group compensation based on their performance and their contribution to their respective organizations. The Board of Directors, with senior management's recommendations, will approve the Bonus Group participants.

- To represent a meaningful incentive, the potential amount of the Incentive Compensation payment must be significant in relation to the participants' based annual salary, say 50%. In some Plans, the amount of incentive compensation may represent 80% or more of the participant's total potential income. Thus, should the participant's performance justify the highest level of incentive compensation, he or she would receive one-third greater annual compensation than if their performance failed to warrant any incentive-based payment. The maximum Bonus Group monetary award would be significant relating to the participant's base annual salary, say 25%.

- Initially, 100% of the potential Incentive Compensation award will be escrowed annually with interest accruing to the Incentive Plan. Subsequently the amount of the escrow will depend of the performance and payment trend, as determined by outside auditors and approved by the Board of Directors.

- Strategic Tasks may change with time. However, Strategic Tasks, which relate to the organization's Strategic Objectives (and Goals) – and on which the Incentive Compensation Plan and Bonus Group plan are based – should relate to the company's Cash Flow and EBIT, even in adverse business, market or global financial and economic periods. Task commitments by specific Incentive Compensation Plan participants may vary during such periods. For example, "Maintaining global marketshare…" may take the place of "Increasing EBIT by X%…" during such periods.

Exhibit '2'

A Strategically Related Executive Incentive Compensation Plan

There are many approaches to incentives, all of which are intended to keep the senior executives focused and their attention on the strategic success of the organization. This is an example of one that has proven to be effective and relatively easy to understand.

Premise I: The maximum potential incentive compensation award can equal the executive's base annual salary, i.e., 100% or a "one multiple."

Premise II: The strategic period for the incentive compensation payout will be three years.

Premise III: The incentive compensation plan participant will receive one-third of his or her strategically based award each year or the degree to which they accomplished their tasks for the applicable year.

Example:

Assume that the annual base salary for the Vice President-Operations, the senior executive who is the subject of this example, is $300,000, i.e., $25,000 per month. Thus, assuming he achieves 100% of his strategic tasks commitments in "Year One" of the Plan, he will receive $100,000 as his incentive award. Assuming, likewise he is successful in years "Two" and "Three," he will receive $200,000 in "Year Two" and $300,000 in "Year Three" (assuming no increases in his base salary during this Three-year period). His potential incentive compensation is escrowed in each of the Plan's second and third year. The numbers would appear as follow:

Year	1st	2nd	3rd	4th	5th
1st Plan	$100,000	$100,000	$100,000		
2nd Plan		$100,000	$100,000	$100,000	
3rd Plan			$100,000	$100,000	$100,000
4th Plan				$100,000	$100,000, etc.
5th Plan					$100,000, etc.
Payout	$100,000	$200,000	$300,000	$300,000	$300,000

This example assumes that the Plan began in the 1st year. If he or she achieves 80% of their second year commitment, the second year payout would be $180,000 instead of $200,000. Examples of Strategic Tasks could include increases in labor productivity, reductions in materials costs, etc. costs, reductions in maintenance or repair costs, improvements in quality (favorably affecting both repair and warranty costs) and improved energy utilization (resulting in cost reductions). This approach provides the flexibility required in the Plan, recognizing that acceptable levels of performance may change over time depending on economic or other circumstances are achieved. It is to be noted that should the executive leave the company of his own volition, future years of his or her payout would return to the general Executive Incentive Compensation Plan fund.

A modification of the above could be could represent a reserve or escrow account for a nominal amount annually to be invested in the executive's retirement plan. This amount would be owed to him or her at retirement or after a certain number of years of service. If the years of service were not achieved, such earmarked amounts would be returned to the general retirement awards fund, and would be available to other executives.

Skepticism is a Necessity

To quote Denis Diderot, the 18th Century French Philosopher, "Skepticism is the first step toward Truth." If incentives are to be effective, and serve the purpose of the shareholders, you as the CEO must exercise considerable skepticism in evaluating proposed tasks on which incentives will be based. The Board is not positioned to do this; you are. Thus among your jobs, this is one of the most important.

Some executives will bite off more than they can chew (or accomplish), suggesting unrealistic levels of performance, perhaps to attempt to prove their worth to you or to bolster their egos. Other individuals will low-ball their aims, attempting to keep something in reserve for the proverbial rainy day. Your reviews with these people should provide you with a sound opportunity – one based on their potential income – to evaluate the extent of their risk-taking or risk aversion attitudes. Also, while listening to **what** is said, stay keen as to **why** it is being said. There are few subjects so important to the future success of your company – and your career – as a solid, well thought out and effectively managed as the corporation's executive Incentive Compensation Plan, particularly in this era of Federal Government intervention in executive pay, well publicized "White Collar Crime," "Fat Cat" bailouts and so forth.

In particular, make certain that the tasks justifying incentive compensation awards focus on the executive's core businesses. All too frequently, you will uncover attempts to plug target holes with such activities as divestitures, new product or system development, acquisitions, purchases of leased assets, etc. being advocated to achieve their target tasks. I am not suggesting mistrust, or an untoward attempt, but I'm cautioning you to be a skeptic in your review with the plan participants of their proposed tasks and how significantly they relate to your strategic objectives and the annual business plan. One approach I've found of value is to decide before hand the minimum number of tasks required – based on your priorities, and to check thoroughly potential "what if" probabilities.

Experience has shown that if all Incentive Plan Participants are required to set "Minimum,"" Maximum" and "Projected" task results, including the impact of anticipated 'what if' probabilities, you as the CEO can compare these without too much time required with a "projected" consolidated plan in excess of what you believe is achievable. This will provide you a baseline to judge initially the executives' proposals and to give them evidence that you anticipate some "stretch" in their performance.

Potential questions in such a review are limitless. However, to get you off the blocks, I would suggest the following:

1. "If you haven't been able to achieve this before, what makes you think you can do it now?" Conversely, "If you have achieved this previously, what factors prohibit you from achieving or exceeding this now?"

2. "What specific factors or influences justify performance in the coming periods which is lower or only equal to performance levels you already have achieved?"

3. "What would it cost to overcome these adverse factors?" "To implement these favorable factors?"

4. "All of your costs, Direct, Variable, or Indirect can be reduced through greater productivity, more astute purchasing, changes in vendors or suppliers, etc. Let's revisit your cost reduction plan and discuss it again."

5. "What are your major competitors doing while you are doing all of this?"

6. "What steps would be necessary to increase your market share in these periods?" What impact would they have on your sales and operating profit?

7. "What actions are you contemplating effecting functions which could impinge – favorably or unfavorably – on your projected strategic results, e.g., increasing or decreasing advertising, leasing versus

purchasing facilities or equipment, employing permanent personnel instead of using temps and so forth?"

Chapter Summary: Motivating people, as in the development of people, is among your major responsibilities. Your objectives in providing motivation are to improve productivity and, hopefully, to strengthen loyalty of the employees to your company and to you. Much has been studies concerning motivation, but, in a nutshell, there are two general types of motivation: Intrinsic and Extrinsic. The first comes from rewards inherent to performing the task or activity itself. The second comes from rewards outside the immediate performance of the task, monetary rewards being the greatest example and the way managers treat employees is key to successful motivation. Extensive studies of motivation indicate that, in terms of what employees desire most from a job, pay, benefits and working conditions trail job security, opportunity for advancement, the type of work and the nature of the company, e.g., one for which people are proud to work.

However, monetary compensation is important. Incentive-based compensation plans span the spectrum from piece-rate as long has been characteristic of the Lincoln Electric Company to executive incentive compensation plans practiced my major S&P corporations. In these latter programs, the incentive plan payments are tied closely to the organization's strategic plans and the payouts to the executives frequently span a three to five-year period. Executive compensation in recent years has become a "hot button" issue with Federal Government politicians. Thus, a business leader must exercise extreme caution in planning, implementing and administrating compensation plans relating to their company's marketing and/or financial results. Based on the Government sponsored bailouts of industrial and finance companies, it has intervened since 2008 as never before in adjudicating salaries, incentive payments, options, etc. relating to the senior executives of companies and firms that received bailout support.

Chapter IX

Corporate Governance: It is Yours to Make it Work.

Corporate Governance is not a new issue, but it surely is one that has gained considerable attention over the past several decades. This attention primarily is tied to the scandalous behavior of senior business executives and government officials or politicians. While surely not a panacea for the problems of the corporate missteps and the stock market "bubble" of the 1990s and the effects of the business-government partnership in ineptitude and greed of 2003 to the present, it is an important subject of corporate-wide impact that demands your serious attention as you assume senior executive leadership responsibilities. Better not to have it, than have it in less than practical perfection.

An important fact in considering this subject is that institutional investors in the early 2000 to mid-2005 period held more than fifty percent of all listed corporate stock in the United States, about sixty percent in the case of the largest 1,000 corporations. Also, as reference, the largest twenty-five pension funds now account for over forty percent of the foreign equities held by all U.S. investors. In effect, institutional investors have assumed the role of quasi-permanent shareholders. The importance of these facts is that institutional investors bring to the market a higher degree of professional diligence than most other shareholders do, and they are aware of how companies operate. They also are more rapidly aware of shortcomings and the nuances of published corporate information and related reports. Hence, while they encourage companies to adopt corporate governance, they also are aware of how close managements adhere to such publicly available pronouncements.

What is Corporate Governance?

Depending somewhat on the backgrounds and interests of the sources, "corporate governance" is defined quite differently, as the following indicate:

- "Corporate Governance is a field of economics that investigates how to secure or motivate efficient corporate management by the use of incentive mechanisms, such as employment contracts, organization designs, compensation and legislation. This frequently is limited to the question of improving financial performance; for example, how the shareholders can secure or motivate executives to deliver a competitive rate of return." *Henrik Mathiesen, "Managerial Ownership and Financial Performance, 2002*
- "Corporate Governance deals with the ways in which financiers or corporations assure themselves of achieving a return on their investment." *Andrei Shleifer and Robert W. Visny, the Journal of Commerce, pp 737, 1997*
- "Corporate Governance is the system by which business corporations are directed and controlled. The corporate governance structure specifies the assignment of responsibilities among different participants in the corporation, such as the board, the executives and managers, the shareholders and other stakeholders, and explains the rules and procedures for making decisions on corporate affairs. By doing this, it also provides the structure through which the company objectives are established, and the means of achieving those objectives and monitoring performance." *Sir Adrian Cadbury, pp. 15, "The Code of Best Practice," 1996; "The Principals of Corporate Governance Paris," OECD, April, 1999*
- "Corporate Governance can be defined narrowly as the relationship of a company to its shareholders, or, more broadly, as its relationship to society." *The Financial Times, 1997*
- "Corporate Governance is about promoting corporate fairness, transparency and accountability."

- *Mr. James Wolfensohn, President, IBRC, the Financial Times, June 21, 1999*
- Some commentators take too narrow a view, and say it (Corporate Governance) is the fancy term for the way it which directors and auditors handle their responsibilities to shareholders. Others use the expression as if it were synonymous with shareholder democracy. Corporate Governance is a topic recently conceived, as yet-ill defined, and consequently blurred at the edges...corporate governance as a subject, as a regime to be followed for the good of the shareholders, employees, customers, bankers, and indeed the reputation and standing of our nation and its economy." *Nigel N G. Maw, "Maw on Corporate Governance", pp1, 1994*

Some of these definitions are accompanied by formulae, quantitative analyses, etc., in support of or to prove the validity of a given definition, some indicating Corporate Governance impact on corporate performance. I would recommend that you review this subject from other sources as well to get the broadest possible perspective. Most interesting. However, you may, as in all things, evidence a degree of skepticism in accepting the results of some of these studies. One research project on this subject, for example, indicates that "investors who bought (stock of the) firms with the strongest democratic (stockholders) rights would have earned abnormal returns of 8.5 percent per year during the sample period," markedly better than others. This may or may not be attributable to merely having Corporate Governance.

We should be able to glean a reasonable working definition of Corporate Governance from the foregoing combined with our own ideas, particularly focusing on the "wrongdoings," etc., of Boards and executives during past, recent decades (I would suggest that Boards of Directors have come off well as compared to the senior business executives regarding media and government attention). There are several factors which I believe the market, the shareholders, the sources of capital and the corporate community would think represent serious, objective Corporate Governance considerations aimed at insuring the integrity and transparency of a corporation's operations. Let's examine these factors in relation to organization and procedural matters:

Organization

- The position and reporting relationship of the internal auditing function.
- The existence of an Ombudsman function, its duties, the nature and content of its reports, its reporting relationship and evidence of follow up of such reports.
- "Pros" and "Con" provided by the Board of (a) a Non-Management Executive as Chairman of the Board of Directors, (b) a "Presiding Director," and (c) staggered election of Board members.
- The size of the Board of Directors and the number of Management seats on the Board.
- Rotation of Independent (outside) Auditors. Why? Why not? If so, proposed frequency?
- Assurance of "Checks & Balances" as relate to reporting relationships and functional alignment.

Procedural Matters

Summary of major (unclassified) subjects and voting records of Board of Director meetings (criteria and identification of "major subjects" to be the Chairman's decision, reviewed by the external auditor). Board attendance and participation in activities of annual meetings.

- Chairman summarizes corporation's general strategic direction (not the plan, etc.)
- Audit Committee Chairman summarizes Independent Audit Report, upcoming annual
- Corporate Auditing Program and the status of the Corporate Governance program.
- CEO and CFO sign off of annual reports, 10-Ks and 10-Qs.

- Position vis-à-vis senior management providing quarterly and annual earnings estimates.
- Qualifications of Independent Directors.
- Criteria for Prospects and Candidates for Board of Director nomination.
- Nature, type and impact of executive compensation plans.
- Expense of exercised stock options, status of previously granted options, and earnings impact of outstanding options.
- Quarterly and annual disclosures of fully funded and non-funded liabilities status,
- Off sheet activities, cash flow sources and applications.
- Board and Senior Executive(s) annual review with debt rating agencies.
- Quarterly and annual report by External Auditors regarding progress against annual, three-year,
- And five-year approved audit programs, particularly attention given foreign operations.
- Independent Auditors provide proposed standards for Audit Committee approval, standards unique to the corporation's specific types of businesses, well within GAAP and FASB, etc., regulations and guidelines.

Relationships

The responsibility for effective implementation of Corporate Governance cuts across several organization lines. For Corporate Governance to be effective, it is necessary that all parties understand the nature of their involvement and act in concert in its implementation. Too often, especially when things are attempted in haste in order to prove to government agencies, to the shareholders or to the media, the relationships required to make it work successfully are overlooked. Such oversight can result in suspicion and ill will within the organization, possibly damaging permanently the very effectiveness of Corporate Governance that is the objective of having such a program.

For example, the Board may decide to plan the implementation of the idea to have a non-executive Chairman of the Board. This action could well be taken—justifiably be scheduled—at the time an individual succeeds the executive who presently is the Chairman, President and Chief Executive Officer of the company. However, if the steps in this action is not well thought out, including such scheduling, bringing a potential successor into the picture before this opportunity is offered the management executive – or the reasons for his or her not being selected—could have seriously detrimental consequences regarding the future faith and trust between the Board and the entire senior management group. The ripple effect of this error in judgment could even influence the relationships of the company with its shareholders, banking interest, etc.

For some time, Boards of Directors have, in the light of media exposure on the one hand, and the practical needs and interests of the business and its shareholders on the other, been attempting to frame Corporate Governance that meets both these and increasing government demands. The Directors of Boards indeed have been attempting to prove that their stewardship places the operations and practices of the respective corporation beyond question. Examples of actions being considered are outlined in Appendix 'H' entitled "The Struggle to Better Pompeia".

The planning and implementation of Corporate Governance is a serious and delicate matter. It is far more than an integrity "Check List" posted on the Boardroom wall. Its implications are strategic and far-reaching. In order for the Corporate Governance to be effective – and not cause more problems than solutions, this action requires 360° thinking and a thorough assessment of potential unintended consequences by all parties before even draft action is considered.

Corporate Governance involves both the Board and senior management. On the Board, the Audit, Compensation, and Finance Committees, as well as the Board's Executive Committee, are primarily responsible. Experience indicates that it may be of value to have the Board's Audit Committee Chairman direct and coordinate this corporate-wide effort. Within management, the Chief

Executive Officer, the President, the Chief Financial Officer and the General Counsel, as well as the senior Internal Auditing executive – are primarily responsible. Here, depending on background of course, I would suggest the General Counsel or the Chief Financial Officer as management's point of contact for this work.

Regardless of the specific executives responsible for developing and drafting an organization's Corporate Governance, frequent reviews should be conducted and include the Independent Auditor. The final draft, including an assessment of possible strategic impacts, should receive combined Board and senior management scrutiny.

Keep Corporate Governance in Context

Corporate Governance is important. As we've referenced earlier, some very intelligent people believe serious management attention and compliance regarding Corporate Governance provisions can favorable affect results. However, while it is more than just another program, don't look for miracles. Many organizations have in place, well developed Codes of Conduct, Ethical Guidelines and so forth that cover most or all the elements of Corporate Governance. Also, Corporate Governance requires commitment not unlike the tasks of the Strategic Plan. You might consider incorporating certain applicable elements of this program in your plan, indicating to your senior people the degree of seriousness, which you give this subject. You also might consider reviewing your Corporate Governance or other similar guidelines annually during the strategic plan review process.

Corporate Governance like all other similar guidelines is subject to change. A caution is to be certain in drafting the Governance you and the Board doesn't permit the elements of the Corporate Governance to force your management to take on more than it can accomplish. Stretch is commendable, but committing your organization to more than is optimally achievable will only cause a loss on interest in such guideline obligations.

Observations

I support totally the purpose and scope of Corporate Governance. In my management experience I have come to consider Corporate Governance as a quasi-legal control document; an executive commitment in providing an ethical, moral and professional guideline on how the organization carries out its operations and its relationships. Nor do I have a reluctance to make this document public. However, as aforementioned, I believe the provisions it includes should be achievable within a reasonable period. For example, when a company is acquired one must recognize – and assess – possible cultural differences in its management's approach to business. Changes in these culture variances may be required, but it also must be recognized that such changes take time to identify, plan and enforce. I would make certain that Corporate Governance provisions recognize such time factors, and is not permitted to limit the talents and ambitions of your management regarding this factor and others such as risk-taking, "Outside-of-the-Box" thinking, innovative initiatives and general business aggressiveness. The ambitious among your executives fight for power, the weak seek validation. Don't make your Corporate Governance provisions be so tight that the weak can, in any way, justify bureaucratic inaction and the ambitious become career frustrated.

An actual ongoing Corporate Governance statement, sanitized to avoid identifying the company, is shown in Appendix 'I'. This statement affords a sound, and practical perspective of the general versus the specific characteristics of such a statement.

Chapter Summary: Corporate Governance is a serious consideration, one with which you should be well informed, particularly in your senior management relationships with the Board and with the company's shareholders. The subject is well publicized globally and I believe it will be gaining in significance, especially now that the Institutional Investor community is referring to it as criteria in evaluating management and the methods it conducts business. It also provides you a single instrument to identify the thinking and, in some instances, proposals being advanced by the market, the financial community, major shareholder groups, and the government. Just keep in mind that, while you may think all of these ideas have merit, your current Corporate Governance does not have to contain them all at this time (see the earlier outline of factors relating to "Organization" and Procedural Matters").

Chapter X

Spouses, Families and Careers: Steering a Balance Through the Rocks and the Shoals

I've always found it puzzling how many senior business executives find more time to spend at their country clubs, trade associations, golf and shooting outings, industry conferences and even alumni association functions than with their families. Inasmuch as one's business career is influenced by relationships, all these extracurricular activities are great, but there is no relationship as significant as those concerning the executive's spouse and family. This relationship is a fundamental element in your career; given the varied aspects of the importance of your spouse and family support; one might say this relationship truly is your "anchor to windward" in terms of both your career and your life. The family relationship, depending on its nature and strength, can prove to be the major support in helping you achieve career success. However, if not well planned and carried out, it can result in the greatest single adverse influence to your career.

The subject is eminently complex and sensitive. Prefacing its discussion, I must admit that I'm not suggesting one needs to be married to be a successful executive. Many CEOs and leaders in other organization venues are not. However, experience has shown that it helps to be married far more frequently than it hinders. As you progress in your career, the air becomes increasingly rarified in several respects, social as well as professional. You will find that several, perhaps most of your career competitors are married, and obviously, the promotion pyramid, which featured many career opportunities at its base, becomes increasingly narrow as it progresses to its point. Indeed, you may already be married. If you are or if you're not, I believe this subject matter may prove a litmus test of relationships.

A career in which you are totally dedicated to achieving your professional potential can be extremely demanding. This is the same whether the career is in business, government, charity or any professional field. Demands are placed on your time and attention; demands which are constant and unyielding. There also is the "variety of unrelated reasons" to which we referred earlier. These pertain to customs and cultures, reflected in social structures and psychological issues.

Incidentally, to these discussions, please excuse my gender usage. "Spouse," as used herein refers either to the male or female partner in a marriage. For ease in writing, instead of repeating such phrases as "his or her," "he or she," and so forth, I have used the male gender – he, him and his. There is no discrimination intended and I hope none is inferred. Also, I am not a marriage counselor, a psychologist, or a sexual relations (or other "male-female" relations) expert. The thoughts and related suggestions expressed herein are based solely of my experience and on that of people I know and respect. These experiences have sufficient breadth and diversity that I believe they should provide you a worthwhile perspective that will help you make your own decisions.

Marriage can be a strong bulwark to a business career. For one thing, especially in the Western culture, a marital relationship is anticipated by most colleagues. While attitudes change over time, a single executive, like it or not, still can be suspect. Sidewise glances and oblique comments abound. Gossip, some born of competitive intentions, often centers on such comments as "It's too bad (you provide the name) isn't married for he is such an interesting person." "I can understand the time demanded of a career, but, after all, he should realize that marriage makes a more complete person, a real asset in business management." Or more daring, "Is there something wrong with (the name again), why isn't he married?" "Can't he 'get along' with the opposite sex? " "Maybe he is too 'self-centered'" and so forth. These are only examples of the "variety of unrelated reasons" referred to earlier. Believe me, the knives will be out, and it should come as no surprise as these and similar types of subjective, parochial, negative thoughts will color the environment as you advance career-wise, and the passage of time doesn't seem to change the situation.

However, marriage also can be positive for other, more objective reasons. The idea, previously expressed, that "no man is an island" perhaps is more true in the business environment that elsewhere. Occasionally at least, you will find that you need counsel from a person in whom you have the greatest trust. Who better (assume the marriage is truly a partnership) than a spouse, a person to whom you confide your greatest life's concerns? An understanding, compatible spouse provides this needed confidentially. The 'operational' words, however, are 'understanding' and compatible.'

This brings us to the first topic on our Check List. One should attempt to identify in a prospective marriage mutual basis for a <u>contented</u> relationship. Forget the flowers and birds of happiness. See contentment. Lust, sexual attractiveness, a "trophy" partner which reflect your ego are not the criteria for a successful marriage, contented or not. The fragrance, cosmetic and personal care industries have developed on the back of people desperately seeking to maintain their sensuous and sexual attractiveness. Physical attractiveness like youth is an ephemeral thing. It simply will not last, and neither will a sound spousal relationship based on such.

The characteristics of understanding and compatibility are many and diverse. Marked differences in ages and social and economic backgrounds are good examples. The family environment of the prospective couple is another. Compatible social and intellectual interests, possibly based on these foregoing factors, are important. Two significant aspects that play increasing roles in a proposed relationship are that (a) personalities and interest – as well as the degree of physical attractiveness – change, and (b), surprisingly, a marriage not infrequently results in children. These aspects of a relationship, one somewhat less obvious than the other, seldom receive adequate attention of its importance to a business career that it should until the marriage ceremony and a good portion of one's life is long past.

To repeat somewhat, the management career is a very demanding mistress or master, over time becoming increasingly so. More time and attention is required. This factor, plus eventual, probable changes in respective interests and desires between the careerist and the spouse, places stress on even of the soundest marriage, which is difficult to foresee at the beginning. The ambition characterized of the careerist requires considerable absence from home, changing acquaintanceships and possibly heightening egocentricity, the magnitude of which seldom was understood or appreciated at the time of the marriage. The interest of the spouse, given the capabilities of desires at the beginning, usually also changes over time, particularly as the couple becomes more affluent and more time becomes available to the spouse to engage in other activities. Considerable maturity and understanding – coupled with constant, objective and sometimes painful communications – are required to hold together successfully these diverse threads. Also, with time, unforeseen changes occur in matters relating to health, energy, vigor, etc., which easily can place additional pressures on a marriage relationship.

Given how busy we all are, even the eventuality of change seldom gets more than a passing mention as we go through day-to-day events. Seldom do we reflect on its possible impact or a marital relationship. I would suggest that, in considering a marriage, you and your prospective spouse might find it of value to consider the following factors, particularly how change might affect them:

1. Difference in age – Consider a delta of 10 to 12 years as the maximum. A wider disparity eventually can result in conflicts in various social interests, friendships, retirement aims, responsibilities for the development of children, economic security plans and so forth. For some reason, women seem to mature more rapidly than men do, at least in through the 20s, especially in the emotion and judgment areas. Thus, all things being equal (which they never are), the edge in age – the older – probably might be the male.

2. The "Like Father, Like Son" Syndrome – In spite of all the romantic prior ideas of compatibility of values, interests, etc., one's family continues to be a significant influence on a prospective couple, unless it is quite dysfunctional – the family, that is. Thus, should the prospective spouse be the male, the careerist should get to know his father and the spouse should do the same with the careerist's

mother. There's far more than a 'even chance' that the person you are considering marrying will, in most cases – particularly in serious matters – act and have the same values, customs and outlook as the respective parent. If the mother is frivolous, there is a good bet the daughter will be the same; likewise the son vis-à-vis the father. This is especially true if the respective family is reasonably wealthy. Compatibility starts here. Take some time to get a good understanding of the environment. How about three years or so? Seems a long time. This is not an inconvenience considering that it's important to your executive career, which took considerable longer to put in place.

3.   "Leader, Follower" – Men or women who are the oldest of several siblings, almost irrespective of age, frequently bring to the party a leadership quality. After all, since they were four or five years of age, they've been the leader; and there are few reasons to expect they will change in a marital relationship.

Conversely, the younger or youngest child, for a variety of reasons, may, even subconsciously, look for a father or mother figure in the spouse or the careerist; a dependency. Should the prospective spouse or careerist be an only child, they could have either of these traits, depending on their parents, their age and maturity. The same aspects relate to gender, the old "Venus," "Mars" factor.

4.   An Exit Strategy? In my opinion, if from the start you rely on an escape route instead of giving reasonable time to test the waters, forget it. If you begin by considering prenuptial agreements, the possibility of divorce or annulments is a likelihood that the relationship will end on the rocks, based on the most insignificant challenges. A relationship with the 'upfront' caveats isn't worth the time and trouble, no matter how beautiful, handsome, brilliant or affluent the prospects. The time required for your career will be seriously impaired.

Changes, over time, may lead to major irreconcilable events leading to a possible separation or divorce eventually. However, you both will be far more mature at that point, enabling you to evaluate things as adults and perhaps capable of thinking of people other than yourselves, possibly your children.

5.   Cultural Challenges – A marriage involving different cultures, native languages, ethnic, religious and political backgrounds possibly may prove interesting, but challenging. While such hurdles should not be viewed as game stoppers, a marriage of like backgrounds – as in interests – will be easier, particularly if a family is in your marriage plans. Again, in like content, a good marriage often requires intellectually compatibility. Look beyond physical beauty or handsomeness; aspects which largely lessen in most people by age 50 or 60, and then the couple is left with little, if these characteristics proved to be paramount in the marriage decision.

6.   Rates of Maturing – I would suggest that a careerist not consider marriage until he or she (there I go again) has achieved maturity, level of judgment and career status. I think there are few things worse or detrimental to a marriage than a careerist who "doesn't know what they want to do," and is jumping periodically from job to job, or company to company. Age benchmarks that should provide sufficient experience and judgment: the male at least 33 years of age; the female at least 28. Go ahead and prove me wrong.

7.   Attitudes and Interests Change with Time – For some relatively inexplicable reason, the female of the relationship at a fairly early age seems to be more aware of the economic, social and intellectual potential of the male than vice versa. However, of equal importance, she appears to be less aware of her own eventual changes in interests and goals. Consequently, at near midpoint in one's career, at a time management and responsibilities are building – and senor career opportunities are beckoning – one suddenly and unexpectedly finds his or her spouse considering departures from

the hereto decided 'norm.' This could be a desire to start a business (or enter the theater), obtain a Degree (or another Degree), become a global tour guide, etc. Adopting a child, volunteering, learning a foreign language, getting a job and travelling represent nothing of a significant change as compared to these. Again, the factor of <u>Change</u>.

While there is, no way, one can anticipate the nature and timing of such change in thinking, one certainly can anticipate and plan for the possible eventuality, and contemplate options. Again, as is true in so many of your executive decisions, your job is to maintain communications – continual communications.

In this regard, encourage your spouse to consider options for future interest. Changes in the direction of their life – fresh thinking – often help both them and you in your relationship. Suggest idea and 'force' them to tell you why or why not. Help to prepare them for options of their interest. These actions will ensure communications and will keep you in the loop. Don't, at your career peril, merely attribute such spousal thinking to "dreaming," "PMS," or some other superficial cause. This is a definite mistake; one that some night might find you coming home to an empty house.

8. Handling "Career Competitors" – You, as the non-career spouse, have spousal competitors for the organization's senior positions, especially that eventually of the CEO. Be constantly aware of this and keep on your guard. It is entirely possible that your careerist, caught up in the challenges of their "work-a-day" world, isn't as aware as they should be of the subtle and intricacies of this often "back biting" competition. You must observe, communicate and keep your careerist informed. Help your careerist in their drive to excel and to set themselves apart. You best can meet and beat the competitors by acting together.

An important facet of this effort centers on keeping informed about your careerist's work and professional challenges. Support his ever increasing, time sensitive accountabilities, many of which will impact you because of the careerist' absences. Again, as in all of the professional and marital relationships, you are a team.

9. The "Partner" Spouse – A responsibility of the non-career spouse is to help the career spouse to better understand the evolution that you both face. The scope of the non-career spouse's thinking must include data regarding the entire business world. He or she must stay informed. Provide updates of articles, references, opinion columns and so forth, including their viewpoints of subject matter to the career spouse. To a significant degree, the non-career spouse is the career spouse's alter ego.

An important function of the non-career spouse is to assist the careerist in the transformation from a "doer" to a "delegator." It is important that the non-career spouse heighten their joint awareness that they are a team, concentrating on their career future. The two individuals should act as partners in understanding and implementing the career path, understanding the nature of the sacrifices required to achieve success. The executive who senses the future and implements what is needed will win.

10. Children and Family – The decision regarding children is a most important one, and should be decided as you consider marriage. The female partner falls heir to this challenge, be it a biological event or adoption. This is a seventeen-year span that will affect her time, interests and life style almost continually, and will require the male partner's time and participation. More than birth or legal processes are involved. Children must be reared carefully, and this requires a partnership involvement as fully as a career. As a careerist sets the example and standard for their people, so they do also for their children.

A two-career marriage, another pre-marriage decision. While, given judicious planning and attention, the responsibilities can be shared, rearing children is going to be considerable more difficult in a "two-career" family. Assigning the job over to a Nanny or a posh boarding school is not an effective substitute.

An important consideration, one related to both the family and the career, is the effect on the female part of the equation following her 15th to 17th year of child dedication. Call it the "Empty Nest" syndrome or whatever, but don't ignore planning for this transition. Whether or not you your spouse enjoy this "breather' is of no consequence. Your partner probably now is in her mid to late-40s. You, the careerist, still are flitting about the globe getting your ego salved at almost every turn, and what now is in it for her? It's Point No. 7, above, in Spades. She, of course, will continue to assist you in your career advancements, but she, too, has a life, and it's your responsibility to help her "fill the void."

11.   Life Style Compatibility – There must be complete agreement regarding the significance you both place on the objective of a successful business career, of the careerist becoming a business leader. Required sacrifices in the career path must be understood and appreciated. Frequent relocations undoubtedly will occur which uproot the family's entire life style. This can become a real rub in a marriage relationship, even though you both agreed on it at the outset. This is one reason, in the uniform military services, it often is said that a "military brat" makes the best spouse for a service member. They have been totally acquainted since childhood how military career requirements impact the family and they've learned personally and vicariously how to cope.

As you sit, enjoying time with your fiancé or fiancée, a valuable use of such time would be to come to agreement about your mutual interests – and the cost – in the careerist member becoming chairperson, president and Chief Executive Officer of a major global corporation. Let's face it we come this way only once. Two people destined for marriage should assess together lives possibly involving problems with frequent and extended absences, increases in the spouse's homemaking, child rearing and concurrent marriage support responsibilities, frequent changing social economic and intellectual milieu, budget constraints, and, yes, boredom at times.

If this soul searching adequate – and relatively frequent – you, mutually, may well decide that your career goal, instead of a corporation's "top spot" should be geared to a somewhat lesser career objective. One that provides sufficient income to live well, assist the children through college, and have funds for travel, investment retirement, and so forth, i.e., an investment-based life. There surely is nothing wrong with such a constructive career alternative, if that's what <u>both</u> of you want.

In considering life style changes, be aware of a possible, eventual "picket fence"-"narcissist" conflict. Not infrequently, and perhaps subconsciously, one spouse over time may become contented in achieving considerably less recognition or material comforts than those desired by their partner – the so-called "picket fence" syndrome. Conversely, and this seems to occur more frequently with males rather than females, the newly crowned 50 to 55 year old president and/or CEO seems to lose his objective bearings or direction. He appears anxious to take on attributes of a younger, more dynamic, possible re-birth of his former self. Increases in physical workouts, tanning sessions and adopting trendy hairstyles are only the beginning. He moves on to motorcycles, sky diving, polo playing and sports cars racing. Celebrity relationships are developed to complement what he sees as his new Adonis-like status – all involved in the "Narcissist" complex. These changes occur, and not too infrequently. Of course, they create considerable stress on the marriage and on the family. To the extent you and your spouse recognize such chameleon-like future possibilities, and alert each party from time to time, you very likely can avoid these occurrences and the inevitable stress.

12.   Think Before Acting – Don't start something – anything – not <u>directly</u> related to your career that you don't intend to do forever. This seems to be such a small thing, but it is the proverbial "molehill" that rapidly will become a "mountain," and it can lead to a bumpy marriage. "Something," in this case, truly means "anything." Attempt early on to define the responsibilities of the career spouse and those of the non-career spouse; and clearly divide them. When one of you steps over this line, the initial response from the other is "thank you." When this action is repeated, it becomes expected and if not performed, a relationship hiccup may well occur. This spans the spectrum from driving the career spouse to the office, servicing the car, caring for the landscape, to the career spouse "dropping off the kids," making the bed, planning the vacation, paying the bills, etc. As mentioned in discussing our Career Guidelines, little credit will be forthcoming by performing the work, much, possibly long term criticism if the work, once started, does not continue. Conversely, never let your spouse undertake a task that you should be performing.

13.   The "Last Word" Condition – It seems necessary that one spouse or the other sometimes believes he or she needs to have the last word in a discussion. The last word being, in their minds the final most important thought. An acquaintance once told me a story about this that I think has both an element of humor and of truth. He related that whenever he had a serious discussion or an argument with his wife, he always had the last word. It was, "I'm sorry, Darling," "You are right, Dear," or something similar. To insist on making the last word is juvenile and can become a habit painful to an otherwise good marriage. It only tends to continue a "you said, I said" dialogue without achieving an understanding or agreement.

An ounce of civility compensates for a ton of apologies. This is certainly true in a marriage. If you address and treat your spouse and your children as you do a friend or perhaps even a stranger, you should be on the way to a great relationship. Let the Golden Rule prevail and let the "final word" be "Good night."

Given the assumed attitude of the reader, I mention this point only as a caution. I've witnessed social instances in which a business executive, attempting to be accepted as "one of the group," will use his spouse or an event in her life as a subject of what he considers as a humorous anecdote. To make a person a butt of a joke is inexcusable. Such acts violate our guidelines regarding discussing personal affairs or saying something about someone which is not complementary. Personally, I would be reluctant to hire a person so inclined, and should they be a member of my company, they would undergo immediate counseling.

14.   You are the Standard, Always – You are the guide for your children and an equal if not a mentor for your spouse. They learn from you. In today's environment, much more than in the nation through the 1950s, you and your spouse must be the examples for your children. No one else is or will be. In matters of disagreement attempt to keep them from becoming arguments or animosities by approaching these situations with calmness, quietude and a reasoned manner. This pattern will be adopted by your children and they will succeed with it. If you are frugal, and they understand the value of that action, chances are that they too will be frugal. You can't very well advocate family, household and social economies by sporting an Aston-Martin and talking about your posh deep sea fishing excursions. Like a business situation, if you can't control your emotions, absent yourself, returning only when you can be the adult they will respect.

15.   Personal Financial Affairs – The subject of money and financial management frequently is a critical challenge to a successful marriage, particularly in the early years of the marriage and of one's career. This subject deserves frequent review between the marriage partners. Early on, you and your spouse must develop a practical plan for expenditures and savings or investment. I might suggest that

you make provisions for savings and investment first, and they practice restricting expenditures for living that will enable you to continually increasing the amount you save. Concentrate on your needs, identify but postpone buying or investing in your wants. Assuming you and your spouse possess the judgment and common sense to make successful lives, ostentation or "keeping up with the Jones" will not hold any interest for you. Only people who lack self-confidence, who have trouble knowing themselves need to make a statement, making show of their material wealth. Practice frugality. Both of you will find considerable pleasure and enjoyment in watching your investments and savings grow.

You also are providing a sound example for your children. An approach to planning and managing personal finances, perhaps more frugal than you would choose is provided in Appendix 'J'.

16. Communicate – Your spouse should be your closest friend, your strongest ally, your intellectual equal and, as a partner, your strongest asset. As such, trust and faith must be absolute, and there should be no secrets, particularly concerning one's health or frustrations. You should ensure that each other is fully informed about your respective conflicts, challenges and concerns; such exchanges frequently go far to solving such. Habitually discuss your thoughts, plans, intentions and schedules with her or him, and in advance, particularly those that may involve finance, health or others, which might involve your partner. Learn early in your relationship those things of importance to your partner, and although they may be minor to you, assiduously attend to them out of respect for him or for her.

From the beginning of your relationship, include your future spouse as often as practicable in your business and social activities. Encourage her or him to overcome whatever reluctance they may have in participating in such activities. After all, as the supporting spouse, they will be an active asset in your career as it progresses. In turn, join them in events of their interest. Also, as much as possible, develop activities that can be done together; things that they enjoy particularly.

17.   "Space" – Recognize the need for independence, for "having some space." This applies to both you and your spouse. Encourage periods in which you each can be alone. Vacation alone occasionally should either or both of you find this beneficial. Avoid the "pumpkin shell" environment. I know that, from time to time, I appreciate getting away and, free of guilt, spend a few days or so just being alone, reading, walking, swimming, sleeping, etc.; a "space" needed to totally "recharge the batteries." All of us benefits occasionally from such personal freedom.

18.   "The Four Horsemen of the Apocalypse" – Remember marriage's *Four Horsemen of the Apocalypse* which alerts you that things are well on their way to "going downhill" for both parties. The *Four Horsemen* are (a) Contempt (Dismissing your partner by sarcasm, facial expressions or other actions, indicating he or she is too unreasonable or stupid for you to take seriously. This is the Lead Horse, and the worst), (b) Criticism (Being continually critical of their speech, dress, punctuality, manners, habits, etc., especially in public), (c) Defensiveness, (always attempting to prove the other party is wrong, interrupting, insistent on "Having the last word," etc., and (d) Stonewalling, (Usually, a male position. Not speaking which translates into "You're not worth talking with or listening to). You would not treat any of your friends or acquaintances, or even your worst enemies in this way. Why would you do so to someone you profess to respect, trust and love?

I have the pleasure of having several long time business acquaintances in various parts of the world, all of whom are married and have successful management careers; some of whom have businesses that involve their spouses. I am frequently amazed how their relationships appear interesting and content yet, because of varying customs, how different are the relations between them. In the Orient, spouses consider each other equals, but accept living and working apart for considerable periods. In the Middle East, the female in the marriage, based on western thought, would seem to be restricted, to be "put upon." Yet they, too, accept their role and enjoy what appears to be a life of contentment and pleasure. However, as referenced earlier, marriages of career-oriented individuals representing significantly different cultures would be challenging at least, difficult at best. Also, more so if child rearing is considered.

A note: This book does not discuss the challenges of single parent families or the severe challenges of making marriages work and achieving family successes when one or the other spouse is burdened with situations involving alcoholism, drug abuse, wife or husband abuse and other deep causes of dysfunctional family relations. I haven't discussed these subjects, not because they are not vital to family and children development, but because people far more qualified than I already have presented much professional literature on these subjects.

Chapter Summary: Sound family relationships are essential to an executive's career success, and a constructive, contented marriage is the Keystone to developing a sound family. Recognizing that severe competition exist, both internally and externally, for the CEO's responsibilities, an executive possessing a sound marriage is in a stronger, competitive position usually than one who is not married. However, to achieve a sound marriage takes as much hard work and constant attention as succeeding in a senior executive career. There is also relative little time for the careerist to relax, given that he or she is the Standard for their spouse and children as well as their professional colleagues. One might say they are "center stage," 24/7/365 on at least Two Fronts, in military jargon. The "mission," in this case, is not only the perpetuation of a better company, but through the executive's children's children, the founding and perpetuation of a better society. Given today's sociopolitical environment, this challenge rests with individuals of this type and their families.

Chapter XI

Consultant: Why and Why Not?

There is an adage I believe it is of Italian origin, which says, *"He learned to shave on someone else's chin."*

In my experience, this sums up today's management consulting industry pretty well. At least it describes quite well the backgrounds of the majority of individuals that today fill the lower ranks of the so-called management consulting firms. Here I refer to firms comprising the <u>general management</u> consulting practice. I'm not referring to individuals or firms involved in advising on specific areas such as research & development, new product development, accounting and auditing, information technology, electronic systems, executive search, project management, legal affairs, and so forth. An interesting transition has occurred in the industry during the past twenty years or so; some of the more specialized organizations have turned to include also general management consulting while some of these general management consulting groups have broadened to include assistance in some of the more specialized areas. As you may have noted, several of the organizations focusing on these niche areas prefer to be known as professional service firms. Some also concentrate on specific major markets such as the *Private Sector* and *Government* or *Defense*.

Before going further, I believe that management consulting firms can serve a most constructive purpose. As the aphorism about other organization indicate, "If they didn't exist, someone should invent them." It is more how the client manages (and controls) their use than a question of their value. The services of a management consulting firm are expensive – by any measure. Thus, you had better know their capabilities and their potential before you retain them.

Organizationally, in most of the current major management consulting firms there are up to five echelons in their structures. These include, from top to bottom, Senior Partners, Partners, Senior Associates or Principals, Associates and Consultants. The Senior Partners, initially the founders of the firms, maintain relationships with senior executives of major client organizations, some still serve on Boards of Directors. The Partners establish and maintain contact with smaller clients. The Senior Associates lead the assignment teams and do most of the actual consulting or advisory work. The Consultants, for the most part, conduct supporting research, perform related analysis work and "crunch the numbers." The Senior Partners and the Partners act as Client Handling Officers, overseeing the progress and quality of assignments. All of these individuals also are marketing focused, seeing additional work or extensions to ongoing assignments. However, the Partners have the greatest responsibility in this area. The organization structure largely is a matrix, although their definitely is a hierarchal relationship within the upper ranks.

My experience indicates that most if not all of these people, including supporting administrative personnel, are the "cream of the crop" in terms of education, intelligence, ambition, character, competitiveness and work ethic (diligent, hard work). I wouldn't necessary characterize them as "brilliant," but some surely are. An important incentive for these traits is the diversity of the assignments and the breadth or scope of the client population, including international travel and its global nature.

Compensation-wise, putting this in terms analogous to an industrial corporation, in addition to base pay based on hours and billing rates, the Partners receive the options, incentive compensation, etc., the Associates enjoy attractive increases in annual base compensation and the Consultants, receive bonuses.

Referring to the previous chapter, given the characteristics of many consulting assignments – the variety, hours, travel, etc., a sound marriage with both partners available to continuously make their contribution is difficult in the management consulting environment. It takes a special, mature, understanding, focused non-career spouse to make it work.

There is no doubt, as aforementioned, that most people in management consulting are highly intelligent. They always have been, and over the years, this level of intellect has improved further. The question about this profession is not intelligence or the other characteristics mentioned earlier. The question relates to experience and the degree of actual management background. To advise a client's management of what to do and how it is to be done, one should have experienced working with and through people – with all of their warts, etc., to know the practicality of one's advice. However, more and more, at least based on my experience, the lack of corporate management backgrounds extend further and further into the upper ranks of major consulting firms.

One is reluctant to mention it, but the politics and inherent inertia of many business organizations can adversely affect the counsel provided by an individual with 4 to 6 years of yeoman-type work and an MBA from the Tuck School (Dartmouth), the David A. Tepper School (Carnegie Mellon), the Kellogg school (University of Michigan) or the Wharton School (University of Pennsylvania).[4]

Over time there are psychological shifts experienced in the approach most people in the consulting profession take to client assignments when new, bright-eyed Consultants or possibly Associates will seek out innovative, different, exciting solutions for their client. As these individuals become more experienced with ongoing businesses, they tend to adopt or incorporate the base line thinking of the older hands such as the Partners, namely "prove to me what really is wrong with what this client currently is doing?" However, unfortunately the rate of increases in the consulting business is outstripping the development of this competence. The "base line" thinking which is so important is not catching up with the challenge. Admittedly, there are values in combining the unalloyed new thinking of the inexperienced with the base line thinking of the experienced "elders" who have "been there, seen that," but there also are opportunities for extreme

---

[4] These institutions in recent years have been ranked among the nation's top graduate business schools by the annual Wall Street Journal – Harris survey.

danger, e.g., the personal computer and IBM, and the advent of continuous rolling and the McKeesport Tin Company.

Along the way, on my career path, I engaged in management consulting for over a decade, working in several countries as well as in the United States. I enjoyed it. It was an education and it was part of my maturing process. But I also was haunted by an awkward feeling; I was hardly old enough to shave.

The dictionary definition of a consultant is a good one. A "consultant," according to Webster's Ninth Edition is "one who consults others," "one who gives professional advice or service, an expert." The operational word here is "expert" not analyst, not researcher but an expert. An expert, by definition, is one who is experienced as well as skilled and talented in a given field or area. He or she as an expert "has been over the ropes," or "through the chairs." They plainly "have been there" and "done that."

Because of the complexity and newness of today's business challenges, no one is self-sufficient. Occasionally, specialized knowledge or assistance is required; a "one time shot," as it were. Recognizing that an organization cannot always afford – nor need – to have unique or specialized talent within its internal structure, consulting, not unlike any out-sourced service, can prove of considerable value. However, considerable thought and planning should be undertaken before retaining such service. Also, you and your management should approach this matter with a reasonable amount of skepticism. You also should emphasize that the use of consultants will continue to be the exception in accomplishing your work.

To better appreciate consulting service, a "thumb nail" history might prove useful. Industrialists, in the United States, dating from the latter half of the 19th Century, occasionally sought advice from individuals in whom they had considerable previous experience and great confidence. Gould, Carnegie, Vanderbilt, Ford and Rockefeller, people with whom you are acquainted, all received such counsel. The Carnegie-Frick relationship is a good example of one that evolved into a business partnership partially due to counsel from finance and legal advisors.

However, it wasn't until the Federal government began intervening in business affairs that professional firms, instead of close personal acquaintances, commenced entering the picture. Legislation and regulations relating to taxation, securities trading, interstate commerce, corporate combinations and trade laws saw professional advisory groups gaining considerable notice. The first largely were financiers, legal firm, tax counsel, plant and property security firms and banks involved in credit and the transfer of assets. Then, in the early 1900s, came the emergence of Efficiency Experts or Scientific Management advisors such as Frederick W. Taylor. "Time and Motion" studies were among the first of such services. The consulting industry grew with Operations Research and Organization Theory entering the lexicon in the late 1930s. By the early 1940s, advisory activities evolved into "general management" consulting organizations, usually taking the form of limited partnerships. In the decade subsequent to World War II, these firms expanded rapidly, partly due to the belief that superior American management practices were due to consulting assistance and partly due to the global industrial and management requirements of many foreign companies at that time. Thus, besides legal and investment banking advisors, we saw the rapid expansion of consulting organizations such as Arthur D. Little (1886), Booz, Allen & Hamilton (1914), McKinsey & Company (1926), Cresap, McCormick & Paget (1938), etc. In addition, specialized advisors, who earlier had formed firms expanded in providing targeted services such as executive recruiting, accounting and auditing (the CPAs), advertising, lobbying or government relations, public relations, project management, and so on.

At this point, in the early to mid-1950s, mainly because of explosive market demands, management consulting firms changed from being comprised principally of experienced executives to organizations drawing largely on younger individuals, college graduates with three to five years of some work experience. Also, due to the postwar opportunities for consulting services in Europe and Asia, the 1950s and 1960s witnessed the next boom in the consulting profession as firms, becoming international organizations and took American management practices abroad.

Subsequently, in the 1970s and 1980s the growth of information technology saw the next expansion, which also was the period in which European consulting firms began expanding. Concurrently, several of the major, global accounting and auditing firms, recognizing the variance in profitability between hourly rates of changes and fee-based businesses, moved into information systoles consulting, and began looking into the general management consulting service opportunities as well. I this same period, the client population sought more specialized global assistance in such fields as mergers and acquisitions, executive compensation, strategic planning (or corporate development), Back Office data processing, and, more recently, corporate governance.

Beginning in the late 1970s, principally with the expansion of the software development market, the dearth of applicable experience found many firms recruiting "consultants" directly from colleges, many with only a Bachelor of Science Degree, some with an MBA, but relatively few individuals with other than academic-related experience. During this period, business problems, particularly those involving global markets, technology development and industry expansion, were becoming more complex, creating an environment in which a consultant's limited practical background was found wanting; requiring the more experienced, mature organization leaders to take more active roles.

This rapid expansion of needs for consulting assistance resulting in several things that caused increased skepticism in the market. For one thing, because of the dearth of consultants possessing tested, practical experience clients were being charged excessive hourly billing rates for people doing little more than data gathering, basic analysis and helping on report writing. Clients in many instances were paying for consulting services when actually they were acting as a "training bed" for inexperienced college graduates, the "shaving on someone else's chin" syndrome. Competitive pressures at times also resulted in some consulting firms hiring client executives to meet partnership needs, particularly in the technology areas. Some firms took advantage of the clients' executive shortages to insert their own Associates and Partners into the client organization. While providing the client some needed executive talent, this action also availed the consulting firm of "rainmakers" within the client organization to develop future work. These practices caused several potential clients to be increasingly wary of consultants and the quality of consulting services during the 1980s and early 1990s.

Another interesting development occurred in the general management consulting field beginning in the 1980s and continuing to the present: That of the consultant performing work, effective as an executive, within the client organization. This practice has been the case for some years in the Government and by services provided by some specialized firms. However, until the late '70s and early '80s, in the private sector general management consultants normally were retained to perform a specific piece of work. This work, a consulting assignment, usually was awarded competitively, had a definite, and committed "start" and "end" and provided an identifiable product or deliverable. Now, some consultants work within a client organization, report to client supervisors and managers, and perform what best can described as regular, ongoing work.

Consulting firms, naturally, are in business to make money – often, they earn considerable money. Most firms charge professional fees based on time provided in carrying out consulting assignments plus expenses. The Hourly Billing Rate – the amount charged the client – of Consultants, Associates, Partners or Principals vary widely, both within and among firms; ranging from $150 to $500 or more. The hourly fee for Senior Partners of major consulting or legal firms easily may exceed $1,500. While the adage often is true that "you get what you pay for," you as the leader of a client organization may want to ensure that your people carefully control the consultant's proposal, the work as it is being done and the bills, being wary of the "incidental" visit or the purpose and time spent in a "status phone call" from a Senior partner, indicating an interest in knowing "how things are going?" Such seeming interest in the assignment can be expensive, costing you the Officers minimum hourly billing rate. When one considers that the personal income of an individual acting in a consulting capacity usually equals about one-third of his or her hourly billing rate, it becomes apparent that this business can be highly profitable; a business in which one could be seriously interested in investing.

In the past, during the same period as one's "hand shake was his bond," the cost and time for proposed consulting assignments were pretty general; approximations, and were accepted by prospective clients as such. Indeed, most ethical consulting firms would keep the client posted on progress and status, but, again, time and cost formed a general commitment. Nowadays, I believe increasingly these arrangements take the form of a legal (or quasi-legal) contract. As the CEO, you should have your people, because of the nature of the proposed assignment and the time and attention being given the work by the responsible company executive, decide which direction is appropriate.

Increasingly, as competition and desire for corporate wealth grew, several consulting firms – reputable in their fields of experience and expertise – began promoting themselves as being qualified to provide services beyond their historic "bill of fare." This thrust into the somewhat unknown was most prominent among CPA firms which, as alluded to earlier, saw the general management consulting field as more lucrative that their traditional tax and auditing business. Three or four of the major CPA organizations have experienced wrenching management, personnel and organizational problems in making this leap. A determination as to which of their Partners would enjoy the relatively greater incomes (and which would not) proved an agonizing experience for these, heretofore well managed organizations. Also, this change from a well-disciplined, procedurally and legally controlled operating environment which characterized the CPA work to a relatively free situation in which general management consulting advice is offered, but is not required to be taken, resulted in reputations being sullied, some fatal to the firms involved.

Retaining Consulting Assistance

With this background and your own experience, let's assume that a problem is believed to have arisen and your management suggests considering seeking outside advice. In such instances, I have found it advisable to ask the executive suggesting outside assistance first to define the problem, and second to bend their best efforts to solve this defined problem before retaining an outsider. They also should be made aware that the costs for such outside service would be borne by their specific unit of the organization, including its impact on their incentive compensation awards.

This approach, the results of which are critiqued by others, for example, the Chief Financial Officer regarding a perceived challenge in the area of finance achieves two worthwhile ends. First, the managers dig in as to what is the exact nature, scope and <u>definition</u> of the alleged problem. Second, in so doing, they develop "first hand" knowledge of the nature of talent and experience required to solve it. They then are in position to identify and evaluate the type of advisory service they will retain and for which they shall pay. An important point to be identified in this approach is one – you and the company – do not want to pay more for the services being retained than the returns to be realized.

A third point is possible and might imply a concern. However, based on what management has learned about you, somewhat irrelevant because I don't think it will happen. That point is, to quote, "Sir (addressing you), I think your idea is great, but time pressures don't permit us to study this matter." In this case, your response and possible action has nothing to do with the alleged problem.

Besides checking references, which frequently is a "sometimes thing," have three or four firms invited that references and related intelligence indicate seem qualified to most successfully handle the work. Have them compete for the assignment. Depending on the nature of the problem, don't ignore individual experts, universities or research center is selecting competitors. The objective of this exercise is to obtain the most experienced, successful sources available. The cost of these competitive presentations, as well as the resulting proposals, is borne by the consulting firms. Require that the presentations be made by the people who would do the work. In selecting the advisory firm or individual, don't fall victim to the now, age-old "Big Blue" syndrome.[5] You're not retaining a name. You're considering retaining an expert that can solve the specific problem your management has identified. Also, in addition to your management ensuring themselves of the consultant's competence, have them guard against any attempt by a firm to get their people directly involved in the management of the company, i.e., the aforementioned "rainmaker" position. Reference checks should help in this regard.

Require written proposals from the prospective consultants, being alert to language and "boiler plate." I realize that some of these cautions may border on "motherhood," but I've frequently found repetition is good for both the soul and the company. These proposals are developed at the consultant's expense. Scrutinize this work, and require it be rewritten if you are not satisfied. A true professional will welcome your attention and your seriousness of purpose. Also, it gives the consultant "up front" an idea of the management-consultant relationship they will experience during the assignment (see Appendix 'K,' *Guidelines for Employing Management Consultants*).

These proposals should include a clear if concise definition of the problem or the purpose of the assignment, the approach (steps to be taken), the product expected – including the implementation and possible "next steps" – the time and cost to do the work, the identity and backgrounds of the consulting individuals to be engaged and the understanding to whom they

---

[5] In the early days of computers, IBM, a company that featured blue color in its equipment, was consider the unquestioned leader in all data processing activities. The company's reputation quite frequently sold its products and services for it. Few Boards and fewer managements would propose any competitor to "Big Blue," even though some outstanding competitors existed. Competitors with equal quality, after sales services, and lower prices. Hence the "Big Blue" syndrome.

will be responsible. Also, it is imperative that milestones be identified and a proposed schedule provided noting required client review and participation.

Closing comments about using consultants: It doesn't take a skeptic to realize that people often tell you what they think you want to hear. Consultants are no exception. Also, remember from your management "side of the fence," that the use of consultants can become a habit or a form of support on which you and your management become dependent. Consultants encourage this relationship for obvious reasons. While outsiders often can be more candid with you than your management, and sometimes may act for you in anonymous ways (for example, suggesting or being involved in acquisition or merger possibilities), they can unintentionally prove disruptive to the organization, causing dissension and harming morale.

Egos sometimes convince individuals that they are qualified to provide advice before they have experience and skills to do so. While education, intelligence, judgment and maturity surely are important management assets, to be an effective consultant or advisor, again, requires experience, if not a few "scars." As an aside, it is interesting to note how often executives who have failed or lost interest in being managers become consultants.

In the selection of an advisor, it is important to assure yourself that the Senior Partners, those who will be responsible for vetting the firm's work, have prior successful management experience in an industrial venue. This is a significant point because as has been pointed out a couple of times previously several of the major consulting firms today are directed by individuals who have come up through the consulting hierarchy without proven industrial experience. Also, be alert to consultants called into your organization or referred to you by outsiders such as by your investment or commercial bankers, creditors, legal firms, stockholders or the courts.

Without prior agreed restraints, adoption of such advice may well lead to poor counsel, conflicts of interest or to loss of confidentiality. This is an area of management prerogative to be acted on by you and your management alone.

Finally, be aware of the motivation of the sources – your own executives – who propose retaining consulting services. Motivations vary, and may be well founded. The motivating thoughts may stem from a justified need for specific expertise that is available only from outside sources. They may stem from a feeling of incompetence or frustration experienced in unsuccessful attempt to "find the answer," or even in defining the problem. However, motivation may originate from the invidious aim of attempting to secure a career position within the consulting firm the executive hopes will be retained for company work. This action represents a blatant conflict of interest, one justifying immediate termination of employment. Inasmuch as you as the CEO cannot possibly vet every potential relationship, I've overcome this threat by requiring any consulting contract being entertained by the company to contain language that it will not hire an employee of the company for at least three years after the completion of the subject consulting assignment and never to employee such an individual in an assignment for our company. This may appear quite severe; possibly "cutting off your nose to spite your face," but it will protect both you and the company from potential conflict of interest charges that could have grave career consequences.

Being a Consultant

Let's now examine the "other side of the coin," that of being a consultant rather than a line manager or executive.

For decades, young people, people possessing a college degree and some practical work experience, have been attracted by the siren's song of the consulting industry. This attraction, in part, results from the perception of the diverse, relatively fast moving nature of work envisioned in consulting assignments. In part, interest has been based on the relatively high salary scale of most consulting firms compared to, for example, basic to middle level supervisory or management jobs in manufacturing, banking, engineering, marketing and accounting firms.

Looking at the overall picture and career challenges in a strategic sense, I would strongly urge that one, particularly in the "near years" seek a line rather than a staff or consulting job. This would be a job in which you are responsible for producing something of value, something useful, and in planning and directing the efforts of others – motivating them to do so. If this, perchance, were an entry level task, I would suggest strongly, as emphasized previously, that you pick a reputable, widely recognized, well-managed company for such initial work. An important factor for your individual psyche and self-confidence is being involved with a product or system that has a technological-based purpose; one that depends little on advertising or promotion, for example an industrial or a medical-related product instead of a largely promotion-based fashion, food, cosmetic or personal care product.

After gaining experience, and enjoying some career success, in a line function, you then have "something to sell," particularly if you have continued for a time sufficient to have supervised or managed people in accomplishing work. You have made a contribution. You have added value. Now, as we discussed in Chapter II, you also have acquired a basis for better determining the nature of your long-term career interest.

Now, with three to five years of recognized success, you may decide to become a consultant, exploiting your experience, your self-confidence, your skills and your success for the advantage of others. Or for similar reasons, possibly having some innovative interest, you may look to a "start-up" opportunity as your major strategic career interest. In the medium to long-term, with such a background, you also have the potential to realize much greater income than would have been possible by initially choosing a consulting post. Overall, an individual who "hasn't been there," is a poor source from whom to seek advice.

A couple of historic quotations seem relevant to this discussion:

> *"Young men are fitter to invest than to judge,*
> *fitter for execution than to counsel,*

and fitter for new projects than for settled business."
- Francis Bacon, *Of Youth and Age* (1610)

"He who would distinguish the true from the false
Must have an adequate idea of what is true and [what is} false."
- Benedict Spinoza, *Ethics* (1677)

Management consulting, as a career, has all the challenges and aspects of interest for which one could wish for in a business career – except one: The confidence experienced through selecting, developing and managing people to produce a product or to directly provide a value added service. Consulting essentially is "advising," and, depending on the background and experience on which the advice is based, it also can provide a value added factor, but it's still advising – it's not doing. Its contribution is indirect.

Chapter Summary: Consultants can be a valuable resource. You should have your own company people identify the problem and determine the skills need to resolve it before considering retaining a consultant. Consultants should compete for your business, and the people making the presentation and drafting the proposal should be the same people doing the consulting work. You manage consultants in the same way you manage your people. i.e., by keeping the objective clearly in mind and by meeting time and accomplishment milestones, and budgets.

Consultants bear all expenses until they involve themselves in the actual consulting assignment. Consultants observe expenses, etc., and comply with all client policies in this regard. Consulting firms contractually commit themselves not to employ your people. If you are going to be a consultant – instead of a line executive, first take the time to "have something to sell." Without "something to sell," you'll probably be little more than an analyst or a "number cruncher."

Chapter XII

Government Intervention: Get Real—It's Only Going To Increase

One may speak of the "free market" system, "capitalism," a "free economy," and perhaps the idea that "The business of America is Business." However, insofar as laissez-faire is concerned, corporate America has not operated in such a relatively hands off environment for the past 30 years or so. Frankly, that isn't all bad."

Government intervention in industry, to the extent that it influenced the business climate, began with the Civil War. Industry, particularly in the north, was drafted into providing the Union with war equipment and supplies, for which it was handsomely remunerated. However, individuals who directed and managed business were taxed for the first time, allegedly to pay for the war effort. This "temporary" tax on income extended into the 1870s.

As the tax was repealed, government began direct intervention in business in the 1880s and 1890s with antitrust legislation and interstate commerce controls. So much for laissez-faire.

However, it is interesting to note that among the principal causes of such intervention was the greed and incompetence of a few leaders of major corporations. "Vision" often is identified as an important strength of successful industrialists. However, the lack of vision, particularly the failure by businessmen responsible for major assets to appreciate the results of expedients and lack of consideration concerning the public and the working populace, has been the principal cause of intervention by most federal and state governments since the 1870s. Reflecting on Taft-Hartley, Sherman antitrust, Equal Employment Opportunity legislation, interlocking directorate laws, the Internal Revenue Service, Federal Trade Commission, the National Labor Relations Board, Securities and Exchange Act, Fair Employment Practices Acts, takeover legislation and more recently regulations regarding the liabilities of directors and executives all have come about or received impetus because of inept management. And soon more intervention can be anticipated.

There's one thing that we can add to "death and taxes" as being certainties: more and more restrictive government intervention. Even if industry attempts to avoid this by "going private," moving abroad or not participating in government-sponsored business, U.S. business leaders – and future CEOs like you – must learn to deal with both state and federal governments. Often times, this will mean dealing with people who do not understand, or who do not want to understand business, refusing to appreciate the essential value of commerce to the future health and growth of the American economy.

An interesting note: while we deplore government intervention in principal, we simultaneously are coming to realize that privatization, subsidization or deregulation are the answers.

There is no doubt that American industrial and economic supremacy occurred and has been maintained due largely to the 19th century's open climate that permitted smart, strong men to exercise aggressive, cutthroat competition. East central coal deposits were developed and exploited for cheap energy using cheap labor, technology expanded exponentially, the factory system exploded, hard-headed competition cut costs, eliminating weak companies and inept managers, industries gained efficiencies through combining asset bases and specializing work practices. In fact, the industrial economy expanded so rapidly that the nation's money supply failed to keep pace with productivity, driving up interest rates and restricting credit availability. The focus was on wealth (which incidentally increased jobs) and increasing national demand. Little thought was given modern day aspects such as pollution, worker safety and preservation of natural habitats.

From the conclusion of the American Civil War to the late 19th century, first the railroads and then the telegraph system, the steel industry and the oil sector provided the underpinnings for the nation's spectacular growth. People like Isaac Singer, Alexander Graham Bell, Tom Scott, Henry Clay Frick,

James Hill, Jay Gould, Collis Huntington, George Westinghouse, John D. Rockefeller, J. P. Morgan, Andrew Carnegie and Thomas Edison were the economic "stem-winders." These people were ambitious, extremely hard working, independent, smart and aggressive. Several started out with less than nothing. This truly was the era of laissez-faire, a "no holds barred" period which saw American industry outstrip the world. Edison's reported belief that "genius is one percent inspiration and 99 percent perspiration" characterized many of his business contemporaries. The self-made success of these men caused great jealousies by those less inclined to work, who in turn gave votes to politicians if they would block the efforts of such businessmen. Hence, government increased its intervention in the nation's business.

Government intervention, given political impetuses because of thoughtless management actions, economic (read unemployment) conditions and the eagerness of politicians to capture votes by pandering to certain blocks of the electorate, took the form of the laws, acts, regulations, etc. (Please refer to Appendix 'I' for a historic background and a chronology of these enactments.)

Initially, Federal Government actions were aimed at limiting economic and political control by individuals or groups of individuals. Gradually, however, government intervention became politically motivated, acting and defending social issues that, directly or indirectly, led to attempting to influence the voting public, favoring the politicians proposing and enacting such legislation, regardless of the possible adverse strategic consequences on the nation's economy or welfare. One result of these Acts and laws, which is being witnessed today, is an increasing number of U.S. jobs moving abroad. It also is becoming politically necessary for the government to provide tariff protection and significant monetary "handouts" to inefficiently managed U.S. corporations to protect jobs and markets from increasingly efficient foreign producers.

It is difficult to appreciate how this deprecating, politically based tide can be reversed. Fortunately, we have it still within our control to "right the ship." However, it will require significant sacrifices on the part of the American public to do so; sacrifices similar to those experienced during the post-Great Depression years of the '30s to '40s. I find it difficult to envision this ever happening.

What to Do?

As businessmen and businesswomen, what can we do to stimulate the growth of our global industrial activities to the benefit of our shareholders and, indirectly, the nation? We can increase our focus and commitment to technological development. We can avoid engaging in government business or activities in which the Government can force on us further intervention and restrictions. We can encourage significantly greater productivity from our people, providing the investment in technology and advanced facilities required to complement their effort and commitment. We can strive through political action to rid ourselves of the self-serving politicians who have brought us to this crisis, electing thinking, sophisticated statesmen to our Congress who put Nation before Party; individuals who realize that the U.S. can and should accomplish such things as energy self-sufficiency. They also, appreciating the need for self-esteem on the part of our citizens, would act to end costly social programs that breed dependency, slothfulness and lack of self-confidence on a large segment of our population. Further, we can personally be much more frugal in our habits, including bringing our compensation more in line with our worth and our contributions. We also can adopt and promulgate philosophies and values in support of such policies.

Are we, and the present generation, too long engaged in "me first" practices – incapable of accomplishing this massive turn around? I must admit that I don't know. If we do, it will be the first time in recorded history that a nation faced with its economic and moral decline has had the spirit and dedication to reverse such trends.

But first, we here must convince ourselves that "it's worth the candle" to enter this strategic conflict, and to encourage others with a like commitment to join us to accomplish these goals. It will be a lengthy struggle, very possibly beyond our professional careers.

A step worth considering, if you conclude that government intervention is affecting, or can, seriously affect your company, the solution would be to adopt the practice of "fighting politics with politics." I don't advocate hiring a separate individual for your company's Government Relations work. However, again, only if government is a real threat, it would be of value to discuss the alternative of joining other like companies to underwrite an experienced individual – call him or her a lobbyist if you will – to make your case in political circles; with both state and federal governments. If this case is not made and the impact of adverse action on jobs in specific geographical voting areas is not realized, business adversaries will continue to win the day. The reason why I would recommend that a company not employ a separate representative for this work is the simple fact that any person hired for a specific piece of work will make a total, 100% time-consuming effort of it, regardless of the job. One must keep in mind that this is an <u>overhead</u> function. It is not directly engaged in making money for the company or the stockholders. These jobs, by their very nature, soon grow until the fee or salary paid to the individual responsible for this work represents the minor part by far of the total expenditures for this function.

Even more important than some other jobs in your company, overhead functions like this one require a well-conceived annual plan, a commitment by the individual. Without such a plan, activities soon swing out of control. Promises are made money is spent and little, if anything, except possibly a salved CEO's ego, results. Remember our organization discussion. Don't permit a "line position" to be created unless you are certain the incumbent will be responsible and accountable for <u>150% of value added</u> output. Don't permit an administrative position (read "overhead") to be created unless you are certain the incumbent will be responsible and accountable for <u>at least two, full-time</u> overhead jobs.

A word about individuals who might best (at least) help you in this work: don't consider Senators, House Members or Legislators. Seek out ambitious, experienced, mature, skilled "staffers" for this assistance. After all, these are the people who really run our governments. Don't give the recruiting job to someone else. Do it yourself. If the actions of government can seriously, adversely affect your business, the talent you retain to enter the list on your behalf deserve your personal attention. Conversely, if you conclude that this step does not require your direct involvement, then you don't need such help.

Lessening the Impact

While "turning back the clock" on the impact of government regulations, acts, laws, etc. probably will not be politically possible, as the senior business executive, you may lessen the impact of government influence on business in several ways.

1. Make certain your management personnel are apprised of regulations, both state and federal, of what they may and may not do, and how to do it. Also, ensure that they are knowledgeable about available assistance.
2. Ensure that records respecting employee relations are comprehensive from your point of view and are maintained in a timely and complete manner. Where practicable, request signatures.
3. Don't make exceptions. Stick to the law, including procedures.
4. Consider including another management individual to sit in on discussions of a disciplinary or corrective nature, including those relating to negative performance reviews, non-promotions, etc. Witnesses and records will prove invaluable.
5. Most importantly, treat your people civilly, fairly and with understanding. Again, no exceptions. This is particularly important in assigning and explaining work. "Exceptions" can be interpreted as "discrimination," an issue you don't want.
6. Should controversial actions become necessary, make certain the benefits more than outweigh possible problems. An example might be considering an "open shop" operation or contract. Seldom are things as advantageous as they first appear.

7. Think long and hard about undertaking government or government-related work. More and more regulations are being promulgated as to how companies must conform to labor and social requirements to qualify for government business. There also is an increasingly number of lawyers seeking fees to question the conformity of such companies, justifiably or not.

As a profit-oriented, constructively driven business leader, one should keep in mind that most government business is motivated to neither achieve profits nor value added results.

At the same time, for the good of your company and your shareholders, take advantage of what few things the government offers which can help you. This isn't being hypocritical. You, your employees, your shareholders and your suppliers have paid their hard-earned money in the form of taxes for these services. For example, the Ex-Im Bank can be used to help finance your exports. Exploit it for all it's worth. Likewise the patent, copyright and trademark services. Also, if your company is so engaged, tap into the governments' various research, development and engineering programs, filling the holes in your technology efforts with their often-superb scientific knowledge and progress. However, again, be wary to avoid "tied in" situations. We are willing to pay to pay for such assistance if necessary (it usually is not expensive for the actual worth seldom is realized), but again, don't become saddled with quid pro quo government requirements, regulations or restrictions on your business.

What Happened to Laissez-faire, Appendix 'L,' provides a historic perspective of the cause and effect of government intervention, interference and/or influence on business, including the creation and changes in taxes and several major Acts, Amendments, regulations and so forth from the nation's beginning until the present, i.e., mid 2010.

A final point: avoid being pulled into political contributions. Your job as CEO is to run a right ship. You are to serve your markets, benefit your shareholders, and fulfill your obligation to your creditors and debt financiers and to provide fair compensation for fair work to your employees. If these individuals wish to use the money they receive from the company to make contributions to political parties or individuals, to "causes" to charitable institutions or for other altruistic or civic purposes, that's their privilege, not your responsibility. You are to stay focused and committed to your corporate job.

Chapter Summary: Intervention, influence or interference by government in business will continue. The challenge for the CEO is to manage it so it does not prove a handicap to the success of the organization. Consideration should be given to staying outside the political arena to the extent practical, limiting participation in government-sponsored business contracts or agreements, insuring all company activities are audited and controlled well within the meaning of government or industrial regulations, Acts, etc., and being as transparent as in competitively possible with the shareholders, the public and the media.

Chapter XIII
"The "Fourth Estate"[6]: Plan to Gain From It

Whatever you may think of the media – and the opinions vary widely, in one form or another, its influence will continue, and you had better learn to live with it. In fact, taking the positive position, exercising astute management, you can make them work for you. I've found that in most instances if you work with them in good times, they will be more considerate and objective when you experience problems in less than favorable times and such bad times <u>will</u> occur. One needs go no further than the Toyota situation in early 2010 to realize this fact.

As a company's CEO, there will be a tendency by you to handle "first things first." When major challenges develop regarding product quality, key executive's departure, a major fire involving injury, or worse, to employees and possibly the public, the discovery of significant bribery, theft or fraud, a major contract problem, a sudden customer or client insolvency and so forth, your initial reaction, somewhat understandably, is to move immediately to resolve the problem. At that moment, you may place a relatively low priority on attention to the media. However, you would be dead wrong.

Before going further, let's define what this is all about. The media involves any channel of public communications, in some cases not-so-public communications. It ranges from global coverage by print and television to the internet. Also, it develops so fast that there well may be several other sources before you read this chapter. Also, as you probably are aware, while most serious journalist, publishers, et al, strives for objectivity, there are

---

[6] When the phrase *The Fourth Estate* first was used in 1792, it was attributed to Edmund Burke and referred to the press because at that time the press was the primary source of news transmitted to the public. However, today it generally includes all mass media, i.e. newspapers, television, radio, magazines and even the recently developed blogs and other internet-based sources. Early on, unlike today, the phrase was used in considerably ill repute.

exceptions and various hues to one's objectivity. There are communications sources that are favorably disposed to business. However, there are also some that are downright hostile.

Media attention, especially national, regional and local print medium, must be constant and unqualified. It should be part of your quarterly activity. Of course, some information is of a propriety and competitive nature. However, transparency should be your guide, and you must make yourself available, treating the people involved as a welcome part of your overall team. Keeping the media informed is just as important as your meetings with financial and industry analysts. Keep in mind: Your shareholders see and hear you once a year, your Board of Directors perhaps eight to ten times annually, your customers and competitors hardly ever. However, you and the company are exposed to them – and possibly, organizations representing acquisition, merger and licensing opportunities every time a press release occurs. Use them.

Always be prepared to know what you want to convey in whatever you are going to report. Changes can be made with varying timing and circumstances, but you should have a central, strategic theme incorporated in your releases. This theme should be developed and periodically reviewed in conjunction with your marketing people and your general counsel. There are experts in the field who can help you in this endeavor.

Stay ahead of the news curve with the press. Television and radio usually come into play after the fact, unless you have acted to draw early reaction, and their sound bites are not of great significance unless something untoward has occurred about you or the company. You should early on initiate contact with outstanding business, industry, financial and economic writers in newspapers such as the *Financial Times, The Christian Science Monitor, the Wall Street Transcript,* and your local and regional papers. In your rush to become globally known, don't forget these local sources. Politicians frequently say that all politics is local. As far as you are concerned, "all business (also) is local," particularly concerning your management, employees, the labor unions, local customers, suppliers, etc. Also, if your company is operating globally, or intends to do so, you should make similar overtures to leading writers in your specific geographical areas of interest. For example, I have found the *South China Morning Post* to be an excellent English language newspaper for China and East Asia.

At your earliest convenience, upon becoming the senior executive of your organization, reintroduce yourself to these people. As indicated in the earlier chapters, you already should have developed an acquaintanceship from the time you succeed to a senior management position, e.g., Vice President of Marketing, Manufacturing, Finance, etc. Take the initiative. Never be too busy to grant such individuals an early meeting.

One method of getting to know leading writers first is to provide comments referencing their articles and columns appearing recently in newspapers and journals. Perhaps surprisingly, I have found many of these writers appreciate your consideration, and respond immediately to your comments. You can take it from there. Given your time pressures, I would suggest scheduling a financial analyst before general news journalist. However, you should not ignore the meeting requests of either.

This is far from a "one way street." Engaging with financial analysts and industry and economic journalist provides you with the opportunity to do some brain picking yourself. Surprisingly, despite all you've heard about investigative reporting, the more you provide reasonable transparency – an openness to meet with these people, the more you learn. This learning can encompass positions and actions by competitors, governments, and political groups positioned to affect business. It also can provide you additional perspective concerning future industry and economic trends, and so forth, which can help strengthen your strategic assumptions and plans. Mutual respect can take you a long, positive way.

There are certain legal requirements regarding press news. For example, being a publicly owned company, immediate disclosures are required regarding anything materially affecting the company's asset base or business. This would include serious discussions relating to possible mergers, acquisitions, spin offs, new financings and so forth. You should involve your General Counsel concerning such matters and keep the Board appraised.

A caveat: You, as the senior officer, are the sole representative of your company with the media (as you, again are the sole management contact to the Board). You might bring other officers and senior executives into specific, well-orchestrated interviews in order to provide exposure for them and to indicate to the reporters or journalists the breadth of the company's management talent, but no release to or interview/meeting with the media is made or held other than through you. This is absolutely necessary. It isn't to heighten your ego. It is to assure that there is no confusion, and that the company is speaking with one authoritative voice. Media exposure to other members of management must be done prudently. Your actions should not permit inferences of anything else but this occasional exposure. Egos being what they are, and assuming your top executives are as ambitious and aggressive as you are, once you open this gate to the media – and permit acquaintanceships – it will be difficult to control. Also, regardless of how well you manage exposure of some people, you will find jealousies undoubtedly occurring which can cause far greater problems within your management ranks than such exposure may be worth. Take care.

Another important point: I would suggest strongly that you, as the organization's senior officer, refrain from providing estimates to the media. This avoidance includes earnings, revenue, future contracts, growth projections, market shares, value of products (both current and those under development) and so forth. Generally, this action did not occur within U.S. corporate management until the 1990s. I realize that in recent years the "estimate" vogue has become increasingly widespread. However, you and your company will gain little if such projections are realized (supposedly the impact already has been credited or discounted) and could experience significant adversity if they are not. Given the eccentricities and fickleness of the future, the probability is that, more times than not, such forecasts (for that is what they actually are) will not be achieved. You may, of course, assuming you know, counsel the reporter or analyst as to the general appropriateness of their own range of estimates, making certain that you preface your remarks with explanations and cautions. In short, let the analysts and reporters do the work for which they are being paid. Drawing conclusions from these interviews, including such things as earnings estimates, is their job. Let them do it.

Also, "know thyself." There is a subconscious aspect to people who have enjoyed career success that, in particular, finds itself notably in the character of many CEOs. These CEOs are "at the top." They have achieved a goal that relatively few executives enjoy. A person, sometimes, as long as the news is good, gets a great feeling in seeing his name in print, his smiling confident countenance on television screens, and being extolled about how great he is. It's not to be denied; most of us simply are built that way. However, it is <u>to be controlled</u>. An interesting addendum: The humbler you appear-or control yourself-to be, the more the media demonstrates their appreciation for you. These are the times to think about – and use-the pronoun "we" instead of "I," and "our organization and "team" instead of "my organization" and "me."

Recall mention made in Chapter II of the media counsel, one of the recommended five professional acquaintances? You should discuss the media management subject frequently with him or her, and stay in touch.

There are several media-centric subjects about which you should be aware, develop findings or have thoughts. Examples include the following:

- Timing of definition and limits concerning disclosures
- The best days of the week, etc. to release "good" news and "not so good" news.
- How does a skilled investigative reporter learn early about such topics as:
  - Senior executives selling their corporate shares in advance of adverse events?
  - Conflicts of interest among auditors and executives?
  - The questionable nature and effectiveness of "China Walls" within professional organizations, e.g., tax and audit firm, legal firms, investment-banking firms, etc.
- What to say and what not to say. Recall Emperor Claudius (Roman leader, AD 41 to 54), "Say not always what you know, but always know what you say." Report what you must, but no more than what is necessary. This is one area in which you should let your

competitors take the lead. You will find that, for whatever reason, these competitors unintentionally will disclose information useful to you.

- How frequently should a company story or a CEO's article appear in order to enhance employee morale or their pride in being a member of the organization?
- Is it wise for a CEO to take public positions on such matters as proposed laws, acts, regulations, etc., which, in his or her opinion, adversely affects business?
- Should a journalist have the legal right to protect (not disclose) his or her sources of information?
- Most journalists refuse to permit you to review their article resulting from your interview, except, possibly to ensure the numbers are accurate. Would you agree with this prohibition?
- Would you encourage journalists to attend your annual shareholders meeting? If not, why not?
- As the CEO, would you agree to be interviewed by Charlie Rose (television interviewer)? Why?
- Decide beforehand several – three to five questions of significance about which the possible answers would be important to your company. Cast them so you can encourage discussion and answers.

Prioritize the following points you would like emphasized as the result of an interview with a financial analyst: charges in EBIT, market share, share price (and multiple), cash flow, debt-to-equity ratio, EPS, return on investment, sales or revenue, operating profit, funded obligations, other (please indicate)?

- Your dividend policy and your related rationale.
- Like so many other instances in which information is shared, rehearse.

Chapter Summary: Given the right thought and plan, interviews with financial analysts, industry journalists and other members of the media can be most useful to you and your business. However, it requires consideration on your part and continual attention. You must develop media relationships before exchanges become fruitful – and such exchanges must be mutually beneficial. Be certain to endeavor to get more from these sessions than you give. Consider using your professional media expert in planning these campaigns. Above all, forget the possibility for celebrity status. Stick to gaining intelligence and creating media relationships better than your competitor does. Be known as being media astute.

APPENDICES

Appendix A

Suggested Information Sources

"A Reading List"

In the practice of keeping informed, first become aware of the background of the source, e.g., writer, medium (newspaper, journal, network, etc.), publisher, etc., principally the political leanings and experiences of these sources. Second, study the article or listen to the subject. Often such material is highly negative, advancing few practical solutions. It frequently is difficult to determine such political leanings or backgrounds, but you at least read skeptically, remembering Diderot's adage, "Skepticism is the first step toward Truth." Most of this material in this Appendix applies to the United States.

I would suggest the following information sources for your consideration:

Books

The following books address several aspects relating to business. These include political philosophies, suggested practices and disciplines, training guidance, economic theories, competition considerations, people development, and factors about which you should be aware, marking you as a knowledgeable, globally aware individual:

- The Elephant's Child - Rudyard Kipling, 1902 (viz., "Six Honest Servin' Men") (from "Just So Stories")

- Toyota Seishan Hoshiki - Taiichi Ohno, 1978 (viz., "The Five Whys")

- The Book of Virtue - William J. Bennett, 1993

- The Fifth Discipline: The Art & Practice of the Learning Organization - Peter Senge, 1990

- The Element of Style - William Strunk, Jr. and E. B. White, 1959

- Security Analysis - Benjamin Graham, David Dodd and Sidney Cottle, 1962

- Atlas Shrugged - Ayn Rand, 1957

- The Innovator's Dilemma - Clayton Christensen, 2006

- The General Theory of Employment, Interest and Money - John Maynard Keyes, 1936

- Sources of Power – How People Make Decisions - Gary Klein, 1999

- The Art of Plain Talk - Rudolf Flesch, 1951

- Rules of Civility - George Washington, 1773

- Memoirs of Hadrian - Marguerite cleenewerck de Crayencour, 1951 (Translation by Grace Frick)

- Gates of Fire -   Steven Pressfield, 1998

- The Tipping Point: How Little Things Can Make a Big Difference - Malcolm Gladwell, 2000

- War and Peace - Leo Tolstoy, 1869

- The Fountainhead - Ayn Rand, 1943

- Gods, Graves and Scholars - C. W. Ceram, 1951

- The Other Side of the Hill - Captain B. H. Liddell Hart, 1948

- The Way to Write - Rudolf Flesch, 1947

- I Ching - Pre-Confucius, Taoists, 1,000-1,500 BC

- The Meditations - Marcus Aurelius Antoninus, AD 173 (Translation by Georg Long)

- Good to Great: Why Some Companies - Make the Leap...and Others Don't   James Collins, 2001

- The Effective Executive Revised, - Peter F. Drucker, 2002 (originally 1967)

Appendix B

Useful Aphorisms

Aphorisms, maxims, adages, axioms or sayings, call them what you wish, always have provided me a concise, sometimes clever way to remember a valuable, self-evident truth. I would suggest, in addition to those with which you already are familiar, the following for one seeking a career in business, or in any other serious career sector where like traits and values are useful:

"Always remember that someone, someplace, is developing a product that will make your product obsolete"

- Gen. Georges F. Doriot (1952)

"Say not always what you know, but always know what you say,"
- Tiberius Claudius Caesar Augustus Germanicus, 1 Aug 10 BC to AD 13 Oct 54; Roman Emperor: AD 24 Jan 41 to AD 13 Oct 54

"God, grant me the serenity to accept the things I cannot change, The courage to change the things I can, and the wisdom to know the difference,"

- Reinhold Niebuhr, U.S. Protestant theologian, 1892 to 1971

"There is nothing more difficult to take in hand, more perilous to conduct, or more uncertain of success, than to take the lead in the introduction of a new order of things, because the innovator has for enemies all those who have done well under the old conditions, and only lukewarm defenders in those who may do well under the new,"

- Niccolo Machiavelli May 3, 1469 to June 21, 1527

"Have no friends not equal to yourself,"

- Kong Tzu (Confucius), Analects, Book I, 8, ii, 504 BC

"I keep six honest servin' men, (they taught me all I knew), Their names are What and Why and When, and

How and Where and Who.
I send them over land and sea, I send them east and west;
But after they have worked for me,
I give them all a rest,"
                            - Rudyard Kipling, *The Elephant Child*, 1892

"Repeating "Why" five times will uncover the root problem and lead to correcting it. Don't stop with the answer to an earlier "why" because you will attempt to resolve a superficial, instead of the root, problem,"
          - Mr. Taiichi Ohno, *Toyota seisan hoshiki*, (Toyota Production System)
                                                                    Chapter 2, 1978

"It is the mark of an educated mind to be able to entertain a thought without accepting it,"
          - Aristotle, Greek philosopher, physicist and zoologist, 384 BC – 322 BC

"It's not the things we don't know that gets us in trouble. It's the things we know that just ain't true."
                    - Will Rogers, American humorist, *The Illiterate Digest*, 1924

"Don't worry about having no position; Worry about that whereby you may become effectively established. Don't worry that no one recognizes you; Seek to be worthy of recognition,"
          - Kong Tzu (Confucius), *I Ching, Book 1; Analects, Book 14, 14, I,* 511 BC

An individual is a man who says: "I will not run anyone's life – nor let anyone run mine. I will not rule nor be ruled. I will not be a master or a slave. I will not sacrifice myself to anyone –nor sacrifice anyone to myself,"
                              - Ayn Rand, *The Ayn Rand Columns, No. 84*, 1962

Appendix C

The Word

Guidelines for a Corporate Career

The principal objectives of this book are to develop, strengthen and broaden one's leadership skills. Key factors contributing to the successful exploitation of one's leadership skills and career potential are dedication, focus, concentration and discipline. Set forth herein are guidelines for your consideration; rules of conduct that experience has demonstrated to be of value, and, should prove useful to you. These also have the aim of strengthening an individual's self-sufficiency and moral rectitude. For some, these rules may appear as "motherhood" truths. However, even so, repetition has value.

Introduction

The single finite factor in our lives is time. Time continues to pass whether we use it well or ill. Time lost never can be regained. Today, assuming a 80-year life expectancy, at ages 30 to 35 most individuals seeking leadership responsibilities and challenges have, on average, fewer than 416,000 hours remaining in their lives; a total of 416,000 hours for professional careers, family relationships, rest, personal care, illness, avocation, possible retirement, and so forth. If one contemplates retiring from a career at, say 60, the working time from this day forward, on average, is cut to fewer than 245,000 hours. Most readers of this book already have spent an equal amount of time just getting to "now". The conclusion is that effective time management is essential to success.

Let's bypass further discussion of the total time available, and concentrate on the maximum hours available for productive use. First, there are needs for which we must provide, needs required to recharge the battery. Let's say six hours of sleep, one or two hours for taking nourishment, a half hour or so for exercise and up to a couple of hours for personal care and related needs. Even at the most efficient, little timesaving is available in these areas. Thus, given the approximate 140,000 or so hours of time remaining for one's productive career, how can we make the most of it?

<u>Guidelines</u>

The following guidelines are aimed both at strengthening executive skills and career potential and improving time management. It is recognized that rules differ in nature and importance, and, given your particular background, I am certain that you can make valuable additions or deletions to and from the following:

1. Eliminate network and cable television and films (movies) from your schedule. Most television programming, including the ads, is geared to audiences below a fifth-grade educational level, and plainly is a waste of time. With some planning, one may find such selections as C-Span or possibly public radio or television provides value-added information, or perhaps music for rest and relaxation. Restrict television viewing and radio listening to early morning or late evening news reporting. Even then, be skeptical as to what motivates the sources as well as to the "facts" being presented. Schedule these times during moments in which you are engaged in activities not requiring attention or concentration, e.g., during meals, exercise sessions or personal care activities.

2. Limit social gatherings. Most such occasions involve extra eating and drinking, neither of which you need. In exchange for the time spent, you gains mostly gossip and so-called "small talk" which is conversational nonsense. None of this adds value to your life or to your career potential. These events only waste time better spent elsewhere. Some people think they need this. You don't. Limit social time spent to your immediate family – your spouse and your children. They are your most important – and most supportive – assets, and, given your career, you'll never see enough of them. Exchange with them information of importance; thoughts contributing to the family's education, contentment, mental "stretch" and future economic wellbeing and security.

3. Some outside social intercourse cannot be avoided, particularly those in which valuable contacts may be made or relationships strengthened. However, again, be selective. It always is necessary to protect yourself and your family from slipping through "the net" of such social events to the level of the "least common

4. Treat all people – everyone – as you wish to be treated – "The Golden Rule." Always be courteous, tactful and civil, but reserved. A smile projects self-confidence provides comfort to others and may be interpreted as friendship or agreement. Such interpretations are positive and may be worthwhile as long as it is not misleading. This takes skill. The way to be civil is to refrain from behavior that trifles with the independence of another. George Washington reportedly wrote, "One should not play with any (person) that delights not to be played with." Civility, decency and propriety all are species of sound manners.

5. Listen more than you talk. Make this a habit. Weigh your words as if each was costing you a gold coin. Use such occasions to learn instead of to teach or inform. Reciprocate only when the opportunity exists for you to learn more than you are divulging, and even then do so sparingly. One never learns when talking. Also, never discuss matters of a personal nature. There is absolutely no benefit in having people aware of your personal or family affairs. Never complain to anyone about anything. Let the other person do the talking. You will be surprised how many people cannot abide silence, and often, because of this failing, you learn things of value that you otherwise wouldn't. Hence, constantly have your communications switch set to "receive" instead of "send." Even your worst enemies cannot bear witness against you for something you never have said or done. Remember, the reason the fish is on the wall plaque – it didn't keep its mouth shut.

6. When you are engaged in conversation, maintain eye contact. This always is important, but is particularly important when you are speaking. This tends to acquire and hold the attention of the other

party. It also demonstrates intensity and interest in the other person and his or her subject; helping them feel that they, at that moment, are the only person in your world. Practice speaking quietly, distinctly and concisely. Limit your body gestures (do anything unobtrusive you wish with your hands, but keep them out of your pockets). Let your voice, countenance and facial expressions project your degree of seriousness, calmness and confidence.

7. Never start doing something for someone that you don't intend to do forever. What you do will become to be expected, and, if you stop, credits will be few, criticisms many. This caution includes everyone – spouse, children, business colleagues, friends and family acquaintances; even your dog.

8. When a change of pace is needed, read, exercise or participate in a physically tasking sport, preferably one of an individual nature that permits you to think at the same time, e.g., jogging, swimming, skiing, rowing, etc. Exercise or "play" to relax and concurrently to strengthen the body and the mind. Golf and team sports require too much time and usually involve non-value-added sidebar social relationships, which waste even more time. An exception could be a serious game of cards –Bridge or Poker, for example – that can improve mental focus and agility. Read constructive materials (refer to Suggested Reading List). Always have a good book with you. It not only will enable you to make valuable use of time, but also will dissuade intrusions. Forget popular and publicized "best sellers" or "blockbusters." Most good writing – fiction, nonfiction, screenplays and theater offerings – occurred before the 1970s. Things that are promoted for sale as being "popular" are directed mostly to people whose shortage of self-confidence causes them to crave being identified with a celebrity or personality other than their own. "Popular" – products or "Causes" – are not for you.

9. Keep business acquaintances and friends separate. Exercise extreme care in entering into a business relationship with friends. Friendship makes an objective business relationship difficult, if not impossible.

Friendship in business leads frequently to suspicion, jealousy, resentment and often animosity, possibly leading to destructive behavior or betrayal. If one finds it not possible to avoid a friendship-related business situation, make certain beforehand that mutually understood and satisfactory working and compensation arrangements are established, and henceforth that your relationship will be on a contractual, professional basis instead of friendship. Also, be certain that a legally binding "exit plan" is in place.

10. "When you arrive five minutes early, you are already fifteen minutes late." Sound familiar? This admonition about being punctual allegedly was given his students by the 5th Century BC philosopher, Produs Diadochus, and is as applicable now as it was in 2400 year ago. To be late is to be discourteous. When you are late, you are telling other people that their time is not as important as yours. Tardiness is the greatest, obvious lack of discipline that is possible to convey to others. From your "Day One", make certain that you always are early, or postpone the engagement.

11. Don't be reluctant to be independent – to spend time alone. Consider the "handle" of being a Loner or of riding single saddle as approbations. Frequently you will find solitude well spent; time with at least an equally intelligent party; often far more useful than time spent with others.

12. Encourage being awarded greater management opportunity by what you accomplish. Be certain that your accomplishments are recognized. However, if you find after some time that you must request additional responsibilities – or greater compensation, you may well conclude that you are working for the wrong person or the wrong organization.

13. If, during the day, fatigue interferes with your thought processes or your physical or mental capabilities, take a brief nap. You may be surprised how refreshing a 30 or 40-minute respite can be, and how quickly you will be able to compensate for the time taken.

14. Peruse newspapers and other press sources over breakfast. Let the headlines guide your interest, then give time only to the first two or three paragraphs of such articles, beyond which usually are details of secondary or tertiary importance. Be conscience of the background of the source of such writings (again, refer to the Suggested Reading List). Also, scan the obituaries. Such data tend to keep you humble, aware of your mortality and conscience of the short nature of time. It should press you to accomplish more within the time you have. Continually strengthen your vocabulary. Learn one new word each day, possibly during breakfast, and use it several times in your daily conversations and writings. In the same manner, complete increasingly difficult crossword puzzles, both to learn and to keep your mind alert. Provide an hour each evening to such pursuits, replacing time possibly given television or some other equally distractive, meaningless activity.

15. Clip and mail or e-mail articles that you believe are of interest to key acquaintances. Given that news is perishable, these transmissions should occur immediately. For reference, purposes maintain electronic or clipping files on people, technologies, organization changes, scientific developments, major economic trends, etc. Keep these current by checking proven sources every day.

16. Make skepticism your partner and make it a habit. Approach information (and people) with measured doubt. Constantly question accepted or established facts, beliefs and institutions. The use of conventional wisdom usually represents an excuse. By suspending judgment, even for a brief period, you provide yourself time to identify and to consider most major aspects of a question. Listen less to "What" people are saying than to "Why" they are saying it. Review their possible motive before responding or deciding. Skepticism – not cynicism – is your helpmate toward objectivity – objectivity is your goal. Healthy doubts can avoid problems. Also, don't rush to define problems. Remember Mr. Taiichi Ohno's "Five Whys." Also, equally important, don't let time constraints push you

into rash decisions, i.e., "Do not take counsel of your fears." Between good sense and good taste, there exists the difference between a cause and its effect.

17. Learn to speak well. Elocution will become an increasingly important asset as you progress in your career. It must be mastered and maintained. To be considered "well spoken" is a major competitive plus, particularly in this age of slovenliness. Speak in a relaxed, convincing style. You might wish to consider joining a group such as Toastmasters to improve your public speaking skills.

18. Plan ahead. One simple step to save time would be to lay out your next-day's wardrobe, accoutrement and breakfast before retiring the previous night. While recognizing that our "biological clocks" differ somewhat, try awaking at 5:00 AM and do 20-minutes of stretching and related light exercises. Shower and shave simultaneously, limiting your cleansing warm water shower to three minutes, followed by a three-minute cold shower. This will awaken you to the opportunities of the day. A 30-minute, end-of-day work out three times per week will help ensure health and a frequent, late evening sauna or steam bath will help make the most of your sleep.

19. Choose a foreign language applicable for your long-term business career and learn new phrase of this language each day. Practice daily while you are driving, showering, exercising, etc. Use language tapes while driving and during your sleep period. Give priority to speaking and vocal understanding. Leave reading and writing to another day. Given China's increasing global political and economic importance, you might consider learning Mandarin, assuming your English already is fluent.

20. Keep a pad, pen or pencil and book on your bedside table and in your dressing room to record "heads up" notes, and for reading. You will be surprised how much better you will sleep by transferring these thoughts from your mind to a writing pad during the night.

21. Your health is paramount. Few of us realize that while we remain mentally keen, well-informed, etc., our body – not only the exoskeleton – begins to deteriorate soon after our fortieth year. It matters not how brilliant you are or how intellectually stimulating. Even if such cerebral dangers as Alzheimer's and apoplexy are not encountered, the pain and suffering of possible osteoporosis, arthritis, adverse heart condition, etc., can materially affect the sharpness of your judgment, reasoning and overall mental attitude. The best for which one can hope is to delay the physical aging process through exercising, eating well and taking reasonable care of ourselves, particularly our weight.

22. Another time consuming but mandatory step is an annual physical examination, including heart stress and bone density testing. If possible, have them conducted by the same physician and have comparable records maintained. Obviously, what one eats and drinks are important. It long has been obvious that a poor diet as well as other thoughtless habits, e.g., smoking, can shorten one's life and damage one's mental acuity. Alcohol and fatty foods have no place in a one's diet. Be sufficiently smart to recognize this and discipline yourself. In this regard, also take care regarding your spouse and the associates you chose. Consider limiting daily meals to two, a light breakfast and a pre-8:00 PM dinner. Restrict beverages to water, non-carbonated juices or soft drinks, and tea or decaffeinated coffee.

23. Most are familiar with the adage, "Never say or do anything about which you, your mother and your immediate family would not be proud to read, view or hear from the media or other people." Avoid gossip. It wastes time and is demeaning both to you and the victim. Another thought, one of long standing, that should be committed to memory, "If you can't say something positive about someone, don't say anything." Establish and adhere to your own high, personal standards of conduct, mores and ethics. Your actions will speak far more about you than slogans, policies, personal relations campaigns,

etc. There's another thought that deserve attention: "Your real character is what you do when you are alone."

24. Don't take comfort or make assumptions that industry, association or government rules, regulations, instructions or practices are guidelines sufficient for you or your organization. Remember that the excuse of "not being guilty of wrongdoing," or of such actions as "taking the Fifth," is tantamount to an admission of sloppiness, incompetence, irresponsibility or worse. By taking time to anticipate problems and unintended consequences will help to overcoming legal and moral challenges. Remember also the caution expressed by Jean de La Bruyere some 400 years ago, "Avoid lawsuits above all things; they pervert your conscience, impair your health and dissipate your property," not saying how much time they waste.

25. "Stay on top of things." Do not assume that someone else will do something of value for you, or in your name. As you progress in your career, you will become increasingly accountable for what happens and for results; you also, like it or not, are becoming the target for other, self-serving, small-minded people. Incidentally, by now your may have come to realize that "assumptions," per se, are questionable in themselves. Make certain that you personally know what is happening, why it is happening and who is responsible, and that you understand the matter thoroughly and are in agreement before action is taken. Don't "assume" or take short cuts or "jump to conclusions," or permit others to do so. Make certain that actions are sufficiently well defined so that a single individual can be held responsible and accountable. Make use of Kipling's "Six Servin' Men" and, again, Mr. Ohno's "Five Whys."

26. Avoid meetings whenever possible. Depend more on the telephone or e-mail. When meetings are unavoidable, such as for security considerations, endeavor to host (manage) them, inform the participants (as few as possible) of the proposed agendum and let them know beforehand how much time will be needed. When it is necessary for you to attend a meeting elsewhere, request the

agendum in advance, and arrive early (remember Proclus's advice), inquire as to time required – seeking to depart before that deadline. As a guideline, endeavor to limit meetings with individuals to 20 minutes, with groups to 40 minutes and, for occasional, multipurpose meetings such as with the Board of Directors, to a maximum of two hours, insisting that these limits are observed. To ensure the participants' attention and to avoid interruptions schedule topics so that 15-minutes breaks are provided every hour. Prior to any meeting, set the agenda goals – "Deliverables" – and ensure that sufficient time and data are provided to achieve them. If any non-agenda topics arise, table them for future attention. A meeting without a "product" is a waste of time. Make certain that participants understand the purpose and the objective of the meeting at its outset.

27. Memories are short. It is important that during the meeting you maintain your own notes on important matters, particularly regarding responsibilities and timing. Given the comprehensiveness of a good agendum, I have found it useful to make notations directly on the copy, and at the conclusion of the meeting review these significant data to ensure understanding and agreement. Never conclude a meeting without a clear understanding and/or a clear conclusion by all participants. The only notes remaining upon the conclusion of a meeting should be those of the secretary. Also, entrust the secretary to keep the participants aware of the remaining time so that time does not become the dictate why understandings or conclusions are not reached, and notes destroyed. Forget recordings. They take more analytical time than the information is worth.

28. In meeting with an individual, remain standing instead of sitting. You will be surprised how fast even significant matters can be resolved in this manner. Forbid interruptions, including phone calls, etc., and stick to your schedule. Another point: in meetings in which you are the host, set the example. These are occasions of necessity. They are

professional talks. They are not "coffee klatches." Thus, as the leader, do not come into meetings with coffee mugs, water bottles, soft drink cans, candy bars, etc. Forego donuts, a refreshment sidebar and so forth. These convey the impression of a relaxed, not-in-a-hurry environment, which should not be your intent. Your subordinates soon will get (and reflect) your message. Also, again, demand punctuality, and make sure that you are the example. Also, the commencement of a meeting is on time when the door is closed.

29. Avoid business meals. Time is wasted "getting to and from," attentions are diverted, interruptions are frequent and the overall environment seldom is conducive to serious deliberation or to confidential exchanges. Also, because lack of formality (for note taking, etc.) and privacy, such a venue easily can result in misunderstandings.

30. Confirm meeting agenda and schedules at least three days in advance. Do this personally if possible. Acknowledge the kind consideration or assistance of the meeting host's secretary, assistant, et al, by note or with a small gift. In all matters, always exceed what is the common, the usual or the expected.

31. Courtesy is a must. You will be astounded by the lasting value to your reputation of such seemingly insignificance expressions as "please" and "thank you." When first meeting, writing or being introduced to people, use their "sir" name, rank or title, and continue to do so until instructed (not "invited," but instructed) to do otherwise. Remember, that in spite of changing times, the use of "Sir," "Madam" or "Miss" is still much respected. Politeness makes one appear outwardly, as one would be, or would hope to be, within.

32. Concentrate of your five key professional acquaintances, viz., your attorney, your CPA, your banker and/or financier, your physician and your media specialist. Identify and become knowledgeable about at least one subject or area of interest to them. Develop and maintain these relationships. Stay close. Keep them informed continually.

These are not people who tolerate or should be subjected to "surprises." Keep them in mind regarding family interests, e.g., career and family anniversaries, birthdays, special events, achievements, etc. Such thoughtfulness is so little observed these days that almost any small consideration you provide shall "set you apart" constructively.

33. Be aware and exploit your personal bearing. Always, regardless of the environment, stand tall, walk erect and with purpose. Always permit yourself time to walk instead of ride. "Power" never hurries. To be hurried or to appear hurried implies lack of foresight or control. Be certain to be properly attired, reasonably in style and superbly in shape. Keep records and rotate your apparel daily relating to the occasion. Avoid being an iconoclast. Let your actions characterize you, not what things you wear.

34. Never evidence fatigue. Force yourself when in public to be sharp, energetic, alert and pleasant. Smile. If illness or fatigue becomes apparent or cannot be overcome, disappear. Don't show weakness or provide people an excuse to sympathize over your appearance or their inferences about your health. Whether or not you want to recognize it, you always are "center stage." If you're not "at the Top of Your Game," reschedule your appearances or meetings. See Point No. 12.

35. You long ago gave up "being one of the boys" (if ever you were). Never indulge in crude humor or use common or course language (either profanity or obscenity), or provide any impression that you approve of it. Never permit your name or your person to be associated with people who do. You long have succeeded because you have "set yourself apart from the crowd." Respect rather than camaraderie is the basis of both your professional and social relationships.

36. Avoid broaching a problem (or an issue) without first having identified in your mind at least one plausible solution – and had

given it at least a preliminary test. Also, have identified a plan by which a solution could possibly be achieved.

37. Limit your position or views to facts, reserving your opinions for family conversations. Remember the adage, "In matters of opinion, the Boss is right." Avoid discussions concerning subjective matters, i.e., political beliefs, religion, community matters, etc., yet another reason to avoid social gatherings. See Point No. 2.

38. Make yourself aware of cultural matters and customs, and the degree to which they may be changing. Review this information with knowledgeable sources before engaging in foreign business travel or visits or meetings with foreign individuals remembering to "triangulate" inputs. Be observant, taking cues from others before you act regarding person-to-person courtesies, being aware always that you are the stranger, a guest in a venue considered as important by the indigenous individuals as your own. Be a student of history and examine current events, applying such knowledge.

39. Control your ego. We each are but one among many. Help yourself to be humble by reflecting personally and frequently on how we, as the human race, are so insignificant in the grand scheme and nature of things, how relatively unimportant is the planet Earth in terms of the galaxy and the universe. Be selfish with your time, but generous in your praise of others. A vain man finds it wise to speak good or ill of himself; a modest man speaks not of himself. When one begins speaking of himself or herself in the third person, one's ego clearly is out of control.

40. Each day, perhaps upon retiring, identify one thing that could be developed or improved, a subject that would contribute to the universal good; a truly new or revolutionary concept, not merely a modification of something already existing. Note these ideas, the challenges they represent and how these challenges possibly could be overcome. Seek to publish the best of these ideas at least annually, refining them to the point that you apply for a patent or

copyright. This practice – this habit –may result in a constructive contribution. At the very least, it will keep you mentally active and alert, and will help to keep you from "In-the-Box) thinking. It also will help to keep your mind open to innovative ideas.

41. Keep appropriate people informed. This includes your superior, your business and professional colleagues, your five key professional acquaintances (see Point No. 28) and, eventually as the CEO, the Board of Directors. This premise also applies to your spouse and your family, with the caveat of respecting as required "the need to know." The watch phrase in all of this, again, is "no surprises, ever." Make certain that individuals such as the foregoing who are positioned to affect your reputation and your career never can say validly that they "never knew" or "weren't informed" or "were not made aware" of your plans or actions. Also, it is important to maintain some type of record of the salient points of such exchanges, agreements (or disagreements), notifications or conversations.

42. In developing people, first look at yourself. While it may be frustrating, train yourself to consider problems as opportunities for improvement or development. Correct or discipline in a positive, quiet and constructive manner. However, first examine yourself. Did you identify and communicate the assignment adequately to the subordinate? Have you followed up, and in a timely manner? Have your attitude and practices ensured that communication channels are open and that free exchange of information and ideas are encouraged? Is this the question of the "right man on the right job," including yourself? Is this the type of problem or challenge requiring a group or an individual solution, or, in turn, one that can be used for management development purposes? Most importantly, have you truly been the "delegator," or are you, for whatever reason, still participating as the "doer?" Discuss disciplinary or corrective matters in private, successes in public. Remember, developing and improving a person with potential; one with who you are professionally acquainted – scars and all – usually is far better than making an

executive change, taking on an individual you don't directly know. Also, keep in mind the constant that all people are different. They develop differently, and consequently must be handled (managed) differently. As a manager, you already should be aware of these differences.

43. Contrary to the management belief that "one size fits all," significantly different business situations often require different executive talents and backgrounds – patience being a talent. An executive who may be excellent in the needs of a relatively one-on-one management style characteristic of a turnaround" situation, a start-up or an incubator environment, may not have "the necessary horses,"', e.g., delegation, planning and control skills, patience, etc., needed to manage a larger, more complex, ongoing organization. A truism is that "all people may have been born equally, but that's where equality stops," is one to be recalled in such management decisions. Consideration always is important, but attempting to change seasoned executives to meet vastly different challenges most often becomes a waste of valuable time when, in reality, a change is needed. The trick, as in poker, is knowing when to hold and when to fold.

44. Release your personal emotions in private. Tensions, stress and pressures often lead to frustration, anger, depression, etc. If they must be released, however, such release must be in private. You never want to project that decisions or considerations are based on or influenced by subjectivity, for example any emotions. Your perceived bearing in such situations must be one of "cool, calm and collected." Recall, that your physician is among your key professional acquaintances and it is he who could assist you at these times. Also, as a leader you may find that providing counsel to others, which is among your major management tasks, helps you relieve some of your own stress. Again, whatever the situation, do not attempt to hold such emotions inside. They must be released or your value as a manager – or spouse or parent – is significantly impaired.

45. Constantly view your company from the perspective of the customer, vendors or suppliers, shareholders, Board members and employers, i.e., significant outsiders. For example, acting in this capacity, occasionally telephone or contact your company's central information or communications system, checking on the quality, promptness, courteousness and professionalism of the response you receive. Follow up. These "first line" employees frequently establish or influence your company's reputation to the outside world. Their performance must be consistent and unquestionably excellent. Such ubiquitous involvement on your part also sends a message to the workforce that you have a personal, serious and continuous interest in such matters. Incidentally, along these lines, avoid telephone answering services or recordings. They are negative at best, insulting at worse. They imply that you are more interested in accruing relatively small – insignificant – savings in administrative costs than you are in the time and concerns of customers or suppliers, etc. Given today's business environment, this also will set your company apart as an organization that cares for its customers.

46. Take care with correspondence. Custom of courtesy dictates that handwritten, posted letters require handwritten, posted responses. Never commit the gaff (or affront) of answering a handwritten letter with a typed, e-mailed or faxed response. While a handwritten, uniquely stamped letter represented the ultimate courtesy in correspondence, one, which you may, chose to employ, it is acceptable that computer processed or typed letters may be answered in kind. However, the method of preparation, responses to facsimiles, e-mail and registered correspondence always should be within one working day.

47. Avoid using your business posting machine for personal correspondence. Your professionalism, seriousness of purpose and consideration are represented in the quality of materials used in your correspondence. Select only high quality bond, embossed

products both for stationery and business cards. Of course, business stationery is not to be used for personal correspondence.

48. Seeking advice from well informed, experienced respected individuals makes sense. However, good people do not appreciate being patronized. Never seek counsel unless your sources understand from experience that you normally use such advice or consider it seriously in your deliberations. "Consensus Building" and "Team Work" also are worthwhile management approaches should you decide that group thinking will be of value in a given circumstance. Be judicious, however, in the use of such tools and take care that you do not appear hypocritical, employing such approaches merely to achieve "feel good" goals. It doesn't take most people long to recognize a phony.

49. Get out of your office and away from that computer. That is not where the organization's principal work is being done. Make frequent "shirtsleeve" tours of plants, offices and facilities a work habit. Start developing this habit early, even in your early career assignments. Before commencing work in the morning, during luncheon breaks, after work or even during normal work hours make your presence known where the job is being done and by the people doing it. Observe what is happening. Show your interest. Become acquainted. It soon will become apparent that you respect and care for others, for who they are and what they are doing; and, being better informed, you will be able to do your job more effectively. It also, most importantly, will demonstrate that you know where the money is being made and respect who is making it.

50. You always are the example. The way you develop and reward people, spend money, reward yourself, control your emotions, plan and carry out your work, hold yourself accountable, respect others, spend your time (and that of others), respect merit (instead of seniority, legacies and other job security and advancement criteria), and the way you establish and project the company's business goals: all will be noted, reflected and, yes, copied in the attitudes and

actions of your people. "We all put our pants on, one leg at a time." In essence, you as the manager or the CEO are no better than the individual cleaning the office or the plant floor. You all work for the same organization. You all are on the same "team." As such, all of you participate in the same programs, are geared to the same policies and enjoy the same types of benefits as everyone else. You all should be enthusiast about the company's future and share a loyalty to the organization. Anything you might do to separate groups within the company is wrong. "Perks" do not exist, or, if they do, you and all employees of the company enjoy them. For example, if there is a public stock offering or a secondary, you and all employees are qualified to participate. You expect nothing less than top quality work performance from them and they expect top performance from you.

Finally, don't take yourself too seriously. Life already has considerable stress and pressure. From time to time a bit of humor helps keep things in perspective, and gives reason for a relaxed moment or two, and usually results in a better working environment afterwards. If "push comes to shove," laugh at yourself. We all, from time to time, do stupid things; things worthy of a laugh, and there's certainly nothing wrong in laughing at yourself.

Appendix D

Comportment

Respect, Civility and Gentility

These points are not all inclusive. However, they should suffice as initial, general guidelines regarding behavior and its major related aspects. Please note there are some subjects duplicated between this document and the previous Appendix. However, the duplications aim at somewhat different purposes. There's no intention herein to insult the reader's intelligence or his or her already well-developed, exceptional behavior. For the most part, these suggestions should be considered as reminders. Some of these ideas may appear "old fashioned," but being a gentleman or a lady never is old fashioned even if current society often ignores this.

It should be noted that manners or comportment relating to subjects such as table or dining behavior, which frequently differ among cultures, largely are omitted; the assumption being that the reader already is aware of these matters or that such information can be obtained from many other, more thorough sources. Thus, the following:

1. Establish and maintain eye contact in discussions with other people to do otherwise projects a lack of confidence, sincerity or interest.

2. Smile. Be personable and relaxed, projecting assuredness and self-confidence.

3. Accord grace and thought – and time – in responding to questions. Make the inquirer feel that his or her question is important, deserving your utmost attention and thought.

4. Speak directly, distinctly and, within reason, slowly.

5. Don't indulge in conversational pleasantries until your host does, and then limit them largely to responses.

6. Dress for the occasion, being fashionably understated.

7. Introduce younger people to older people or to individuals of superior positions, e.g., "Dr. Elder may I introduce [to you] Steve Clark? Steve, this is Dr. Elder."

8. Stand when being introduced to or meeting older people, individuals of superior position or women, or when such people enter your room. Remain standing until the other person departs or until they are seated or ask you to sit. Women are the exception; they may remain seated.

9. Open doors for women, and generally assist them in passing through the door – ahead of you. This includes entering automobiles, offices, residence, etc. also, assist them.

10. When seated, keep your feet on the floor, or cross your legs <u>at the knees</u> so that the sole of <u>your shoe faces downward</u>, not being visible to others.

11. Sit straight with your back erect in the rear of the chair. If you must do something with your hands, fold them in your lap. Remember to limit your gestures while speaking.

12. Don't sit or stand behind your desk when greeting or meeting guests. Get up, get out and meet them. You are not a Pasha; you are a businessman or businesswoman. Arrange chairs or, if not practical, schedule another room, one without obstructions or

conversational subjects. Remember, by remaining standing, you shorten time spent in meetings. Beverages are not required. Set the standard. Don't take beverages into meetings (or conferences, Board sessions, etc.). These are business meetings, not coffee klatches.

13. Assist in seating women and older people. Remain standing until these people or individuals of senior position are seated, only then take your seat.

14. Meet alone with a guest who has requested a private meeting. If others in either of your parties should attend, invite them to participate following your initial meeting with your singular guest, and by her or his leave.

15. At table, do not take your napkin, or partake of any food or beverage, until all the people are seated, and the host or person of superior position at your table does so.

16. When required to leave the table during a meal, place your napkin on your chair seat. At the conclusion of the meal, when departing your place, place the napkin loosely folded on the table at your place. Again, be prepared for different customs.

17. Never use a cellular 'phone or similar communications device in a non-private environment, e.g., in management meetings, theaters, hospitals, aircraft, etc. Within a public area use it only "out of the public flow," i.e., out of the presence, movement or traffic of other people.

18. Follow the actions of other, more experienced individuals in observing customs, etc., e.g., removing shoes, addressing people, handling of business cards, greetings used, seating arrangements, male-female distinctions, etc. Keep your eyes open, your mouth shut, and prepare yourself beforehand.

19. Unless you are fluent both in speaking and understanding, don't attempt to use a foreign language or expression. Do this only if circumstances permit or it become necessary.

20. In moving from place to place <u>take care not to cut off</u> people. Keep your head on a swivel and use your peripheral vision. If, by accident, you disrupt another's movement, apologize immediately for such boorish behavior.

21. Take care not to dominate conversations. Practice listening more than you speak.

22. Be particularly careful regarding humor or subjective conversational topics.

23. When approaching a door simultaneously with another individual, open it for whomever, it is, permitting them to enter before you. This is to be done for a child, an adult or one's worst enemy. A slight, "by your leave," flourish might even be appropriate.

24. When introducing a person into an open social environment, move them gently, perhaps lightly by the elbow, from party to party, personally introducing them, taking care not to interrupt

Appendix D | 233

or to permit conversations to develop. The idea is to get them introduced, not to get involved in conversations.

25. When walking with an older person, a female or a person of a superior rank, occupy the outside position i.e. that nearest the street, curb, road or balcony.

26. Habits are for lemmings (or for people wearing baseball caps indoors, and rings in their ears or noses, or in or on other parts of their anatomy). Avoid doing anything "out of habit," particularly faulty habits. Make reason, judgment, civility and gentility the catalyst of what you do – the factors on which your reputation is – or will be – based. Doing things or purchasing things because they are "popular" or "cool" usually indicates a lack of self-confidence or self-esteem. Such people find comfort in being one of the crowd. This is not in character for individuals such as you.

27. Chewing gum? Never, at least never in public. This is as gross as chewing tobacco. However, <u>if chewing anything, do it with your mouth closed</u>.

28. Endeavor to make anyone with you think, at that moment, that they are the most important, most interesting person you know. Your actions should lead them to feel most comfortable and secure in your company. Be reserved, but civil, courteous and chivalrous to all. Assume every person you meet to be your equal or your better. Let them prove you're wrong (if, indeed, you are).

29. When driving, be it an automobile or a golf cart respect your passengers. Some people prefer greater caution than others. Respect their preferences. Speed and recklessness gains you only disrespect and demonstrates your immaturity. One may lose

much, other than life, in how one drives a vehicle. Be cautious and courteous.

30. Be optimistic, enthusiastic and project a positive attitude. Be skeptical, but never cynical. However, control your exuberance, avoiding flamboyance and irrational impetuosity or impulsiveness. Project a calm, rational, reasoned grace; your respected *persona grata*.

31. Practice behavior reflecting "noblesse oblige;" refinement, consideration for others and quiet confidence. Avoid actions that can be interpreted as arrogant, loutish, common, boisterous, boorish or inconsiderate, or attitudes that may be inferred as reflecting a superiority complex. Remember, the title of "gentleman" or "lady" must be earned, and then maintained. Never assume that such are given just because of your title or rank. **A rule:** When in doubt, rethink what you are about to say, and then be quiet.

Appendix E

Entrepreneurship: A Different Career Path?

The question has arisen as to how our CEO Career Path – both responsibilities and the Time Line – would change if one's business situation and interests concerns a Start-up or an Entrepreneurship situation instead of a career with an established corporate organization. In summary, given the extent of most of your business experience, I would say, in general, "not that much."

However, in support – or in refutation – of this point, let's examine the situation. In a new business, a start-up, or, in some instances, a knock down and a complete turnaround, what is needed?

First, an idea, a new product, process or service, including how it will be produced or provided, with what ongoing factors will it be competing.

Second, The acquisition as early as possible of at least a patent, copyright and/or a trademark-pending certificate. Be certain your patent is as "iron bound" as circumstances permit.

Third, A sound, practical determination of the market, how it will be approached and served, i.e., exploited, and "Max," "Avg,"(or "Expected") and "Min" projections of revenue (sales), cost of sales, expenses, pre and after-tax profits, cash flow and investments, including lease, "make or buy" requirements, etc. These must include how the product is to be produced, or the service provided competitive considerations and well thought out "what if" scenarios and their potential impacts. And the whole thing must be sound, practical and convincing, particularly so for your banks and venture capitalists. Don't be afraid of annealing your thoughts by seeking people who can ask the embarrassing questions. To make this work, you'll have to answer them soon or later, and it might as well be sooner.

Fourth, A convincing description of the management talent needed and how these "holes" will be filled and by whom. And when. Also, an idea as to who will direct who, i.e., an organization concept

Fifth, your business objective, i.e., a quick success, take public and sellout, an expanding business with a long-term business strategy, etc. Your aim.

Sixth, money. Funds or a commitment for funds to carry the new business for a period of time; at least until favorable cash flow is established to cover the cost of such funds. Don't forget, all during these three to five years – yes, three to five years – you and your family have to live and this will require money and time away from family obligations. Thus, it is necessary that your spouse is totally supportive of this venture.

Seventh, politics. You may have the best, most practical idea in the world; an innovation for which there is a present and long term "crying need'" However, if it in any significant way conflicts or competes with products or services currently in the market sponsored by major companies, you will face a challenge.

Eighth, flexibility. Fight to the greatest extent possible for your idea and for the management and financial control of your company. However, realize that you may well have to take a licensing approach or some other oblique direction to success. Don't despair, necessarily, because history is replete with situations in which corporations have acquired start-up situations only to spin them off in the future at considerable discounts from their acquired cost. Thus, be flexible. If "push comes to shove," go with the acquired company – the one possessing your idea – in a senior or senior management position, and wait out the possible divesture. It's happened many times.

Finally, patience. Every step in a start-up will take at least twice as long as one initially estimates. A simple critical path method analysis often is a good idea. You may find that, given the time of the people involved, that some of these steps may be carried out concurrently.

Now to our question as to relevance of this course to the entrepreneur. Assuming you have individuals with sales, marketing, finance and money raising and, if required, production experience – and enough cash flow to keep your alive and to provide for basic legal assistance, you probably don't need a CEO Career Path of the type we're discussing.

However, and this is a major caveat if you don't have these management assets in place, and are independently capable of lasting three or five years with zero income. I would strongly suggest that you strike for a responsible job in a key company of the type we have discussed, and proceed with a career path plan – yours, ours or someone else's. This move will provide you income, it should certainly provide you additional, valuable management experience, and it will give you time to further strengthen your entrepreneurial plan – organization. Financing, etc.; also you'll have additional experience with a recognized company, which will provide you further bona fides with venture capitalists, potential key employees, etc. However, every option or alternative bears a cost. and this one is no exception: you and your colleagues will have to work doubly hard, doing two jobs successfully to get your new enterprise off the ground and concurrently fulfill your corporate career responsibilities temporary though they may be.

A start-up is no picnic. The number of failures to successes is extremely high. Patience, considerable energy and immense understanding are requisites. However, of course, the payoff can be significant.

Whatever you do, don't even come close to giving away a significant amount of your company in order to expedite a start-up. Watch such ideas of debt conversions to equity. If the opportunity can be developed, attempt to obtain legal, financial and other services on a contingency basis. However, AGAIN don't even discuss approaches that come close to surrendering ownership or management control. A reading of Henry Ford's early days in putting together the Ford Motor Company is a worthwhile primer for you to study.

AND DONT GO IN FOR AN ENTREPRENEURIAL OR START-UP IDEA IF YOUR MAIN GOAL IS TO MAKE A "FAST BUCK". IF YOU DONT HAVE A PASSION FOR THE BUSINESS AND TAKE A LONG TERM INTEREST IN IT. YOU WILL FAIL.

Appendix F

What You Want in a Director

Much has been written over the years about the qualifications of a Director for the Board. These criteria usually focus on the requisite that the prospect must be the leader of a major company, that the company which he or she heads should have complexities and industrial challenges similar to the subject organization, possess outside Board and Board Committee experience, and no potential conflicts of interest. These all are valuable criteria and should play a significant role in the selection process. However, I would suggest that several others may take precedence. These include:

1. Demonstrated reputation for the truth, and possesses the courage and confidence to speak up. This encompasses integrity, honesty, morality, accountability, ethical thought and behavior, etc. One who asks the "tough questions," and is not satisfied with other than sound answers.

2. Time. Should an individual not be comfortable in providing at least 25 working days annually to your Board's affairs, he or she should not be considered a prospect.

3. Is an objective individual, evidencing constant, sound judgment – Inherently and quickly determine the important from the relatively unimportant. Stands on his or her own feet.

4. Welcomes unanticipated, changing conditions. Looks beyond the present, identifying potential unintended consequences, their impacts, and how they may be managed.

5. An ability to contribute based on experience in which he or she has failed as well as succeeded. An ability to provide practical counsel evolving from empirical lessons learned.

6. Possesses compatible management, economic and financial beliefs (their social belief can be whatever it is, but conviction to meritocracy and economic and financial conservatism or liberalism must be unequivocal to that of the other Board members and the objectives of the company).

7. Respect for others based on what they do (accomplishments), not who they are (titles, wealth, families, fame, etc.). You don't want "celebrities." You want "contributors."

8. Absolutely no business relationships with the company or any of its affiliates, nor should a candidate's family have such connections e.g. financial, economic or social.

9. An enthusiastic, positive attitude. Not initially limited or mentally confined by procedures, processes, regulations, laws and/or other "barriers." Mentally flexible. Thinks "outside the box," concentrating on "how to get the job done," not on "why it can't be done."

10. An almost innate drive for success in everything they do and in everyone, they manage.

11. Patience, mental maturity. Experienced in the necessity sometimes to "take two steps back to achieve three steps forward."

12. Of an age and possessing an interest permitting at least five years of future Board participation before retirement or other possible departure from the Board.

13. Possesses an industrial or professional background adding to, complementing or "filling a gap" in the Board's make up.

Appendix G

What You Want the Board to Do

The responsibilities – and the exposure or liabilities – of the Board of Directors, particularly their legal aspects, are broadly defined and relatively well known. However, an equally important subject to the Chief Executive Officer is how these broadly defined responsibilities are met. I would prioritize what I want the Board to do as follows, several relating directly to how effective the CEO does his job:

1. Be totally prepared prior to the meetings, including possible discussions with Board Colleagues. Have questions or comments prepared beforehand, providing such to the CEO.

2. Oversee the developing of key operating and administrative policies, including those relating to Corporate Governance, approving such and monitoring their implementation.

3. Oversee the management of the company, but not managing the company. The Board delegates the management function to the senior executive, i.e., the CEO, Chief Administrator, Managing Partner, etc., and holds him or her accountable for results.

4. Evaluate the performance of the senior executive, reviewing the senior executive's evaluation of the executives reporting to him or her. Establish, approve and authorize prior to payments or grants the compensation of these individuals.

5. Critique and approve the organization's strategic plan and its annual business plan; authorize and approve major expenditures needed to effect these approved plans. Among other criteria, ensure that optimum credit ratings are protected and that the company's

strategic debt-to-equity position protects its corporate and financing interests.

6. Identify principal and/or unique management challenges involved in achieving the strategic plan, and determine of the senior executive's skills and experience – capabilities – are adequate to meet the challenges of the approved plan. Evaluate the senior executive's assessment of such capabilities of the company's other key executives, overseeing management development or changes, if required.

7. Ensure that compensation policies and management's compensation plans are adequate, strategically focused, performance-based and competitive. Also, ensure that no financial relationships beyond the approved compensation plan exist between the company, its executives and its employees, e.g., loans, grants, advances, services, etc.

8. Approve independent auditors and legal counsel; ensuring that such outside firms are not related in any way to organizations whose executives are on the Board of Directors and are not engaged by the company in other activities which may be construed as representing conflicts of interest, e.g., consulting, financial advisory activities, outsourcing engagements, etc. Ensure that corporate policies are carried out concerning such retained services, e.g., rotation of firms, managing partners, etc.

9. Review proposed annual and strategic audit and tax plans – both internally and externally developed; Approving such plans, including the individuals responsible for their implementation; conducting interim reviews with independent and internal auditors, internal and external legal counsels and with investment bankers, satisfying the Board that agreed objectives and timelines are being accomplished. These reviews will be requested through the senior executive, and will be conducted by the entire Board, which may delegate certain

functions to appropriate Board Committees. Reviews to include adequacy of control and reporting procedures and systems.

10. Keep informed through open source data as to the company's performance, competitive actions, and government and industrial practices and actions on which the company's success depends, including visits to company's business sites, advise the senior executive periodically concerning such findings and conclusions.

11. Approve capital expenditures, acquisitions, mergers, divestitures and all actions relating to changes in assets in excess of a certain "hurdle" value level; ensuring that such proposed plans provide complete cost information, including renovations, upgrades, maintenance and repairs, etc., and that their relationships to the strategic plan and annual business plan is specified and quantified, and that proposed performances are being realized.

12. Ensure that identities of qualified Director prospects and candidates are maintained; working with the senior executive, to keep such candidates appropriately informed and interested in company affairs.

13. Review and approve materials to be provided shareholders and the public, including press releases, draft quarterly and annual statements, reports, articles for publication, etc.

14. Review and approve annually the company's Statement of Ethics and appropriate management compliance of related policies.

15. Ensure that the company's financial and financing plans protect its assets, the shareholders' interests and the financing capabilities of the enterprise – equity as well as debt financing – and optimum overall costs.

16. Oversee the sale or "spin off" of assets, including ongoing Business Units, operating units, subsidiaries, etc. (reference point No. 11, above), ensuring that optimum value is realized, and that potential liabilities are accommodated.

17. Review annual meeting plans, materials and presentation methods, participating in the shareholder meeting as requested by the senior executive.

18. Provide support to management in implementing approved policies, plans and procedures, striving for unanimity in all major Board decisions; assist the senior executive and his senior management in continually strengthening employee morale and loyalty to the company.

Appendix H

The Struggle to Better Pompeia?

Today's corporate Boards of Directors are struggling in their efforts to "better Pompeia" and project that their future deliberations and actions are "above suspicion."[7] In addition to preparing for the influences of Federal and State government Acts, proposed Acts, legislation and newly introduced regulations of the Exchanges, etc., on their businesses, Boards are considering many internal steps to achieve the goals of transparency, trust, honesty and propriety. Examples of actions Boards are considering include the following:

- A non-management executive to be the Chairman of the Board

- The Chief Executive Officer, the President and the Chief Financial Officer to be legally accountable for "signing off" company audits and related public and government-required reports

- Professional (external) auditing firms to be rotated every three to five years

- Eliminate practice of staggering the election of Director of the Board

- Name a Director of the Board as the "Presiding Director"

---

[7]Julius Caesar reportedly said, "I wish my wife to be not so much as suspected." This was said by the Emperor in the 62 BC trial of Publius Claudius when asked by the Judge involving the Bona Dea scandal why he had separated (later divorced) from Pompeia, a relative of Pompey. This quotation eventually evolved into the traditional and famous aphorism that "Caesar's wife must be above suspicion," from *The Parallel Lives of Famous Greeks and Romans,* by Plutarch, AD 90, Section 10, page 9.

- Involve shareholders in the development of compensation plans relating to senior management executives

- Expense stock options

- Appoint an Ombudsman who will report directly either to the Chief Executive Officer or to the Chairman of the Board of Directors

- Directors of the Board and/or Chairmen of Board Committees to participate directly in shareholder meetings

- Restrict nominees for Director of the Board to individuals completed independent of the company and/or its management

- Shareholders to be privy before the fact to three-year or five-year Professional Auditing firm's audit programs

- Internal audit function to report directly to the Chief Executive Officer or to the Chairman, Audit Committee of the Board of Directors

- Discontinue the practice of providing outside parties quarterly and annual "earnings estimates"

- Limit management members of the Board of Directors to fewer than one-fifth of the Board of Director seats

- Retain only Investment or Merchant Banking firms that do not provide Analyst or Specialist services or Investment reports to or pertaining to the company

- Restrict the services of Professional audit firms solely to auditing and tax services

- Ensure that a company's auditing and reporting standards are well within the scope and meaning of those of GAAP, FASB and so forth

Appendix I

Corporate Governance Guidelines

(An Example)

I.   DIRECTOR INDEPENDENT AND QUALIFICATIONS

Independence
A majority of the Directors shall meet the New York Stock Exchange listing standards for independence. All of the members of the Audit Committee, Compensation Committee and the Nominations and Governance Committee shall be independent.

Qualifications
The qualifications for the company's Directors are set forth in the Qualifications for Directors.

Change in Affiliation
Directors are expected to report to the Chairman of the Board and the Chairman of the Nominations and Governance Committee when they experience a significant change in their business or professional affiliation or responsibility and offer to resign from the Board. The Nominations and Governance Committee, in consultation with the Chairman of the Board, will determine whether the Director continues to adequately meet the requirements for service on the Board of Directors and whether or not to accept the resignation.

Limit on the Number of Other Directorships
Directors are expected to devote sufficient time to fulfill their responsibilities as Directors in accordance with the criteria set forth in the Qualifications for Directors. Accordingly, Directors may serve on the Board of Directors of other public companies, but shall limit such service to that reasonable

number of companies, which will not conflict with his or her responsibilities as a company Director.

New Directorship

Directors are expected to inform the Chairman of the Board and the Chairman of the Nominations and Governance Committee of any public company directorships that they have been offered before accepting such directorship. In addition, no Director shall serve on the Board of Directors of any company competitor or in any other senior relationship with such a competitor.

Term Limits

Company Directors are not subject to term limits because the Board of Directors has determined that the knowledge, expertise and continuity provided by those Directors who have company experience and who continue to meet its Qualifications, as Directors are valuable to the company and its shareholders.

Tenure

A non-management Director may only continue to serve as a Director until Directors are elected at the annual shareholders' meeting immediately following the Director's seventieth (70th) birthday. Management directors shall retire from the Board of Directors on their retirement from the company.

Chairman of the Board and Chief Executive Officer

The Board of Directors believes that it is important to retain the flexibility to allocate the responsibilities of the offices of Chairman of the Board and Chief Executive Officer in any manner that it determines to be in the company's best interest. The Board of Directors specifically reserves the right to vest the responsibilities of Chairman of the Board and Chief Executive Officer in the same individual, and currently believes that it is in the company's best interest for the Chief Executive Officer to serve as the Chairman of the Board.

II.   DIRECTOR RESPONSIBILITIES

Preparation for and Attendance at Meetings
Directors are expected to prepare adequately for and regularly attend meetings of the Board of Directors and Board Committees on which they serve.

Special Meetings
Recognizing that situations arise requiring prompt Board action, Directors shall make themselves available for special meetings and shall promptly return documents requiring their signature. Directors shall receive prompt notification of such special meetings.

Disclosure of Potential Conflicts of Interest
Directors must disclose to the rest of the members of the Board of Directors any potential conflict of interest they may have with respect to a matter under consideration, and, if appropriate, refrain from voting on a matter for which such potential conflict exists.

Board Review
The Board of Directors shall review and, where appropriate, approve fundamental operating, financial, risk management and other corporate strategies, as well as major plans and objectives, and shall monitor the effectiveness of management policies and decisions, including the execution of plans and strategies.

Public Statements
Absent unusual circumstances, the company's senior management, as opposed to individual Directors, provides the company's public voice.

III.   BOARD AND COMMITTEE MEETINGS

Meetings

The Board of Directors generally meets at least seven times a year, on dates selected by the Chairman of the Board. Directors will receive as much advanced notice of such meeting dates as reasonably practical.

Agenda

The Chairman of the Board, in consultation with the other Board members, shall set the Board of Directors' meeting agenda. The Chairman of the Board, in consultation with the Chairman of each Committee, shall set the agenda for the meetings of the applicable Committee. Directors and Committee members may suggest addenda items and may raise other matters at meetings.

Executive Sessions

The independent Directors generally meet at least twice a year in regularly scheduled Executive Sessions and may hold such additional executive sessions as they determine necessary or appropriate. The Chairman of the Nominations and Governance Committee normally shall preside at these Executive Sessions.

IV.   BOARD COMMITTEES

Audit, Nominations and Governance, and Compensation Committees

The Board of Directors shall at all times have an Audit Committee, Nominations and Governance Committee and a Compensation Committee. All of the members of these Committees shall be independent Directors. Each of these Committees shall operate in accordance with applicable law, its Charter and the applicable rules of the Security and Exchange Commission and the New York Stock Exchange. The Chairmen of these Committees should not serve in such capacity for more than five consecutive years.

Executive Committee

The Board of Directors also shall have an Executive Committee with the power to act on behalf of the Board of Directors, except for powers reserved to the full Board of Directors pursuant to (applicable State) law, the company's by-laws or any standing Board resolution. The Chairman of the

Board shall be the Chairman of the Executive Committee, a majority of members being independent Directors.

Public Policy

The Board of Directors shall have a Public Policy Committee that will advise the Board of Directors with respect to public policy, and regulatory and government affairs issues which affect the company. A majority of the members of **this** Committee shall be independent Directors.

Other Committees

The Board of Directors also may establish such other Committees as it deems appropriate, and delegate to those Committees any authority permitted by applicable law and the company's by-laws as the Board of Directors sees fit, other than the responsibilities delegated to the Audit Committee, Nominations and Governance Committee, and Compensation Committee in their Charters or reserved to the full Board of Directors.

V. DIRECTOR ACCESS TO MANAGEMENT AND INDEPENDENT ADVISORS

Access to the Company's Management

Each Director shall have complete access to the company's management. The Company's management will make itself available to respond to Directors' questions about the company at times among Board meetings.

Independent Advisors

The Board of Directors and Board Committees may engage and consult with financial, legal, or other independent advisors at the company's expense.

VI. DIRECTOR COMPENSATION

Role of the Compensation Committee

Each year, in accordance with the terms of the Charter, the Compensation Committee shall review the compensation paid to the members of the Board of Directors and provide recommendations to the Board of Directors regarding both the amount of Director compensation that should be paid and the allocation of such compensation between equity-based awards and cash.

Indemnification
In accordance with the terms of its Articles of Incorporation, the company shall indemnify the members of the Board of Directors to the fullest extent of the law.

VII.   DIRECTOR ORIENTATION AND CONTINUING EDUCATION

Director Orientation
Following their election, every newly elected member of the Board of Directors shall participate in an orientation program established by the company. This orientation program shall include presentations designed to familiarize Directors with the company, its strategic plans, significant financial, accounting and risk management issues, the company's Code of Conduct, compliance programs and other controls, its senior management and its internal and external independent auditors. The program also shall address procedures of the Board of Directors, Directors responsibilities, the Board's Corporate Governance Guidelines and Board Committee Charters.

Continuing Education
The Board of Directors encourages its members to participate in continuing education programs sponsored by universities, stock exchanges or other organizations specializing in Director education. Directors may attend continuing education programs at the company's expense.

VIII.   MANAGEMENT EVALUATION AND SUCCESSION

Evaluation of Chief Executive Officer and Other Management
The Nominations and Governance Committee annually shall report to the Board of Directors on its evaluation of the Chief Executive Officer's

performance. The Board of Directors shall review this report; including discussing it outside the presence of the management Directors, to satisfy itself that the Chief Executive Officer is providing the strategic (long term) and tactical (short term) leadership that the Board of Directors deems necessary for the company. In addition, the Nominations and Governance Committee, with input provided by the Chief Executive Officer, shall conduct an annual assessment of the performance and development of the company's other officers and senior management.

Succession Planning

Succession planning for the company's officers and senior management positions is critical to the company's strategic success. The Nominations and Governance Committee shall annually review the company's succession plans and report on them to the Board of Directors. The Nominations and Governance Committee also shall identify potential successors for the Chief Executive Officer position; although this does not mean that it must at all times have selected a particular individual as the designated successor to the Chief Executive Officer. The Chief Executive Officer shall participate in this process by providing the Nominations and Governance Committee recommendations or evaluations of potential successors and identifying any development plans that the Chief Executive Officer recommends for such individuals. The Chief Executive Officer shall recommend to the Board of Directors on an ongoing basis one or more successors in the event that the Chief Executive Officer unexpectedly becomes incapable to continue to serve in such capacity.

VIII.   ANNUAL PERFORMANCE EVALUATION OF THE BOARD

Self-Evaluation by the Board of Directors

The Board of Directors annually shall conduct a self-evaluation to determine whether it and its Committees are functioning effectively. The Nominations and Governance Committee shall be responsible for seeking comments from all Directors and reporting its evaluation of Board and Committee performance to the Board of Directors on an annual basis. The full Board of

Directors will discuss the evaluation report to determine what, if any, action could improve Board and Board Committee performance.

Statement of Principles

These Guidelines are a statement of principles and intent. The Board of Directors reserves the right, unless otherwise required by law or the rules of the New York Stock Exchange or the Securities and Exchange Commission, to make exceptions to these guidelines where it believes such action is warranted due to special circumstances and is in the company's best interest.

Evaluation of Corporate Governance Guidelines

The Board of Directors recognizes that these Corporate Governance Guidelines must continue to evolve to meet the changing needs of the company and its shareholders, and changing requirements. The Board of Directors, with the assistance of its Nominations and Governance Committee, periodically will review these Corporate Governance Guidelines to determine whether changes are appropriate (it is noted that changes will be incorporated effective fourth quarter 2004 and first quarter 2005 as new laws and regulations become better defined and are implemented).

IX.   STOCK OWNERSHIP GUIDELINES

Stock Ownership

Directors and officers are encouraged to make a substantial investment in the company's stock, depending on individual circumstances. From time to time, the Board of Directors shall set minimum stock ownership guidelines.

Appendix J
Managing Personal Finances

After several years of education and career-oriented work experience, you either are in the management ranks or shortly will to be. This phase of your career brings on new responsibilities and increasing time pressures. It also brings on important ancillary challenges about which you must give time, including one that you probably already have experienced some impact: how best to manage your own personal finances. To achieve success in your corporate career you must give attention to this challenge – planning and managing your own financial resources. If this isn't done, and done well, tensions and turmoil easily can result which can prove to be a significant distraction to one's career, may seriously and possibly irreparably affect one's marriage and possibly one's health. I know that this is nothing new to you, but money long as been the greatest obstacle to a constructive marital relationship, which, of course, is required for a most successful career.

To date in your career you probably have enjoyed increases in income beyond the needs of you and your family. This may even have come as a pleasant surprise. However, herein lays the danger of euphoria. For example, those cute children in the not too distance future will grow into teenagers and candidates for college. This will require money. Another example, a marriage and children probably will require a larger residence. This will require money. Eventually, you and your spouse might wish to consider retirement and look forward to travel. This will require money. I believe you get the picture. Even so, if you are like many of us, advertising and promotion of luxurious goods surely may begin taking its toll on you, or on you and your family. Visions of owning Aston-Martins or yachts, taking foreign ski vacations, frequenting four or five-star restaurants, occupying palatial estates, purchasing haute couturier apparel and booking 'round-the-world cruises may crowd out your better – frugally-oriented – judgment. Hopefully, as we discussed in Chapters X, you and your spouse, or your spouse-to-be seriously share ideas about money.

Let's talk about the sobering subject of "first-thing-first" in managing money.

Assume you earn on your present job $144,000 (U.S.) per year and your exceptional contributions garner you a bonus for the year of an additional, say, $15,000. How do you make the most of this? Well, first off, let's accept the fact that your frugal life style should continue for a while, say three or so years. Second, this wonderful amount of money is not yours. Actually, it hasn't been yours, or of people like you in the United States since 1905.

OK. Pencil to paper…

$144,000 ÷ 12 = $12,000 per month. Forget the bonus for the moment.

Total	$12,000.00
Less Income Tax (Est. 28%)	$ 3,360.00
Other (Est. 8%)*	$ 960.00
Net	$ 7,680.00

*Social Security, health benefits, retirement benefits, etc.

Thus, the amount we have to work with approximates $7,700 per month, or about $92,400 per year. Big difference from where we started.

Now, in our financial statement, we've our "Where Got," what will be our "Where Gone?" Here, we are assuming two individuals. Of course, a single person will be less expensive, more than a couple, more expensive.

- Estimate that your dwelling – mortgage payment, apartment or condo lease, etc. – will require about one-fourth of your net money, viz., between $1,900 and $1,950 per month. The amount remaining – $7,700 less $1,925 – now approximates $5,800. Note: The "one-fourth" figure has evolved over time from data provided the public from banks, real estate experts, etc.

- Now our real discipline sets in. Let's bring in the bonus. Of the foregoing bonus, remember the $15,000 – that amount, after taxes and so forth, is now $9,600. I suggest that you fold into this amount about $6,000 from your annual net income and put the resulting $15,000 or $16,000 in the bank. This isn't a fortune, but it is of sufficient significance to get a bank's attention, another aim for your financial plan. Purchase a CD, a treasury note or a money market fund, corporate bonds or something similar that places your savings at little risk and affords you something above inflation and the changing value of the currency. Inflation, as Warren Buffett explains, is a greater tax than any tax legislation every enacted. Unless you come into this position with wealth beyond that based on your career income, or your spouse has a professional knowledge of the market (or is a "wiz bang" investor), I would avoid common stock. Yes, I know, "how conservative can this guy get?" However, the real aim in all of this is to strengthen your discipline while, concurrently, not needing to give your investment program too much attention (see point No. 7). Again, the time you give to this subject takes away from the time for your career and your "partner" – your spouse and family.

- A good objective in this initial facet of your financial plan is to set a goal. For example, you and your spouse might decide that within three to five years you will want to accumulate enough funds to finance, at least, a down payment for future personal real estate. Keep on the lookout for unimproved property for sale in a good, residential zoned area, one with a fairly stable tax base and improving values. This you could purchase as an investment or for your own, expanded use. Another goal could be establishing a college fund for your spouse or for your children. Again, the discipline in making a plan and sticking to it is the aim. Perhaps your spouse might find this an avocation of interest.

- Now you have $1,700 per month or $20,400 annually for such things as food, clothing, transportation, utilities and, to some degree, entertainment and diversion. Discipline now becomes part of your entertainment, and it costs you nothing buy thinking and perhaps a challenge within the family.

Important, Related Actions

Please consider the following as suggestions or proposals for your consideration:

1.   Make a three-year, monthly budget, a plan that keeps you within your resulting net figure (for example, the above $1,700 per month. As your income increases, put the amount of the increase in savings. You might be surprised that, by the end of the thirty-six months, you can survive comfortably on less than the amount of the monthly budget. Also, negotiate with your utilities supplier to get your payments on some form of quarterly budget payment plan.

2.   Adopt an Individualist's attitude. One that reaffirms that you and your spouse are self-reliant. You don't need affectations or material show of "keeping up with the Jones." Develop the challenge of having fun in beating your budget, in being frugal. Remember, you are "Needs" oriented, not "Wants" driven.

3.   Use cash or employ debit transactions – not debt. Save until larger items can be purchased. Don't get on the "slippery slope" of debt financing. Of course, prudence indicates the need to establish a credit rating. However, you can accomplish this by a Line of Credit agreement, but you don't have to use it.

4.   Re-locate your dwelling within walking distance say a half mile to a mile, from your place of employment. This will eliminate the need to drive to and from work – saving money, and also
Provide you exercise, which we all need.

5.   Attempt to arrange a lease-purchase agreement on your dwelling. Your dwelling is the best investment relating to your direct life type you can make. Over time, instead of depreciating it usually will gain in value, exceeding by far inflation and the impact of any possible negative exchange rate. In investing in structures, I have found it is

wise to obtain advice and guidance from <u>two</u> inspectors or licensed construction experts. Also, check zoning provisions and the political environment regarding such in the area of interest.

Don't neglect the possibility of acquiring repossessed property. Your bank (or another bank) or your Credit Union (see below) often have such real estate, vehicles and similar opportunities, which they want to remove from their books as fast as possible. And normally will consider any reasonable offer. Check these sources before making a final decision in such matters.

6.   Purchase used furniture. The markups on costs of the U.S. furniture industry, with its rather archaic marketing and distribution structure, are second only to that of the financial sector. By purchasing used items, you let someone else pay the top price while you enjoy furniture that largely will be covered anyway. The exception to this recommendation would be genuine antiques that grow in value with the passing years, examples being an antique upright clock, an antique breakfront or a piano.

Relating to household and related purchases, a good buy is the magazine, *Consumer Reports.* Many of the magazine's "fillers" are exaggerations or meaningless, but the principal articles, particularly those dealing with big ticket items such as white goods, tools, automobiles, etc. are valuable references in considering certain purchases. At least these notes provide you sound bases for asking questions. However, consider renting equipment for one-time or periodic jobs. You don't need a tools inventory hanging on the wall.

A couple of years now have passed, and your savings discipline is well established – a habit is created.

We now move to the next steps:

7.	Begin putting away at least one-third of your combined after-tax income. As the parlance goes, "Save 'till you squeak." Determine which can become the greater savings masochist, you or your spouse.

Develop a plan for a reasonable balance among various investment classes, viz., Cash or Equivalent, Money Market Securities, Corporate Bonds, Common Stock, Real Estate, etc. Review the status and soundness of your plan at least annually. Your commercial banker will help you accomplish this for little or no charge. After all, you might pick up a CD from them occasionally.

Don't ignore securities paying dividends, particularly if they represent leading companies in sound, growth industries, having good earnings' and cash flow trends and reasonable multiples. There sometimes are methods in dealing directly with these companies to increase your dividend income substantially.

Consider small-cap situations for about a third of your securities investment. Look for opportunities in this area having (a) a reasonable three-to-five year "staying power" history, (b) significant insider ownership, say 20% plus, (c) better than 12% Return on Assets, (d) companies receiving little analyst attention, say less than four individuals, and (e) institutional holdings of less than 15%.

A couple of caveats: First, tax efficiency is paramount. It's more important to avoid what could amount to 2 to 3 percentage points annually than it is to outperform your benchmark by 1%. Second, long-term investment is key; unemotional, disciplined rebalancing, making consistent contributions (after maximizing your retirement contributions) and staying invested. Third, don't attempt to "Time the Market." Lastly, similarly, returns usually come in concentrated "spurts," so being out of the market" can destroy all the good that you've accomplished.

8.   Join a Credit Union. Sometimes in making such a selection, there are in-state and out-of-state considerations. Membership is a reputable organization can provide several benefits for little investment or cost, among which is establishing your credit position (see point No. 3).

9.   Avoid Credit Cards. The convenience they afford covers a most virulent and deathly plague. The usurious rates charged and the vague and confusing provisions are universal. Always consider, in using Credit Cards for purchases, you are underwriting the cost of the slime with which these firms chose to deal and their own credit evaluation ineptitude.

10.   To the extent you can, without risk of damaging your credit standing or reputation, arrange to delay the retirement of whatever education debt you may have. Usually, the debt to banks for education needs, universities, parents, relatives and so forth carry a much lower interest rate than other debt. Take advantage of it.

11.   Avoid acquiring an automobile if possible. Use public or "Mass" transportation, or, again, walk. Recall *The Word* (Appendix 'C'). An automobile results in insurance, garage costs, fuel, maintenance and, regardless of age, depreciation; considerable expense for the dubious privilege of possible and needless flexibility and convenience. Also, remember, second only to furniture (see point No. 6), an automobile has the greatest depreciation of all household assets.

12.   If you find that an automobile is absolutely necessary, seek out a vehicle model at least three years old, with a little or no damage

record and one having several years warranty remaining. In today's market (2010), this means approaching the "car thing" looking for a top price in the neighborhood of $15,000. In this regard, check the availability of "leased cars" being turned in, and prospective purchases on the Internet. These often can represent better deals than the conventional "pre-owned" market and in most cases, good warranties remain. Let's face it. The only purpose of an automobile, if such cannot be avoided, is to get from "Point A" to "Point B" (and return) safely and in reasonable comfort. One might consider Mr. Warren Buffett as a good example in this and in several other aspects of frugality. You don't need a shiny Porsche to prove your value or your worth.

Incidentally, as you may already be doing, use New Car Dealers or Distributors only for warranty work. You will find far greater economies, as, again, you probably already realize, in handling all other related purchases and service through repair garages and stations with which you have established relationships.

13. Avoid the Sirens' Song of "Sales" – any sales. Also, the "come ons" of hawkers who promise "no payment or interest for the Eternity." These ploys are intended for the naïve. All that is happening in these cases is that merchandise is marked up to cover profits and cost of capital before the "Sales" commence.

14. Purchase generics. Most private bands involve costs including the producer's advertising and promotion, which are of little use to you. You might consider a foods club or purchasing club in which quantity purchasing reduces the cost, but, again, study before you act.

15. Recall the career value of being informed? Spend your time and money on well-researched newspapers, journals, periodicals and books. As pointed out earlier, television programming largely is a waste. However, if home schooling, music appreciation, sports events, theater and/or serious literary discussions are of interest, an

investment in a Blu-Ray player and an OLED television may be a valuable asset for you and the family.

16. Club or Association memberships are expensive, their services and events are costly and such associations tend to channel you into the same groups and though processes which usually can become staid and boring. Tennis, golf and card games can be of interest and to an extent beneficial, but you don't have to join clubs to participate.

17. Don't load up on mortgage debt. While it is better to borrow against your home that to assume most other types of debt, mortgage interest still will cost you a bundle of money. For example, if you are in the 28% Federal income tax bracket, you'll save 28 cents in taxes for every $1.00 you incur in mortgage interest, but what about the other 72 cents? That's out of pocket – your pocket. There is an equal peril in purchasing a larger home, hoping for exceptional appreciation in value and in refinancing a present mortgage. Also, don't forget maintenance, repairs, modernization costs, insurance, and so forth. Over time, these expenses largely can offset what you anticipate in price appreciation. Again, just examine the numbers before you join the lemmings.

18. Special Days such as birthdays, anniversaries, Christmas, Ramadan, Hanukkah, Passover, Easter, New Years, Spring Festival, Mother's Day, Father's Day, etc., are great to remember. However, they have become excessively commercial and increasingly expensive. Today, five or six greeting cards with postage can cost as much as a "night on the town." Consider drafting your own poems and themes for such occasions. Remember, it really is "the thought that counts." Who knows, you might even become a poet.

The same rationale applies to vacations. Entire multibillion-dollar industries exist – and are expanding, drawing entirely for their profits on the emotions of prospective customers. However, considerable savings can be realized through closely budgeting these events. The principal value of a "vacation" should be a "change of pace" for you and your family – a diversion from the day-to-day life. It is not necessary to incur the costs of expensive air travel and hotels or resorts to enjoy a diversion. Time with your spouse and children, a couple of good books or rented films and possibly practicing your hobby will accomplish this purpose, and you all can pursue you individual interests, and , concurrently, achieve relaxation. You might, should such interest exist, contemplate organizing or participating in a play reading group or an investors' club, both worthwhile and broadening diversions.

19.   Let your colleagues and acquaintances know, through your actions, your attitude toward expenditures of your time and money for other than required things. You will gain their respect and admirations, and perhaps several adherents.

20.   A most important and often sensitive subject is Estate, Inheritance and Gift taxes. However, regardless of the sensitivity, you and your parents, or you, your spouse and your respective parents should address these issues early on. To preserve the estate, and reduce (hopefully eliminate) inheritance and gift taxes require planning, time and trust to fully implement a plan to accomplish these objectives. The assets of the family estate have been created and expanded largely due to hard work, frugality and astute planning. They should remain in the family for its use and further development otherwise in spite of your wishes it will be garner by the government for whatever political purposes it elects. Protection of these assets can occur only if all parties concur and work together. "The sands are constantly shifting" in these matters, and it is one area in which skilled, experienced, impartial counsel can well pay for itself. However, as in the earlier discussed, before retaining counsel, gain some perspective of the challenges independently. However, plan early. In these issues, in which personal feelings become important, time can slip by quickly and someone else can well enter the situation to your detriment.

21. Throughout this entire managing subject, look to the future and fully engage all members of your family. This not only is a vital matter to your career, but can become a valuable learning experience for your children. By your examples, those of you and your spouse, the children and learn and appreciate the importance of discipline and the fact that being frugal does not impair a constructive and pleasant life style.

Appendix K

Guidelines for Employing Management Consultants

In reaching for outside counsel – or <u>considering</u> retaining outside counsel, there are several steps that should be taken to ensure that you have the best talent on the job and that the "product" will approximate the value you expect.

1. Identify the real problem requiring possible outside assistance:

    ▪ First, "drain" the capabilities of your own people in identifying and in attempting to solve the problem – apply the "5 Whys." This will acquaint your people with the challenge being faced and will stretch their abilities in their effort to resolve it. It will also gain respect for you inasmuch as you had confidence to first task them with the challenge. This action will also convince your people that an outside view probably will be beneficial in resolving the issue, i.e. that a consultant is needed.

    ▪ Obtain a draft definition of the problem from your management. Get consensuses regarding the challenge, the resolution of which will need outside help.

    ▪ Obtain a general plan from management as to what it believes would be required by outside counsel to do the job and the product it would expect. This shows sound management on your part because next, you are going to solicit management thinking and assistance about what individuals or firms should be considered by the company to provide such outside help. In other words, you have brought them into the picture, and again have shown them your respect in asking their now experienced opinions.

2. Solicit proposals from qualified outside counsel. Have the senior management which is most involved with the problem identify consulting prospects.

- Check with acquaintances in other companies in identifying several prospects that appear to have the qualification for this specific piece of work, for example, four to six individuals or firms.
- Provide these prospects with a written description of the job and what is wanted in terms of a product, determining their degree of interest. Obtain "Conflict of Interest" statements and "nondisclosure agreements."
- Arrange presentations by the prospects, preferably with all key members of management in attendance, having the prospects emphasize (1) their understanding of the problem and its significance to the company, (2) how they would approach the work, including management involvement, (3) who specifically would be involved from their firm and their summary backgrounds, (4) their experience with this type of assignment, (5) references and (6) nature of noncompetitive protection. Make sure the people who would perform the work make the presentation and participate in discussions.
- Check references (and sub-references). (1). Verify the job, the approach taken, who did the work, confidentiality, etc. (2). Degree of success, client satisfaction, time and cost, comments. (3) Transition and implementation, counsel "post-job" involvement. (4) General comments, views, etc. The degree to which management was disrupted? Were they more interested in this job or in getting the next job? Would you hire them again (if not, why not)? Were you, in effect, training their people? Was there evidence of personnel 'bait and switch,' etc. (5) Importantly, to what degree did the consultants endeavor to take an active management role in future activities of the client organization? (6) After all of

this, take the results of such references with "a grain of salt. " Remember be skeptical.

3. Request bid proposals from consulting candidates, i.e., your highest rated prospects.

    - A written proposal including the points (above), plus review and control points (meetings, etc.), profiles of people to do the work, the amount of client participation, estimates of consulting fees and business expenses, payment schedule, implementation schedule, and next steps. Be wary of "boilerplate" and "estimates." Require maximums for both time and costs, and detailed billings. Determine costs, etc. of cancellation.
    - Be wary of proposals developed in phases. Suggested phases of work are not bad in themselves in that they can be used effectively as control points or milestones for checking progress or for possibly changing the direction of the assignment. However, sometimes they are used to obfuscate the competitive nature of fees and costs for the entire assignment and/or get the consultant's "foot in the door" for additional work.
    - Due date for decision (beyond which consultant's staffing may change). Remember, your company is hiring individual talents, not retaining a firm.
    - Decide on the company manager and personnel to work with consultants.

4. Select Outside Consultant

    - Meet with primary candidate and review the company's revisions to the candidate's proposal. Don't be deluded by the "Big Blue" syndrome.

- Require a contract – this is a business arrangement. Don't be put off in this by professions that tell you "we don't require contracts."
- If the primary candidate doesn't accept the job, go to number two, etc.

5. Conduct Periodic Review and Control sessions and Commence Implementation

- Require periodic reviews during the assignment, the first of which should be scheduled within four to six weeks after the work begins. This meeting essentially is to ensure that the consultants are on track.
- Subsequent meetings depend on timing of work in progress. Sessions should occur at the completion of the findings, analysis, conclusions and recommendation points of the work. This will save time, enabling the company to begin initial implementation steps before the study is formalized. It will also ensure that conclusions and recommendations being developed are not the result of "one size fits all" thinking of the consultant, as innocent as this thinking may be.
- Be certain in reviewing the work that "things hang together." Have they followed your "One-third, One-Third, One-Third" plan? Is the problem well defined at the outset? Do findings, Analyses, Conclusions, Recommendations, Implementation and Next steps build upon each other? Given what should be the consultants' understanding of the problem and your company's characteristics, do the recommendations make sense? Given competitive and economic conditions – both tactical and strategic, are their conclusions and recommendations practical, or are they "blue sky?"
- If the consultants are staying in contact sufficiently with you, the client, you and your people should know the conclusions,

recommendations, etc. before the job is completed, and the report received. Did they "bring along" your people?

6. Critique Consultant's Work, including three or six-month Post-Assignment Status Review. Be "up front with them in your evaluation of their work.

A word of caution: Some firms, indeed, some of the larger, more renowned general management consulting firms, attempt to place their personnel within the client's organization. Sometimes allegedly, this is "to assist the client during the implementation phase of the assignment," but actual intent eventually is to have them assume permanent management roles. You should be wary of such attempts. These people may be highly qualified, but the intent and the question of where their strategic loyalties lie make this a practice that represents a risk and a conflict to you and to your company.

Appendix L
What Happened to "Laissez-faire"?!

History is a great teacher, that is if we can obtain a relatively unvarnished version of it, and, then, if we chose to determine what we can learn. Among the things, we may learn and to apply in our management responsibilities is how and why the U.S. governments, both Federal and State, began intervening in our business and personal lives. Essentially, the factors that motivate the politicians in the U.S. government are the same that motivate politicians in most other governments. How to keep their jobs and how to find money to pay for things to keep their jobs. For instance, consider the history of how these governments began taxing our income and what has occurred since we or rather the Supreme Court permitted the politicians to do this. **One important lesson to learn and to keep in mind: Once the governments enact an idea about money, particularly one beneficial to its Congressional or Legislative members, it is there forever and its benefits to them always increase.** Hence, the way to stop these actions and change directions is to actively participate in the system and by changing the politicians.

However, this provides only momentary relief; the new politicians, regardless of what they profess they will do about cutting, costs, reducing the deficit, end often not accomplishing or doing what they claimed they would do. Knowing something of the history may provide us reasons to ask "why?"

Wars and the increasing attention given by the politicians to social support and protection of the voting potential of minorities and the less affluent population, has been the bases of taxes on income, profits, dividend and inheritance in the United States since 1862. Progressive income levies against individuals who have worked harder and hence realized higher incomes began in 1932. The politicians have been playing with the rates and the system since the beginning, reducing tax rates somewhat following considerable increases, thus taking advantage of the public's short memory, allowing the people to believe that it is receiving advantages. However, the net of all of this always is a resulting increase!

Income Taxes – In 1943, a significant change in the collection method on taxes on income – renewed in 1913 – was introduced with the withholding system on salaries and wages. While the high Federal tax rates restricted somewhat the expansion of State rates during the 1940s, the cities, especially in such states as Ohio and Pennsylvania, increased the use of income taxes on salaries and wages.

Corporate Taxes – The first U.S. tax on corporate income occurred immediately prior to the Civil War to generate funds to pay for the war. This so-called "temporary" tax wasn't repealed until five or six years after the war ended (note the speed with which the Congress acts when loss of money to it is at stake!).The first rate imposed, also in 1913, was 1%. It continues to increase reaching a high rate for the period of 13.5% in 1926. It was reduced to 12% two years later, and then increased again in the 1930s. During the latter half of that decade limited rate progression was introduced primarily," as we were told, "to lessen the impact on the growth of small businesses." For example, in 1936 the rates ranged from 8% to 15%.

During World War II, the corporate tax rate reached 40%. In '46, the tax structure was simplified with a two-tier approach, i.e., 23% applying to all corporate income with a surtax of 19% on income exceeding $25,000. In 1951, the basic rate was increased to 28%, and in 1952 to 30% – the maximum effective rate being 52%. The 1964 Tax Reduction Act, one of the few times in which the Congress demonstrated awareness that companies could use funds for economic improvement and job growth far better than governments, reduced the maximum rate for larger corporations to 48%.

Double Taxation of Dividends – The double taxation of dividends also first occurred in 1936, at which time dividend income of individuals was subjected both to normal income tax and surtax. Congress rejected a proposal to apply the corporate tax only to undistributed profits, favoring a supplementary tax on such profits in addition to the regular levy. This tax was strongly protested, and was abandoned in 1927, showing that the public can achieve results!

Estate and Inheritance Taxes – One's sense of independence or freedom from government power is the knowledge and assurance that one's possessions can be passed on to his or her children, spouse, parents or any designated party. In the United States, the Federal tax is dependent entirely on the size or value of the estate, while the State taxes widely are patterned on the remoteness of the heirs' relationship to the deceased. Those who oppose inheritance of property believe such property is acquired without work or contribution, and causes further inequality of income within society. This position is a characteristic of socialism.

There are two types of "death taxes": One, an estate tax imposed up on the privilege of transmitting or transferring ownership of property at the time of death, and two, an inheritance tax imposed upon the privilege of receiving property from a decedent at death. The first is based on the entire capital value of all property changing hands at death, the second being calculated based on the amount of each benefit and on the relationship (if any) of the beneficiary to the deceased.

Death taxes are imposed for two purposes: One, to collect revenue, and two, as a social policy, to lessen the aforementioned "inequalities. " As far as revenues to the government are concerned, death taxes are relatively insignificant. Federal estate tax revenue has never amounted to more than 7% of total tax revenue of the U.S. Federal Government, frequently much less. However, it carries considerable clout for the politicians with these socially based programs aimed at breaking up large estates and limited the accumulation of wealth with little or no regard of how it was achieved.

The first U.S. Federal government death taxes were imposed in 1798. However, they were opposed strongly and failed to become a permanent part of the Federal tax system until the Federal Estate Tax – the only Federal death tax in effect –was adopted in 1916. Only Nevada among all the states does not have a death tax. All of the others have such a tax, most being on inheritance, some on estates, and some on both. After 1926, the states were encouraged to enact death taxes because the Federal estate tax permitted a credit to the estate if it pays a death tax to the state.

Estate tax rates in the U.S. have varied greatly over time. For example, in 1962 rates ranged through some twenty-five brackets from 3% on the net value of an estate of $5,000 or less to 77% of the amount by which a taxable estate exceeded $10 million. By the early part of this decade, the rates and deductions changed considerably. However, seldom has there been an equal interest by an Administration and The Congress to reduce or eliminate them. Four further, current data refer to the following two websites: www.virtualology.com'virtualpubliclibrary/halloftaxes, inheritancetax.org.

Social Security – Prior to the 1800s, family independence and responsibility being highly regarded, the primary relief of poverty was left to private charities, workmen's provident associations, church groups and one's own family or relatives. In essence, people took considerable pride in caring for their own, many out of necessity.

In 1889, under Otto von Bismarck's leadership, Germany became the first European nation to introduce what was then a modern form of social security consisting of a contributory health insurance program, a national compulsory accident insurance program and pensions for the elderly. At that time, the country's retirement age was set at 70 (lowered to 65 in 1916). Germany's actions were followed by Austria, Hungary and Great Britain which, in 1911, adopted a compulsory health insurance program and became the first country to establish a national system of unemployment insurance; the former being extended significantly in 1920.

In the United States, recognition that social welfare could be best handled by the government was rather late in coming. This was due to four reasons: The U.S. economy during the 1700s, 1800s and early 1900s was largely agricultural and there was little unemployment, at least in the present sense of the term. Family groups were fairly large, and they traditionally assumed responsibility for their members who were aged or in need. This was supported by an 19th Century belief that personal initiative and hard work were all that were necessary to achieve material success and, conversely, indigence was synonymous with incompetence or laziness accompanied by a cultural stigma attached to any government-sponsored aid to the poor. In fact, many extremely poor individuals and families refused such aid as a reflection of their pride, self-worth and values.

Workmen's Compensation, which had begun in the U.S. in 1908, was the nation's first type of social insurance. With the exception of Wisconsin, which passed an unemployment insurance bill in 1932, the 1908 version was the only form of social insurance that existed in the U.S. until 1935 when the Franklin Roosevelt administration proposed a broad national social program.

The Social Security Act of 1935, based on the Federal government's idea that it could care for citizens better than they, was part of Roosevelt's "New Deal" program. This was a national system of social security for which was paid by taxing business enterprises and individuals. It consisted of the following:

- Federal old-age benefits for workers
- A Federal and State system on unemployment insurance
- Financial aid to help the states provide public assistance to dependent children, the needy aged and the needy blind
- Provision for maternal and child health services
- Services for crippled children (Polio was still a rampant and wide-spread disease)
- Child welfare services
- Vocational rehabilitation
- Federal aid to the states to assist them in establishing public health programs

The definition of "needy" has become increasingly broad over the years. From 1935 to 1954, the number of groups and member of workers covered by old age, survivors and disability insurance expanded considerably. The use of food stamps and other benefits paid by taxes to benefit the poor and needy no longer required that efforts were made to find and engage in work, even though jobs were found for many of them. Today, it is increasingly ironic that many of these individuals receive tax rebates even though they do not pay taxes! Within the last three decades these benefits including free (tax-paid) medical attention, housing assistance and preferences regarding education, have been given illegal immigrants as well as to America's "disenfranchised." The rationale for this is difficult to appreciate inasmuch as illegal immigrants do not yet have the privilege of voting (except perhaps in some of the south western and western states), nor do they pay taxes.

Today, in an attempt to "roll back" the tide which, given the present political climate, appears as an extremely difficult task, increasingly vocal groups are advocating a Flat Tax, a Fair Tax, a VAT Tax, and/or an increasing use of a Consumption or Sales Tax; all aimed at lessening or eliminating the present onerous income tax, to be combined with significant cuts in government spending.

The hope, at least is to dissuade The Congress and State legislators from any further increases in progressive income tax actions. The dream is to reverse the trend, attempting to prove that the present thinking regarding approaches to gaining tax revenue will materially damage the incentives for Americans to work harder and do better, thus strengthening the nation's strategic economy.

Taxes and Their Possible Effects on Incentive and Tax Revenues

Most people agree that if one's total income was taxed, i.e., a 100% tax rate, there would be little incentive to earn money or to work for that purpose. This, of course, would necessarily assume that no "loop holes," etc., existed. Many economist, financiers, social scientists and so forth have studied the impact of this relationship for years, possibly beginning with Ibn Khaldun around 1380. More recently, sources you may wish to reference include Jude Wanniski, John Maynard Keynes and Arthur Laffer as well as such studies as the Congressional Budget Office's 2005 *Analyzing the Economic and Budgetary Effects of a 10 Percent Cut in Income Tax Rates*.

The question – one highly hypothetical – is how high can be a tax rate on income before the incentive to earn money is adversely affected, and, hence, adversely affect tax revenues to the government? Complexities such as possible differences among various income groups about the incentive to work and the subject of progressive taxation will significantly affect the estimates. However, you should be aware of this subject in planning your business. A good place to start in order to obtain a broad understanding of the issues, probabilities, etc., is the subject of the Laffer Curve and the theories and analyses relating to it. However, I'm of the opinion that until empirically based statisticians replace or are positioned to seriously influence lawyers, little will change in the attitude of politicians toward taxation.

The power to tax is not the only approach used by politicians to intervene in business affairs. In fact, it is but one among many as will be reviewed subsequently in this chapter.

Business law is beyond the scope of this book. However, you must recognize that it is important for you as an aspiring industrial leader to have a working understanding of laws and regulations that may affect your business; also an appreciation for the background that nurtured such important influences.

You, as an advancing business executive, should become informed about major laws and regulations so that possible violations do not occur from ignorance. With sufficient counsel, you may even determine ways in which these laws, possibly their vagueness, might work for you, thus minimizing their time and cost impact on the progress of your businesses. To paraphrase a combined thought of Euripides, Thucydides and Santayana, "Those who cannot (or don't) remember the past are condemned to repeat it."

Also, you should ensure that you are sufficiently informed about the backgrounds and changes in relevant Acts and regulations to at least be able to discuss them intelligently with your general counsel, outside lawyers, etc., as to their effects on your industries and companies – and how you stay out of trouble!

It is interesting, when reviewing the chronology of U.S. government actions, to note that there were few, if any, major interventions or obstructions by government of business through the administration of the first twenty or so of the nation's Presidents. In fact, just the opposite appears to be true. From George Washington, the first president, to Rutherford B. Hayes, the twentieth president, most of the actions taken resulted in factors favorable to business and business expansion. Between President Jefferson and President Polk, the size of the nation almost doubled. Subsequently, during President Franklin Pierce's administration – the President, Japan was first opened to the west for trading purposes. Actions by Presidents Lincoln and Grant resulted in the completion of the intercontinental railroad. With the exception of the income tax enacted during President Lincoln's term and continued until General Grant's second term, tariffs and other non-income related revenue sources provided almost the entire nation's funding. The early administrations of Jefferson, et al also sponsored forces to protect America's transoceanic commerce and the banking system steadily was strengthened almost from the time the country was founded.

Indeed, it was not until the advent of President Benjamin Harrisons' administration in 1899 that a major legal action occurred and that being the signing of the Sherman Anti-trust Act of 1890 – some 115 years after the birth of the United States. Even the Sherman Act was not adverse legislation aimed at business, but actually to increase competition through eliminating coercive combination practices. However, there continues to be considerable debate about the value of this legislation

Events rather than political motivations have led to most government actions. The chronology of Federal government Acts, laws and regulations over the past 140 years which have influenced American business or the business environment, as well as the underlying events which were the catalysts for such actions, is as follows (*an asterisk precedes those actions or events which strategically – and directly or indirectly – affect U.S. business, favorably or unfavorably*):

President – George Washington (Elected 1789)
- *Tax enacted on the Sale of Whiskey, 1791 (Resulted in the "Whiskey Rebellion")

President – George Washington (Re-elected 1793)

President – John Adams (Elected 1797)

President – Thomas Jefferson (Elected 1801)
- *First Barbary War, 1801-1805 (For protection of U.S. ships and international commerce)
- *Louisiana Purchase, 1803
- Lewis and Clark Expedition, 1804-1805

President – Thomas Jefferson (Re-elected (1805)

President – James Madison (Elected 1808)
- *Strengthened Constructionist definition of The Constitution

President – James Madison (Re-elected 1812)
- *The War with England, 1812 (The results of the War ushered in entrepreneurship, the Industrial Revolution in America and higher tariffs to protect emerging American industry)
- *The Second Barbary War, 1815-1816 (Ended the threat of piracy in the Mediterranean)
- The collapse of the Federalist Party
- Louisiana admitted to the Union, 1812
- The Treaty of Ghent in 1815
- Indiana admitted to the Union, 1816
- *Bank of the United States Act, 1816

President – James Monroe (Elected 1816)
- *Florida acquired (1825)
- The Missouri Compromise (1820)
- *Advanced The Monroe Doctrine (1823)

President – John Quincy Adams (Elected 1825)
- *Assisted in formulating the Monroe Doctrine

President – Andrew Jackson (Elected 1829)
- *Opposed the Bank of America
- *Increased powers of the Presidency

President – Martin Van Buren (Elected 1836)
- Financial Panic of 1837

President – William Henry Harrison (1840)
- (Deceased after one month in office)

President - John Tyler (Succeeded Harrison in 1841)
- *Tariff increase (1842)
- *Annexation of Texas (1845)

President -James K. Polk (Elected 1844)
- *Establishment of the 49th parallel as the nation's northern border (1846)
- *Walker Tariff of 1846 (substantially reduced the Tariff of 1842)
- Oregon Treaty, 1846 (became Washington, Oregon, Idaho and parts of Montana and Wyoming)
- *Independent Treasury System Act of 1846 (government funds were held in the Treasury rather than in banks and other financial institutions
- *Treaty of Guadalupe Hidalgo, 1848 (became California, Nevada, Utah, most of Arizona and parts of New Mexico, Colorado and Wyoming)

President – Zackary Taylor (Elected 1848)
- *Clayton-Bulwer Treaty of 1850 (Replaced by the Hay-Pauncefote Treaty, 1902)
- (Deceased after less than two years in office)

President – Millard Fillmore (Succeeded Taylor, July 9, 1850)

President – Franklin Pierce (Elected 1853)
- *Commodore Perry opens Japan to Western trading
- *Gadsden Purchase, 1854

President – James Buchanan (Elected 1857)
- Financial Panic, 1857
- South Carolina secedes, December 20, 1860

President – Abraham Lincoln (Elected 1861)
- *Morrill (First and Second) Tariff Acts, 1961
- *Revenue Act of 1861 (The nation's first Income Tax law; a 3% Flat Tax on annual income above $800 ($19,307 in current Dollars)
- *Revenue Act of 1862 (change to a Progressive Tax structure)
- *Homestead Act of 1862
- *Morrill Land-Grant College Act of 1862
- *The Pacific Railway Act of 1862
- Legal Tender Act of 1862 (the first currency since the Continental of the Revolution)
- *National Banking Act of 1863

President – Abraham Lincoln (Re-Elected 1864)
- *National Banking Acts of 1864 and 1865
- *The Pacific Railway Act of 1864

President – Andrew Johnson (Succeeded Lincoln, April 15, 1865)
- Civil Rights Act of 1866
- *Alaska Purchase, 1867
- Tenure of Office Act, 1867
- Impeachment attempt failed, 1868

President – Ulysses S. Grant (Elected 1868)
- *Transcontinental railroad completed, May 1869
- Public Credit Act of 1869 (Assurances to repay Civil War debts)
- Enforcement Act of 1870

- *Patent Act of 1870 (17-year term adopted in 1861 covered trademarks and copyrights)
- *The first Federal income tax expires, 1872 (This tax was imposed in 1862 to finance the Civil War)

President – Ulysses S. Grant (Re-Elected 1872)
- *Depression – 1873-'79 (Caused by overextended debt and speculation)
- Specie Payment Resumption Act of 1875 (Dropped the Silver dollar, began drive to the Gold Standard)
- Civil Rights Act of 1875

President – Rutherford B. Hayes (Elected 1876)
- *Pendleton Civil Service Act of 1883
- Supreme Court invalidates the Civil Rights Act of 1875
- Pacified the South by removing Federal troops, 1877
- Bland-Allison Act of 1879
- *Federation of Organized Trades and Labor Unions established, 1881
- *American Federation of Labor (AF of L) established, 1886
- *Interstate Commerce Act of 1887 (Primarily aimed at Federal oversight of railroad activities)
- *Currency Act of 1890 (Commits the United States to the Gold Standard)
- *McKinley Tariff of 1890
- *Public Lands Preservation Act of 1891
- *State governments involved in demise of the AAIS strike at the Homestead Works, 1892

President – James A. Garfield (Elected 1880)
- (Assassinated only six months after his presidential inauguration)

President – Chester A. Arthur (Succeeded President Garfield September 19, 1881)
- *Pendleton Civil Service Reform Act of 1883
- *Shufeldt Treaty, 1882
- *Standard Oil Trust, 1882
- Chinese Exclusion Act, 1882

- Civil Rights Cases, 1883
- International Meridian Conference, 1884
- *Wabash, St. Louis & Pacific Railway Company vs. Illinois, 1886

President – Grover Cleveland (Elected 1884)

- *Interstate Commerce Act of 1887 (A major business-related legislation; the resulting agency (ICC) became template for most ensuing U.S. Government agencies, etc.)

President – Benjamin Harrison (Elected 1888)

- *The first Pan-American Conference occurs (1889)
- *Dependent and Disability Pension Act of 1890
- *McKinley Tariff Act
- *Sherman Anti-Trust Act of 1890 (based on Congressional power to regulate Interstate Commerce)
- *Sherman Silver Purchase Act of 1890
- States of North Dakota, South Dakota, Montana and Washington admitted to the Union, 1889
- States of Idaho and Wyoming in 1890
- Panic of 1893

President- Grover Cleveland (Elected 1892)

- Depression, 1893-'97
- *Wilson-Gorman Tariff Act, 1894
- *The Supreme Court holds that the Constitution forbids Federal Tax on individual's income, 1895; A 5 to 4 decision that the Wilson-Gorman Act, placing a 2% tax on annual individual income over $4,000 (equivalent to about $55,000 today), was unconstitutional.
- *A Proportional Tax (2%) imposed, 1894 (In part this was to offset losses from reduced tariffs. The Supreme Court found this unconstitutional because the tax was not entirely apportioned according to population)

President – William McKinley (Elected 1896)

- *Dingley Tariff, 1897
- Spanish-American War, 1898

President – William McKinley (Re-elected 1900)
- *Annexation of Cuba and the Philippines, 1900
- *Gold Standard Act of the United States, 1900
- (Assassinated September, 1901)

President – Theodore Roosevelt (Succeeded President McKinley Sept. 1901)
- *Coal Mining strike mediated by the Federal Government, 1902 (The first involvement of this kind)
- National Reclamation Act, 1902
- *Elkins Act, 1903 (Strengthens penalties against railroad rebates to favored shippers)
- *Bureau of Corporations, 1903, established
- *Construction of the Panama Canal, 1903
- *The Perdicaris Incident, 1904 (Informed the world that America would protect its citizens, regardless of their global location; helped insure the President's election)

President – Theodore Roosevelt (Elected 1904)
- *Supreme Court dissolves the Northern Securities Company, 1904
- *Pure Food and Drug Act, 1906 (Prohibits adulterated foods and drugs; requires labeling)
- *Meat Inspection Act, 1906 (Requires sanitation standards; requires Federal inspection of meats)
- *Hepburn Act, 1906 (Tightens further existing railway regulations)
- *The U.S. Navy's "Great White Fleet" accomplishes a global circumnavigation showing the emerging naval power of the U.S., demonstrating its industrial prowess, and its capability to protect its commerce and territories, December 16, 1907 to February 22 1909

Resident – William Howard Taft (Elected 1908)
- *Payne-Aldrich Tariff Act, 1909
- *A levy first imposed on corporate profits in the technical form of an Excise Tax, 1909

- *Mann-Elkins Act of 1910 (Extends the authority of the Interstate Commerce Commission to include communications, and further strengthens regulations of the railroads)
- *ICC Regulation of Telephone Service - 1910
- *Wisconsin imposes an income tax, 1911 (First state to do so)
- *Triangle Shirtwaist Company fire, in New York City, 1911 (over 140 deaths)
- *Supreme Court orders dissolution of the Standard Oil Company, 1911

President – Woodrow Wilson (Elected 1912)
- *Clayton Antitrust Act of 1914 (Strengthens law by defining specific practices)
- Federal Reserve Act, 1913
- Underwood-Simons Tariff, 1913 (Reduces tariff rates, imposes an income tax)
- *Sixteenth Amendment, 1913 (Grants Congress authority to tax income; Congress that year imposes a graduated Federal income tax, maximum of 7% on annual income over $5,000)
- *Federal Trade Commission (FTC) Act, 1914 (Replaces 1903 Bureau and increases span of Laws)
- *Federal Farm Loan Act, 1916 (Farmers qualify for low interest Federal loan using their land as collateral)
- *Federal Estate Tax Act, 1916
- *Federal Warehouse Act, 1916 (Federal loans available by providing inventory and crops as security)
- *Workmen's Compensation Act, 1916 (Provides Federal employees accident and/or injury protection)
- *Adamson Act, 1916 (Limits straight time hours for interstate railway workers to an 8-hour day)
- *Keating-Owen Act, 1916 (Prohibits products made by child labor from interstate commerce)
- The United States enters World War I

President – Woodrow Wilson (Re-elected 1916)
- Nineteenth Amendment to the Constitution, 1920 (Provides women citizens the right to vote)

President – Warren G. Harding (Elected 1920)
- *The Transportation Act of 1920
- Recession, 1920-'21
- Sheppard-Towner Act, 1921
- Washington Naval Conference, 1921 ("Normalcy" sought in global weapons production)
- *Fordney-McCumber Tariff, 1922 (Restores higher tariff rates)

President – Calvin Coolidge (Succeeded President Harding, 1923)
- Supreme Court strikes down minimum wage law for women, 1923

President – Calvin Coolidge (Elected 1924)
- *Teapot Dome scandal, 1924 (Interior Secretary leases Federal land to oil wildcatters for personal loans)
- *National Origins Act, 1924 (Limits foreign migration to the U.S. to 164,000 annually)
- Federal Farm Board established, 1928
- Robert F. Wagner elected to U.S. Senate, 1926 (Becomes a principal labor and welfare advocate)

President – Herbert Hoover (Elected 1928)
- Kellogg-Briands Pact, 1928
- Federal Farm Board, 1928 (Authority is broadened)
- "Black Thursday" occurs, October 24, 1929 (Stock market crash commences eventually contributing to the Nation's "Great Depression" 1929-1940 – unemployment was still 11 million in 1938, i.e., approximately 20% of the U.S. population)
- Smoot-Hawley Act, 1930 (Raises sugar tariffs, resulting in Cuban government upheaval)
- *Glass-Steagall Act, 1934 (Forces a "Chinese Wall" between Stock Analysts and Investment bankers)

- *Reconstruction Finance Corporation (RFC) established, 1932 (Provides loans to businesses)

President – Franklin D. Roosevelt (Elected 1932)
- Tennessee Valley Authority (TVA) established, 1933
- Federal Deposit Insurance Corporation (FDIC) established, 1933 (Insures deposits up to $50,000)
- Agriculture Adjustment Act, 1933
- Emergency Banking Act, 1933
- Railroad Retirement Act, 1934
- *Security Exchange Act , 1934 (among several other things, assigned guideline responsibilities , through the American Institute of Certified Public Accountants (1936), to the Committee on Accounting Procedures (1936)
- Works Progress Administration (WPA) established, 1935
- Committee for Industrial Organizations (CIO) established, 1935 (Largest Labor Union to date)
- *National Labor Relations (the Wagner Act) Act of 1935 (Establishes the National Labor Relations Board, greatly strengthening labor's position)
- *Rural Electrification Administration established, 1935
- *Social Security Act of 1935
- *Banking Act, 1935 (strengthens the control over the money supply)
- *Public Utilities Holding Company Act of 1935 (Regulates interstate transmission and restricts gas and electric companies to a single geographic region as defined in the law)
- *Revenue Act of 1935 (Increases tax rates at the higher individual incomes, on corporations and on estates and gifts)

President – Franklin D. Roosevelt (Re-elected 1936)
- *Robinson-Patman Act of 1936 (Restricted pricing practices related to monopolistic market strategies)
- *Taxation of Dividends paid and received commences, 1936 ("Double Taxation")
- National Housing Act, 1937
- Wagner-Steagall Act, 1937

- *Union organizes General Motors UAW) and United States Steel (USW) with Federal government providing oversight
- Attempts to "Pack the Court" foiled, 1937
- Bankhead-Jones Farm Tenancy Act, 1937 (Establishes Farm Security Administration)
- *Wheeler-Lea Act, 1938 (Relates to product and services advertising and promotion)
- CIO of 1935 becomes Congress of Industrial Organizations (CIO), 1938
- Congress reduces taxes, 1938
- Agricultural Adjustment Act, 1938 (Curtails certain crops and provides farmers subsidies and financing)
- Chandler Act of 1938 (Introduces Chapter X to the Bankruptcy Act)
- Hatch Act of 1939 (Forbids Government employees from participating in election campaigns)
- Impact of "Great Depression" continues – U.S. unemployment in 1939 above 15%

President – Franklin D. Roosevelt (Re-elected 1940)
- *Investment Company Act of 1940 (Also known as the Investment Advisers Act of 1940)
- *Fair Employment Practices Commission (FEPC) established, 1941
- Ford Motor Company (UAW) and Republic Steel Corporation (USW) organized by the Unions, 1941
- *War Powers Act, 1941
- Japan initiates War against the United States, December, 1941. Congress declares War (War got U.S. out the "Great Depression")
- *Revenue Act of 1942 (Expands graduated income-tax rates and system)
- *United States Export-Import Bank established, 1942 (Provides export financing for businesses)
- *Smith-Connally War Labor Disputes Act, 1943

President – Franklin D. Roosevelt (Re-elected 1944)
- United States Export-Import Bank reorganized, 1945

President – Harry S. Truman (Succeeded President Roosevelt, April 1946)

- Employment Act of 1946 (Establishes the Council of Economic Advisors)
- Office of Price Administration (OPA) abolished, 1946
- AT&T's Bell Laboratory produces the first transistor, 1946
- ENIAC, the first electronic computer comes on line, 1946
- *Labor-Management Relations (Taft-Hartley) Act of 1947 (Outlaws Closed Shop, Walkouts)

President – Harry S. Truman (Elected 1948)

- Marshall Plan enacted, 1948
- McCarran Internal Security Act, 1950
- *Celler-Kefauver Act, 1950 (Further strengthens anti-trust legislation)
- *Patent Act, Title 35, 1952 (Broadens patents, trademarks and copyrights legislation)

President – Dwight D. Eisenhower (Elected 1952)

- Atomic Energy Act, 1954
- AFL-CIO merger, 1955
- Iranian leader, Mohammad Mosadegh, deposed; destroying U.S.-Iranian relationships to date.

President – Dwight D. Eisenhower (Re-elected 1956)

- World's first atomic energy plant comes on line in Pennsylvania, 1957
- *Public Law 86-750 enacted, 1957 (Authorized the SEC authority regarding maintaining books, reports and records)
- *The President notes the dangers of the "Military-Industrial Complex," 1961
- *Accounting Procedures Board established, 1959, replacing the Committee on Accounting Procedures, 1936

President – John F. Kennedy (Elected 1960)

- United States sends Special Ops troops to Vietnam, May 1961 (beginning of "number of U.S. troops" there)
- (Assassinated November, 1963)

President – Lyndon B. Johnson (Succeeded President Kennedy, November 1963)

President – Lyndon B. Johnson (Elected 1964)

- *Civil Rights Act, 1964 (Creates the Equal Employment Opportunities Commission)
- *Economic Opportunity Act, 1964
- *Tax Reduction Act, 1964 (Reduces corporate and Upper Bracket individual income taxes)
- *Federal Health Insurance Program, 1966 (Creates Medicare)
- *Medicaid established, 1966 (1966 cost equaled $800 Million; 2000 cost approximated $95 Billion)

President –Richard M. Nixon (Elected 1968)

- Fannie Mae established, 1968
- *Occupational Safety and Health Administration (OSHA) established, 1970
- *Racketeer Influence and Corrupt Organization (RICO), 1870 (Title 18, U.S. Code, Section 1961-1968; especially Section 1964(c))
- *Wage and Price Freeze instituted, 1971
- *U.S. withdraws from Bretton Woods system – End of the U.S. Gold Standard
- *Federal Contract Compliance Act, 1972

President – Richard M. Nixon (Re-elected 1972)

- *DDT use banned by Federal Government, 1972
- *Financial Accounting Standards Board established, 1973, replacing the Accounting Procedures Board, 1959; putting in place the Generally Accepted Accounting Practices (FASB), 1973

President – Gerald R. Ford (Succeeded President Nixon, August 1974)

- Recession, 1974-'75
- U.S. troops withdraw from Vietnam, April, 1975

President – James Carter (Elected 1976)
- *Export Controls Legislation, 1976
- Department of Energy created, 1977
- *Court breaks up AT&T
- *Foreign Corrupt Practices Act, 1977
- *The Community Reinvestment Act of 1977 (encouraged providing mortgages to higher risk markets) Iranian "students" take over American embassy, taking hostages
- Inflation hits in 1979-80; 1980 bank interest rates reach 20%
- Attempt made to free U.S. hostages being held in Iran results in a complete failure

President – Ronald Reagan (Elected 1980)
- Recession, 1980-'83
- *Surface Transportation Assistance Act of 1982

President – Ronald Reagan (Re-elected 1984)
- Immigration Reform and Control Act, 1986

President – George H. W. Bush (Elected 1988)
- *Federal Clean Air Act, 1990
- Oil Pollution Act, 1990 (Evolved and based on the 1989 *Exxon Valdez* incident)
- *Proxy votes, which may add value, and voting rights are subject to the same fiduciary standards as other plan assets per Department of Labor, 1988 – Rendering of Court opinion
- *Honest-Services Fraud Addendum, 1988 (Addendum to 18 U.S.C. 1346)

President – William J. Clinton (Elected 1992)
- *North American Free Trade Agreement, 1993 (Negotiated by President Bush)
- IRS adds section 162(m) limiting corporate executives' compensation regarding tax deductibility (1993)
- PRC Most Favored Nations' Trading Status, 1994

- *Driver's Privacy Protection Act of 1994
- World Trade Organization (WTO) Agreement, 1994
- *Private Securities Litigation Act, 1995 (Large shareholders may be named controlling parties in class-action shareholder suits, see Bragdon vs. Telxon)
- Proposed Health Care Reform Plan of 1994 fails passage

President – William J. Clinton (Re-elected 1996)
- *Export Administration Act, 1999 (Important for U.S. exporters)

President – George W. Bush (Elected 2000)
- Eight-year Securities' market "bubble" burst, 2000
- Regulation for fair disclosure (FD) Act of 2000
- *South China Sea Agreement of 2000 (to resolve control issues. U.S. not a signatory)
- Terrorists bomb New York World's Trade Center and the Pentagon, September 11, 2001
- Sarbanes-Oxley Act of 2002
- Enron, Worldcom, Tyco International, Arthur Andersen, ImClone Systems, Ernest & Young, HealthSouth, Merrill Lynch, etc., management and financial scandals
- Financial "bail-out" of U.S. Airlines industry, 2003
- *Check 21 Act, 2003

President – George W. Bush (Re-elected (2004)
- *Enactment of H.R. 1424, as amended. (See Public Law 110-343) (A modification of The Emergency Economic Stabilization Act of 2008; includes Troubled Asset Relief Program (TARP) (A bailout of the U.S. Financial system. Subsequently broadened to provide $17.4 Billion to the automobile industry, viz., GM and Chrysler)

President – Barack Obama (Elected 2008)
- *Lilly Ledbetter Fair Pay Law, 2009
- *American Recovery and Reinvestment Act (ARRA), 2009 (Provision of $862 Billion. Inasmuch as the Federal Reserve already had cut interest

rates to zero, it was thought wise to use fiscal policies instead of monetary policies such as most economists believed to be better. The aim of this Act was to create jobs and promote investment)

- Expanded Hate Crimes Law, 2009, folded into the 2010 $680 Billion Defense Authorization Bill, 2009
- *Credit Card Accounting, Responsibility and Disclosure Act, 2009
- *Weapon Systems Acquisition Reform Act of 2009
- *Healthcare Overhaul Law, 2010
- *Employee Free Choice Act, 2010 (pending)
- *Preserve Access to Generics Act of 2010
- *Financial Reform Act of 2010
- *Consumer Financial Protection Bureau created, 2010

Appendix M

Acknowledgement

The book is based largely on the author's personal management experience over the past several decades. However, not unlike his career, his thoughts, actions and life have been guided by his religious faith and psychological beliefs. They also have been positively influenced by several intelligent, thoughtful and considerate individuals with whom and for whom he has had the privilege of working and associating. There also have been negative influences, the sources of which shall remain anonymous. He has learned from these experiences as well. Thus, in acknowledging the people who have provided the author their positive influence, he thanks the following individuals who demonstrated their confidence and trust in helping to make his career possible. However, it is to be emphasized that these people may or may not agree with the opinions and premises expressed in this book (The order of this listing is alphabetical, the positions and years indicated are those when the author first became acquainted with these individuals):

- Mr. James L. Allen (1957), Senior Partner, Booz, Allen & Hamilton

- Mr. Philip F. Anschutz (1984), Chairman, CEO, President, Anschutz Petroleum Company

- Mr. Norman R. Augustine (1985), Chairman, CEO, Martin Marietta Company

- Mr. Robert W. Austin (1952), Professor, Legal Aspects of Business, Harvard Business School

- Mr. Arthur Bailey (1930), Maternal Uncle

- Mrs. Mary M. Bailey (1928), Maternal Aunt

- Mr. John W. Barton (1982), Corporate Attorney; Dravo Board member

- Dr. Ilker Baybars, Deputy Dean, Graduate School of Industrial Administration, Carnegie Mellon University

- Dr. Ronald G. Campbell (1949), Professor, Oregon State University

- Mr. Frank C. Carlucci (1982), Senior Member of The Packard Commission

- Mr. Philip L. Carret (1952), Manager, Pioneer Fund

- Dr. Thomas P. Detre (1974), President, University of Pittsburgh Medical Center (UPMC)

- Mr. E. Mandell "Del" de Windt (1983), Chairman & Chief Executive Office, Eaton Corporation

- Mr. Robert Dickey, III (1974), Chairman, CEO, President, Dravo Corporation

- Mr. Michael D. Dingman (1974), Chairman, CEO, The Henley Group

- General Georges F. Doriot (1952), Professor, Manufacturing, Harvard Business School

- Dr. Douglas M. Dunn (2000), Dean, Graduate School of Industrial Administration, Carnegie Mellon University

- Mrs. Jessie V. M. Faught (1928), Mother

- Mrs. Lynda C. Faught (1983), Spouse

- Mr. Thomas F. Faught, Sr. (1928), Father

- Mr. Joseph H. Flom (1984), Senior Partner, Skadden, Arps, Slate, Meagler & Flom

- Gen. Alfred M. Gray (1987), Commandant, United States Marine Corps

- Mr. Richard R. Hough (1978), Executive Vice President, AT&T; Dravo Board Member

- Mr. H. Frederick Hutchinson, Jr. (1991), Director, Senior Advisory Panel, Central Intelligence Agency

- Mr. Donald E. Jahncke (1953), Manager- Engineering, Lincoln-Mercury Division, Ford Motor Company

- Mr. Michael D. Kadoorie (1997), Director, Sir Elly Kadoorie & Sons Ltd.

- **Mr. Joseph A. Katarincic (1976), Attorney**

- Miss Patricia L. Larson (1944), Classmate, Salem Senior High School; Oregon State College

- Mr. Louis K. Lawrence (1943), Manager, Reid Murdock Canning Company

- Dr. Harry Levinson, PhD (1984), Industrial Psychologist, Levinson Institute

- Mr. Jack M. Lyons (1954), Manager, Engineering, Ford Motor Company

- Mr. Bernard P. McDonough (1956), Chairman, McDonough Corporation

- Mr. Malcolm McGregor (1951), Classmate, Harvard Business School; Partner, Boyden Associates

- Mr. James H. Manges (1951), Classmate, Harvard Business School; Partner, Lehman Brothers

- Dr. Allan H. Meltzer (1999), Professor, Graduate School of Industrial Administration, Carnegie Mellon University

- Mr. John A. Miller (1931), Maternal uncle

- Mr. Roger H. Morley (1967), Vice President, Gould Incorporated

- Gen. Tai-Joon Park (Retired) (1979), Founder-Chairman, Pohang Iron & Steel Company (POSCO)

- Mr. F. Newton Parks (1959), Vice President, Booz, Allen & Hamilton International

- Ms. Leta Jean (Faught) Parker (1947), Spouse

- Ms. Herma C. Pfister (1939), Sixth Grade Teacher, Bush Elementary School

- Cpl. William E. Rasnik (Hansing), (1946), Drill Instructor (DI), Recruit Depot, United States Marine Corps

- Mr. Martin Roberts, (1992), Managing Director, COGENT Northern Telecom.

- Mr. Rong Yiren (1992), Chairman, China International Trust & Investment Corporation

- Mr. Rudolph J. Schaefer, Jr. (1970), Chairman, Schaefer Brewing Company

- Mr. William A. Scott (1939), Circulation Manager, Capital Journal newspaper

- Mr. Paul L. Sliper (1948), Upper Classman, Phi Delta Theta Fraternity, Oregon State College

- Mr. Ralph E. Smiley (1957), President, Booz, Allen & Hamilton International

- Mr. Edward J. Smith (1953), Supervisor- Engineering, Lincoln-Mercury Division, Ford Motor Company

- Mr. James W. Taylor (1957), Senior Partner, Booz, Allen & Hamilton

- Mr. Eric M. Warburg (1964), Partner, M. M. Warburg, Brinckmann, Wirtz & Company

- Mr. James H. Webb, Jr. (1987), Secretary of the Navy, Department of Defense

- Ms. Wu Yi (1993), Minister, Ministry of Foreign Trade and Economic Development People's Republic of China

- MGen. Yang Qian Li (1995), Army, Peoples Republic of China

- Mr. Richard A. Yocom (1934), Fellow Member, YMCA

- Ms. Zhang Guangdi (1984), Vice Minister, Ministry of Communications, People's Republic of China

- Mr. Zhu Rongji (1982), Senior Member State Economic Commission, People's Republic of China.

www.ingramcontent.com/pod-product-compliance
Lightning Source LLC
Chambersburg PA
CBHW030800150426
42813CB00068B/3297/J